Praise for Maria Bartiromo's Use the NEWS

"Maria Bartiromo's new book provides a tour of the key factors that move stocks . . . Highly recommended for readers who want to enhance their knowledge about the stock market."
   —Jack Schwager, author of *Stock Market Wizards*

"Maria Bartiromo's unique role, along with her candid views, gives ordinary Americans a valuable insight into this little-understood world, so that you can become a better investor."
   —Ric Edelman, bestselling author of *Ordinary People, Extraordinary Wealth*

"Maria offers a fresh and vibrant approach to financial journalism. Her unique and provocative style is surpassed only by her clear, thoughtful, and thorough presentation of market news and insights."
   —Richard A. Grasso, Chairman and CEO, New York Stock Exchange

"This book contains dozens of powerful investment nuggets, each of which is worth 1,000 times the price of this book. If you're an investor in the stock market, you need this book."
   —Robert G. Allen, author of the *New York Times* bestsellers *Nothing Down*, *Creative Wealth*, and *Multiple Streams of Internet Income*

"*Use the News* is a valuable resource for investors, from novice to expert. Thanks, Maria, for educating your viewers and, now, your readers."
   —Arthur Levitt, Jr., former SEC Chairman

"This book serves as a primer for the average individual investor to choose the news to use in making investments."
—*Booklist* (Starred Review)

"In a friendly, hands-on style, [Bartiromo] offers readers a view of the stock market . . . from her vantage point as a reporter on the floor of the NYSE."
—*Publishers Weekly*

"Bartiromo is adept at illustrating the double crosses, contradictions, and wrong turns awaiting all but the most savvy investor."
—*Business 2.0*

Use the
NEWS

Use the
NEWS

How to Separate the Noise from the Investment Nuggets and Make Money in Any Economy

MARIA BARTIROMO

with Catherine Fredman

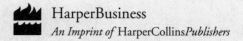

HarperBusiness
An Imprint of HarperCollinsPublishers

USE THE NEWS. Copyright © 2001, 2002 by Maria Bartiromo with Catherine Fredman. All rights reserved. Printed in the United States of America. No part of this book may be used or reproduced in any manner whatsoever without written permission except in the case of brief quotations embodied in critical articles and reviews. For information address HarperCollins Publishers Inc., 10 East 53rd Street, New York, NY 10022.

HarperCollins books may be purchased for educational, business, or sales promotional use. For information please write: Special Markets Department, HarperCollins Publishers Inc., 10 East 53rd Street, New York, NY 10022.

First HarperBusiness paperback edition published 2002

Designed by Stratford Publishing Services

Library of Congress Cataloging-in-Publication Data has been applied for.

ISBN 0-06-662086-4
ISBN 0-06-662087-2 (pbk.)

02 03 04 05 06 RRD 10 9 8 7 6 5 4 3 2 1

*This book is dedicated
to the memory of my grandmother,
Rosalia Maria Morreale, who I feel is always with me,
and to my parents, Josephine and Vincent Bartiromo,
for a lifetime of encouragement*

Contents

Foreword

In June 1995, Maria Bartiromo became the first reporter to broadcast daily from the floor of the New York Stock Exchange. In doing so, she broke new ground for journalists and, most significantly, set a new standard in reporting on financial markets. Maria is a true pioneer in bringing Wall Street to Main Street.

Maria offers a fresh and vibrant approach to financial journalism. Her unique and provocative style is surpassed only by her clear, thoughtful, and thorough presentation of market news and insights. Then, too, Maria's drive for innovation and professionalism is exceeded only by her commitment to keeping the investing public informed. A simple approach perhaps, but one that has clearly been of great value to America's 85 million investors.

The participation in today's market by an increasing number of investors has been fueled, in large part, by the equally dramatic increase in market information. Now 85 million strong, American investors are no longer casual bystanders. They demand and deserve the latest news and developments from financial markets and the enterprises in which they entrust their savings and futures. With access to more resources than ever, investors "use the news" to make highly informed, more knowledgeable investment decisions. Ultimately, this serves to boost investor confidence in our markets and contributes to the economic well-being of America and, increasingly, the world.

Richard A. Grasso
Chairman and CEO
New York Stock Exchange

Preface to the Paperback Edition

The world of investing has changed dramatically since this book was first published.

Use the News came out at the beginning of a recession that claimed more than one million jobs in 2001 alone. Then we were hit by the terrorist attacks of September 11th, which occurred barely ten minutes into my morning broadcast from the floor of the New York Stock Exchange, just two blocks away from the World Trade Center. A few weeks later, Enron, the seventh-largest company in America, declared bankruptcy in the midst of an accounting scandal that shook the investment community to its roots.

The mood of the markets has changed, for sure. Professional and individual investors alike have been humbled. They lost a lot of money—and, unlike during the optimistic days of the roaring bull market, they weren't going to make it back any time soon.

People are much more skeptical these days—of news from companies, news from auditors and rating agencies, and news from anyone pushing stocks, whether analysts or brokers. At the slightest hint of financial confusion, investors promptly punish the company's stock, driving down the market, increasing market volatility and further exacerbating mistrust of Wall Street.

Investors have become skeptical of news from the media and from independent watchdog organizations. They've even become skeptical of Alan Greenspan for his handling of the economic downturn. In short, they've become skeptical of investing in general.

But while investors' attitudes have changed, what hasn't changed is the fundamental forces that move the markets. What hasn't changed is the basic nature of news that you can use. The noise has changed, but not the news.

The noise has gotten much louder in the past year, making it even more difficult to sift out the news nuggets. It's hard to see clearly during this kind of maelstrom. It's hard enough to think clearly when you're caught in the emotional whirlpool generated by the events of the past year. No one can, which accounts for the seemingly illogical trading patterns that boost the Dow 100 points one day and then take it right back down the next. But if the events of the past year have taught any single lesson, it's that it's more important than ever to take the time and trouble to separate the nuggets of news from the overlying noise. At the end of the day, the current uncertainty and confusion over accounting and how companies recognize revenue in their quarterly reports is positive. The beauty of America is that there are naysayers. There are those who will stand up and raise their hand and say "this doesn't look right."

I'm not saying that it was easy to see through Enron. How did Enron, the seventh-largest company on the Fortune 500 list, manage to convince everyone that the company was as strong as Fort Knox? It hid $40 billion in debt scattered in thousands of limited partnerships that only showed up on the balance sheet as a series of cryptic footnotes. It allegedly hid billions of dollars of loans from Wall Street firms by counting them as financial hedges instead of debt. The partnerships were private, so they didn't need to disclose their balance sheets. Plenty of companies use hedging activity to protect themselves from volatile trading.

If Enron had disclosed the true nature of its debt, then credit-rating agencies, industry analysts, and investors would have known earlier that the company was riskier than it appeared. But it didn't have to.

Perhaps one of the most stunning revelations of the Enron debacle was that some of its accounting treatment conformed to existing recommendations from the Financial Accounting Standards Board, the nation's accounting rule-maker. Clearly there were some issues where Enron's partnerships crossed the line of legalities; however, using outside partnerships to transfer debt and other liabilities to off-balance sheet partnerships is actually legal.

That's not to excuse Arthur Andersen, the accounting firm responsible for auditing Enron's books. Such independent auditors are now being questioned about being independent at all. Some charge once again the conflict of interest issue, making it almost impossible for the auditing side of an accounting firm to remain independent in the face of huge fees being generated on the consulting side. In the case of Andersen this remains to be seen, however, since the investigation into Enron continues as I write this. We cannot judge exactly what went on until we hear from all of the principals.

Having said that, Enron, in my opinion, represents what may be the peak of an era now as infamous for conflict of interest as for skyrocketing stock prices fueled by the people who knowingly participated in that game: analysts of investment banks promoting companies that their firms solicited business from, accounting firms approving auditing statements that wouldn't rock the boat, and companies that let only a few top officials know what was really going on.

This era also reflected the sheer force of public opinion. While there were some isolated reporters and analysts who raised red flags and challenged Enron's practices, for the most part they were ignored as investors watched the stock soar yet higher. Even investors who had doubts couldn't justify them when a respected outside auditing firm signed off on the company's financial statements. By a combination of bravado and financial sleight of hand, the company managed to fool just about everyone from analysts to the media to investors. It even managed to fool its own employees.

In retrospect, there were some very simple questions to ask if one were to have been an unfortunate investor or holder of Enron stock. The first and most obvious was how is the company making money? It is such a simple question, one almost feels silly asking it. But that was one of the easiest ways to determine that this was not an easy-to-understand investment. As I have written many times throughout this book, follow your instincts. If you don't understand it, maybe it is not what it seems. To be realistic, there will be other Enrons. There will always be other Enrons, most smaller, some equally as large. Unfortunately and particularly during bull markets, people, companies, and investors seem to take things to the edge. The Enron debacle may have been fraudulent, but what has occurred in the marketplace is less about fraud than it is about fundamentals. As a result of Enron, investors today will scrutinize the way companies report earnings and account for revenue, earnings and debt.

One example occurred in January when Tyco International was criticized for failing to report what had amounted to $8 billion worth of small acquisitions over the past three years. To be fair, Tyco had at the time a market capitalization of well over $60 billion. It is a huge conglomerate and many of these deals were small in comparison. Did it do anything wrong? Did it need to disclose every small deal publicly? The markets decided yes and took the stock down considerably. The investment community questioned whether Tyco stock should be trading at 15 times next year's earnings if, in fact, the earnings picture was not what it seemed because the growth was skewed by additional acquisitions. So in reality, the issue is a fundamental one. How much have earnings grown and how are companies achieving that growth? The true quality of earnings has been put up for debate and thus so has the level of stock prices. That is the fundamental issue with which we are all dealing. It is not one of fraud on the part of American corporations. That is the good news. Why shouldn't we question valuations? Why shouldn't we push companies to become more transparent? It is important to be skeptical in an environment where conflicts of interests arise.

The results of this debacle will also be good news. What happened to Enron is a major wake-up call for the investment community. As a result, we're likely to see far-reaching reforms in the auditing business and an increasing amount of regulatory oversight. Companies will be pressured to present more transparent financial statements. And investors will have learned some valuable, if painful, lessons about things not always being what they seem. Auditors have begun closer scrutiny of the appropriateness of write-offs. Investors today need to be just as skeptical. How can they take the lessons learned from Enron and apply them to make smarter, more informed investment decisions? How can they tune out the noise and focus on the news?

The Enron story has proved that certain nuggets are more newsworthy than ever.

Financial Fundamentals

Back when Enron was high and I was working on Chapter 4 of the hardcover version of this book, I wrote, "The news is all in the financial statements." Since then, we've received the equivalent of a bucket of icy water thrown in our faces. Your reaction is probably, "But, Maria, even if the news is all in the financial statements, what good is it to us if the company's financial statements are not what they appear to be? How can we know when to trust a company's cash flow statements, its balance sheet, and its statement of operations?"

Cash flow doesn't lie. I describe the cash flow statement as a company's checkbook: It reveals exactly when and what money is going out, and when and what money is coming in. One of my hedge-fund manager sources, who declines to be named, says that his favorite—and the easiest—way to check up on companies is to see whether the cash flow matches what the company is saying. If the product is so hot, the cash flow should be consistently strong. Do not invest in a company without understanding how much cash is coming from operations.

Another way to check on whether a company's financials are what they seems is checking on how often the company raises cash from the public markets. Enron had constant problems with its operating cash and would come to the marketplace every six months to raise money through the sale of stocks and bonds. It didn't make sense. If the company was doing as well as it said it was, if the cash was there from selling the product, whatever the product may be, we should all have been asking ourselves, why was there a consistent need to come back to the public markets to raise more money?

Debt, as discussed throughout the book, can be another bad sign on a company's balance sheet—assuming that the signpost is standing up and the sign is legible. In the example in Chapter 4, we show you Wal-Mart's balance sheet. What you don't see is what's key: you don't see any footnotes, pro forma numbers, goodwill write-downs, or other extraordinary items. Enron masked its mounting debt behind myriad footnotes, rightly assuming that few people would take the trouble to attempt to decipher them.

What it all comes down to is: If you have any doubts, check it out. One of the most important elements of a company's financial fundamentals to check is the quality of its earnings.

Quality of Earnings

Quality of earnings simply means: How did a company achieve its earnings? If it's reporting 20 percent growth every quarter, despite competitors seeing declines, what is it doing to accomplish that feat? And how do those earnings hold up when put in the context of any underlying debt or other significant costs on the balance sheet?

To be fair, the ten-year bull market also created an urgency to meet growth expectations. During the 1990s, companies felt an urgency to meet or beat analysts' expectations—the "whisper number" that's one of Wall Street's most enduring forms of gossip. It became the norm for management to do whatever it took to report profits that matched or exceeded the consensus on the Street. This created an opportunity for management to look for creative ways to achieve growth, whatever it took.

The crux of what we're talking about is the GAAP gap, the ability of a company to stretch generally accepted accounting principles, or GAAP. Things happen during bull markets that relax rigid standards, and many companies took advantage of that flexibility to push their accounting to the edge.

Today that GAAP gap remains, even now that the bull market is definitively over. When IBM reported its fourth quarter earnings for 2001 in a conference call in mid-January 2002, it announced that it had beat Wall Street's profit forecasts. It did not disclose that the sale of its optical unit to JDS Uniphase had generated $300 million that the company used to lower its operating costs. It did not account for the transaction as a one-time gain, as is the practice. Instead, it claimed that profits had grown, even as revenue in most categories had declined, because of increased productivity and higher sales of certain products.

Such one-time gains are often identified as nonrecurring charges. Skeptics have said using them to offset expenses does not create a fair representation of the company's operations. Having said that, it was not illegal that IBM did not tell us that a major reason for the drop-off in expenses was the sale of a unit. Some analysts said they did know about the sale and had been told on conference calls but not to the extent that it had helped expenses so considerably. They say IBM could have been more specific. Cisco has also come under scrutiny for its use of stock-option grants and executive compensation. Option grants were stratospheric for the second straight year in the year ended July 2001, despite big losses in that time period. The company had an operating loss of $2 billion and a net loss of $1 billion, but the CEO was awarded option grants worth an estimated $121.6 million. The CFO, who also serves as senior vice president, was awarded $13.2 million. When should a company recognize such option grants? When they are vested or when they are given to the employee? It is another gray area that has been put up for debate. Who is to know the value of that option grant once it actually vests and the employee actually sells the stock? These are discrepensies currently being disputed, when it comes to accounting practices.

GAAP gaps can breed accounting scandals and, in fact, the Securities and Exchange Commission has recently begun cracking down on companies that have incomplete or misleading disclosures, even in their press releases.

Do You Understand How the Company Works?

Can you honestly and simply explain how the company makes money? As Jonathan Cohen, managing director of Wit Soundview Capital, says in Chapter 4, "The quality of the business model should be the number-one point: Is this a company that can make money, that can generate real profitability over the long term?"

During the initial Congressional hearings on Enron, Enron executive Sherron Watkins, who had warned then-Chairman Kenneth Lay about the improper partnerships, quoted former CEO Jeffrey Skilling: "Jeff Skilling said that if it doesn't make sense, don't buy it." Enron didn't make sense. All we knew was that every year it reported great earnings growth. But no one really understood how they achieved it. And whenever anyone questioned it, he or she would be laughed at.

Personal Attacks Against Naysayers

A red flag that has nothing to do with accounting is when the management of a company launches a personal attack against a skeptic. Enron's management did it against a reporter at *Fortune* magazine who questioned the company's accounting practices. Gary Winnick, the head of Global Crossing, and the top management of Qwest both did it to Morgan Stanley's telecom analyst. In Chapter 9, we describe how Ed Crutchfield, the then-CEO of First Union, publicly ridiculed analyst Tom Brown because

Brown criticized First Union's dilutive acquisitions. We learned later that Tom Brown was right in doing so as First Union stock tumbled over too many dilutive acquisitions.

One money manager says, "The moment the company starts acting that way shows real weakness. I expect management to be minding the business and not spending their energy yelling at analysts."

Pay Attention to Business News

What you see in the headlines of the business press is often a news nugget that can lead to a mother lode. Some examples:

- *Secondary offerings.* Any time a company announces a secondary offering or a bond offering is a reason to hoist a red flag. Remember that the companies that keep coming back to the market have the coziest relationships with the investment banks, because the investment banks are underwriting the stock and bond sales and, in the process, are getting huge fees. Not surprising, those are often the companies that the investment firm's analysts are pushing the hardest—another good reason to be skeptical.
- *Insider transactions.* It's important to watch what the principals of the company are doing with their shares of the company stock. As we explain in Chapter 8, sometimes insider transactions are a bunch of chicken guts but sometimes they can also be portents. Many of the Enron principals sold stock aggressively in 1999 and 2000 before the company imploded. Conversely, Michael Dell bought millions of shares of Dell Computer when the market bottomed out in the fall of 2001—four months after, he had doubled his money.
- *Unexplained departures.* What does it mean when a CEO or an important manager resigns "for personal reasons?" Enron's Jeffrey Skilling resigned after only six months on the job. Anyone on Wall Street who was watching the company, myself included, said, "Huh?" I had interviewed Skilling on my show many times. He seemed passionate about

his work. Then, all of a sudden, he bowed out "for personal reasons." It didn't make sense—and raised a red flag.

Short-Selling

Economic conditions change. Competitive conditions change. Companies respond—or don't. That's the reason you want to check out what the short-sellers are thinking.

You should ask yourself on a regular basis, "Is the reason that I bought this stock in the first place still there?" But, to be honest, what we should do isn't what we actually do. That's why it's a useful exercise periodically to check out the top five stocks being shorted. Try to figure out why. Is there something the experts see going on at these companies that could be prevalent throughout the sector or that could have an impact on the stocks in your own portfolio?

Markets change, events evolve and what's news and what's noise shifts with the times. A year ago, the actions taken by the board of governors of the Federal Reserve banks—the Fed—were so anxiously anticipated that they actually spawned "the Fed effect" in the market. As I write this, the issues of the day are about accounting practices, not about whether the Fed will raise interest rates. I still think we should watch what the Fed does, but right now, monetary policy has taken a backseat to corporate earnings.

I know that just as it's easy to ignore the red flags when everything is going well, it's equally appealing just to bury your head in the sand when things take a turn for the worse. But it's more important than ever to trust your instincts, heed your doubts, and pay attention to the red flags that may signal trouble for a stock. I've said it before and I'll say it again: Your judgment is your ultimate investing tool.

The Enron debacle represented a turning point for investors. Believe it or not, that's good news.

Because of what happened, we're going to see real change in accounting regulations that will make it tougher for companies to hide behind obscure financial statements and hopefully easier to root out the relationships between accounting firms and their clients that often lead to conflict of interest. The SEC is proposing new rules, and so is the Federal Accounting Standards Board. No auditor wants to become the next Arthur Andersen, so they're going to think twice before signing off on practices that might once have been fine.

Coming on the wake of the dot-com crash, Enron's collapse has reinforced a healthy skepticism of the analyst community. Few analysts are going to commit themselves to rave reviews of companies as they did routinely in the past.

All of these developments will provide greater transparency of information and further level the playing field for the individual investor. If nothing else, the lessons of the Enron story should make us into smarter investors.

True, there will be more noise to tune out. But there will be more news that you can use.

Acknowledgments

I have one of the greatest jobs of all time. Every day I go to work as an anchor at CNBC and absolutely love what I do. So I want to thank Bill Bolster, Bruno Cohen, and Pamela Thomas Graham, who run such a phenomenal ship at CNBC. I also want to thank Bob Wright, CEO of NBC, and Jack Welch, outgoing CEO of General Electric, CNBC's parent company, for giving me the chance to do what I do. A special thanks to David Friend, Ted Shaker, and Elyse Weiner. It makes me so proud to be part of that company.

It would be difficult to find a more hard-working group of people than the team of *Market Week:* my co-producer Diane Galligan, segment producer Lori Ann Larocco, and my assistant Diana Cabral. They track down and book the CEOs and market experts whom I interview on the show, dig up background research, and put together a weekly investment calendar just like the one I discuss in this book. Their experience makes *Market Week* the show it is—and provided a sounding board for many of the ideas I present in this book.

I could not carry the workload I do were it not for all the producers, writers, and segment producers with whom I work: Matt Quayle and Nick Dunn on *Squawk Box,* Andy Hoffman and Joanne Po on *Street Signs,* and Rich Fisherman and Petra Wright on *Market Wrap,* as well as all the other members of the team, including production assistants, editors, directors, and camera operators, who are too numerous to mention here. A special thanks to Anna Levitan, who has provided me with valuable assistance at the New York Stock Exchange every morning.

I have the luxury of being able to pick the brains of many of the investment community's top traders, analysts, market strategists, and money managers. Getting inside their heads has helped me become more adept at separating the news from noise. I'm especially grateful to those people who generously gave their time and shared their expertise in interviews for this book. In alphabetical order, they are Joe Battipaglia, Arnie Berman, Charles Biderman, Tom Brown, Amy Butte, Denney Cancelmo, Jessica Reif Cohen, Jonathan Cohen, Bob Gabele, Tom Galvin, Jerome Heppelmann, Chuck Hill, Arthur R. Hogan III, Robert Hormats, Jonathan Joseph, Lawrence Kudlow, Arthur Levitt, Nick Lobaccaro, Robert Loest, Kevin McCarthy, Dennis McKechnie, Henry McVey, Paul Meeks, David Menlow, Bruce Meyer, Dan Niles, Joe Ricardo, Jeff Rubin, Steve Shobin, Ravi Suria, George Strachan, Dana Telsey, Deborah Weinswig, and Edward Yardeni.

A big thank you to everyone at the New York Stock Exchange, especially Dick Grasso, chair of the exchange, for opening his home to me and allowing me to broadcast from there, and also for agreeing to write the foreword to this book. He is a pioneer and a friend.

Many, many thanks to my viewers, all the men and women who in their telephone calls and e-mails to me prove over and over that the individual can invest just as wisely and responsibly as the professionals—if not more so! You deserve all the market information you can get.

The truth is, I've been trying to write a book for five years. I sat on one idea after another until Wayne Kabak, my longtime agent at William Morris, told me that the best time was right now and pushed me so aggressively that I realized I didn't have a choice. He oversaw the entire process, tirelessly reviewing every chapter and noting every single typo. The fact that this book exists is in no small part due to him.

Wayne found the perfect editor, Adrian Zackheim of HarperBusiness. Adrian made sure we were on the right track and then stood back and trusted us to stay on it. His enthusiasm for the project was sincere and unwavering.

Then there's Catherine Fredman. She made the process of transforming an idea into a book seem natural and enjoyable. Her understanding of the subject matter, her ability to follow my thoughts and capture my voice, and her incredible organizational skills were immensely valuable. In addition, she enthusiastically interviewed many of the sources and researched many of the facts quoted in these pages. I could not have written this book without her.

My family—my mom and dad, Josephine and Vincent, my brother, Pat, and my sister, Theresa—kept me going with constant encouragement. I speak to my mom sometimes twice a day, but when Catherine and I were working, she refused to call, for fear of interrupting us. I can't count the number of times she came over at night with homemade chicken soup to keep me going.

I've saved my deepest, warmest thanks for last. My husband, Jono Steinberg, never complained when I turned our living room into an office and he, along with the dog, was relegated to the bedroom almost every weekend—and many weeknights—for the past eight months. Even though he didn't need to hear every last detail of the process, he always listened attentively, let me bounce ideas off him, and gave me sound advice and unstinting support.

Introduction:
The Information Explosion

We live in an extraordinary time for ordinary investors. Wall Street has gone from an institutional club admitting only select professionals to a game that's wide open to individuals.

In the past two decades, equity ownership in the United States has soared. In 1983, some 42.4 million Americans owned stocks directly or through mutual funds. By 2000, Richard Grasso, chairman of the New York Stock Exchange (NYSE), estimated that the number had grown to eighty-five million, an increase of more than 100 percent. Today, CNBC pegs the number at one hundred million. To be sure, one of the major reasons was the record-breaking bull market. Another no less important reason is the bonanza of information that's now available to individual investors.

In the decade or so that I've been reporting on Wall Street and business news, we have seen an explosion of information about investing, the stock market, the economy, and personal finance. We see it in the myriad of magazines and newspapers, in the skyrocketing number of Internet websites—more than 352,000 web pages on investing, at my last count—and in television programs with reporters like me who make it their business to ensure that the news that will affect your investments tomorrow is in front of you today. Together we've created an extraordinarily rich information library that is open to everyone.

Every week, it seems, a new website debuts, offering individual investors ever deeper and more detailed data that was once available only to professionals. Do you want to get a sense of the amount of money flowing into—or out of—the market, a vital statistic that professionals use to predict whether the market is heading into bull or bear territory? Do you want to check a chart of the performance of a certain company's stock for the past ten years? Do you want to scrutinize the track records of various research analysts to see whose calls have been on the money—and whose have missed the mark? All this information is readily available with just a couple of mouse clicks. And it won't cost you a cent.

Similarly, you can get an idea of the personality of a company's chief executive officer (CEO) or the thought processes of its senior management. No longer are canned CEO speeches the only source of information for the individual investor. In addition to magazine profiles and television interviews, conversations and conference calls with company executives are increasingly being broadcast live on streaming video on the Internet. You can tune in and form your own opinion of the management team.

I think the explosion of information is terrific, and I'd be the first to say that it's detrimental not to take advantage of it. I'd also be the first to say that there is information overload. And it's only getting worse.

I know, because I deal with it every day. I get to my office in the CNBC studio overlooking the floor of the NYSE by 7:00 most weekday mornings and immediately I'm swamped with information. My first report is live at 8:05 a.m. eastern standard time on CNBC's *Squawk Box* morning show. After that I have exactly eighty-five minutes before the opening bell rings to sift through faxes, e-mail, phone calls, newspapers, and the wires and decide what's news and what's not.

I flip through the newspapers—the *Wall Street Journal,* the *New York Times,* the business section of the *New York Post.* There is a great column covering the markets in the *Financial Times* that I typically glance at. If there's a story I've heard about in the *Washington Post,* I look at that too. Then I go through the wire services on the Internet: Reuters, Associated Press (AP), Dow Jones, Bloomberg, Bridge.

I'm mostly looking at the headlines for the big stories in business that might be influential in moving the markets. If Royal Dutch Shell released earnings in Europe overnight, will that news move the stocks of other oil companies like ExxonMobil and Chevron here in the United States? If two insurance companies announce a merger, then overall insurance stocks might react.

I check Reuters to see what the international markets did overnight. If there's a big story affecting stocks in Europe and Asia, the U.S. market will usually be affected too. When major European and Asian companies trade actively on their local exchanges, the movement normally triggers big moves in their American Depositary Receipts. When Japanese cell phone maker Kyocera cut its global mobile shipment target in the winter of 2001, Nokia, Ericsson, and Alcatel all traded down on world exchanges. A day later, Motorola preannounced similar news, sending the group down further. A year earlier, Germany's Deutsche Telekom's acquisition of VoiceStream made waves overseas that spilled over to the U.S. markets. Similarly, if something happens in the U.S. market, Europe and Asia will take their cue from the United States.

Most mornings there are no fewer than twenty faxes waiting in the fax machine and fifteen e-mails from different brokerage firms, hedge funds, and other companies that have opinions on the market, and analysts noting their take on certain stocks or sectors. There could be something from Deutsche Bank Alex Brown about the banks or from Goldman Sachs's leading analyst, Abby Joseph Cohen, about the broad market or from a trader or analyst who has his own market sheet, such as *Bulls, Bears and Bloch,* which is analyst Ralph Bloch's morning note. Some items contain news that will move the markets that day. A big call in the bank sector is important because banks have been a leadership group and the market often follows the cue of the bank sector. Cracks in the health of financial institutions can have great impact.

Certain analysts rock stocks with a single report. Abby Joseph Cohen's comments can do that, as can remarks from those analysts who are the "axes" in certain stocks—so called because a negative call from them will chop the stock's price, most of the time because they have a long history of being right. So if Henry McVey at Morgan Stanley Dean Witter or Amy Butte at Bear Stearns makes a call on banks or brokerages, he or she will likely move those stocks. If Merrill Lynch's Henry Blodget says something about Internet companies, particularly something negative, he will move those stocks. In early 2001, former Federal Reserve governor Wayne Angel and his fellow economist John Ryding told clients that there was a 60 percent chance that the Federal Reserve would cut interest rates between its regularly scheduled meetings to stave off a profit recession. Those comments reversed an all-day sell-off in the National Association of Securities Dealers Automated Quotation System (Nasdaq) and helped the Dow halve a 200-plus-point sell-off. They then upped the ante, days later calling for an 80 percent chance the Fed would cut that same week. It didn't happen until the Fed met during its regularly scheduled meeting about 3 weeks later.

These people have built reputations on their calls for the groups they follow and have become almost cultlike leaders. Because investors listen and react to their calls, I also listen to what the axes in certain groups are saying each morning.

There are reports or analyses that might not do anything to the market that day but are worth keeping in my files to look at later. John Murphy of MurphyMorris.com might notice a breakout of a particular stock, or Steve Shobin, a technical analyst and chief portfolio manager at Americap Advisers, might have been going through different charts and discovered a pattern in a particular sector over a certain time frame. That could make an interesting interview after the morning rush.

Then there are some releases that just aren't important. That trader with his own market sheet often won't have broad impact. His sheet contains his own opinions, which may be worth considering but may not make a big splash.

Other reports are what's called maintenance. Maintenance reports are pretty common and they work like this: Let's say that after the markets closed yesterday, a company preannounced that its earnings would fall below analysts' expectations. Consequently, the next morning the analyst community announces that it is lowering *its* expectations. The analysts want to have the same earnings estimate as the company so that their estimates and the company's profits match when the company reports earnings. If the company says the consensus estimates are too high or too low—a statement known as corporate guidance—the next day analysts will lower or raise their estimates accordingly to "maintain" the estimates that the company believes are doable. For my purposes, maintenance reports are merely a repetition of news that I already know. I pay attention to them but try not to waste too much time on them. A change in earnings estimates is much more newsworthy to me if it breaks away from the consensus and predicts something different.

Other news that's *not*? Often a company will publish a press release and make a big deal announcing some new product when, in fact, the product won't have any effect on the company's earnings. The press release is just a way for the company to keep its name out there, to keep people buzzing about its products. It goes right in my wastebasket.

There's plenty of information that comes my way and—don't get me wrong—I need plenty of it. After the morning show, I anchor two more shows on CNBC—*Street Signs* at 2:00 p.m. and *Market Wrap* at 5:00 p.m. Every Friday at 7:30 p.m., I coproduce and anchor *Market Week,* in which I preview the coming week on Wall Street. All of these reports demand that I deal with a constant information flow. I go in early and work late and am constantly on the go. I love what I do, but I don't have the time and energy to waste on insignificant research, unimportant press releases, and e-mail that are at best a distraction. Those I toss.

Okay, by now, it's 7:45 a.m. and I'm on the phone.

I call Instinet, an electronic communications network (ECN) to get real-time quotes of stocks trading before the opening bell rings at the NYSE or Nasdaq. I want to know which stocks are trading in volume in the premarket. Telecom stocks might be jittery in anticipation of an analysts' conference about the sector. Cisco might have reported earnings after the market closed the day before and I want to see what the reaction was. Instinet volumes tell me that if people want to trade Cisco so much when the regular trading session isn't open, then clearly it will be one of the more active stocks when the opening bell rings.

I don't check for stock quotes online because most websites don't give real-time quotes; there's a fifteen- to twenty-minute lag. Markets move fast, and I need to know what the stock is trading at *now.* Fifteen minutes ago, the stock might have been trading 5 points higher and then I'd be in danger of seeing the wrong information. Instead, I check the CNBC ticker, which is in real time. It airs live trading, so I can glance at my television and see the most recent trade, whether it was on the NYSE, Nasdaq, Instinet, or one of the other ECNs.

I call all the big investment banks—Merrill Lynch, Deutsche Bank Alex Brown, Credit Suisse First Boston, Goldman Sachs, Prudential Securities, Lehman Brothers, J.P. Morgan Chase, Morgan Stanley Dean Witter, Salomon Smith Barney. All of these firms, commonly called "sell-side firms" because they sell research and ideas and execute trades for a commission, have what they refer to as a morning call. This is a conference call with thousands of each firm's brokers and research teams or analysts across the country. One trader runs the meeting and various analysts make a case for the way their sectors or individual stocks may trade. One analyst may be pushing a certain stock, another may downgrade a sector, or still another may have new information from company managers with whom he had dinner last night. Perhaps the analyst received proprietary information from an industry trade group like Information Resources Inc. (IRI), which tracks volumes in the food and beverage sector. IRI's information isn't available to individual investors, but it really moves stocks. Institutions pay for it. You often hear analysts citing IRI when talking about Anheuser Busch, Pepsi-Cola, or any of the major food companies.

The analysts' comments are broadcast through speakers, or "squawk boxes," on every trading desk in every office from New York to London to San Francisco to Tokyo. The morning call goes on anywhere from 7:00 a.m. to 8:30 a.m., and there are often so-called break-ins, or specific calls based on that day's market activity. Then the firm's brokers start selling that call. They call their clients and try to sell them ideas: "Say, our analyst thinks PC stocks will go higher, so you'll want to own IBM and Dell and Hewlett-Packard." If the salesman convinces his client to make the trade, his sales trader will negotiate the best price on the basis of the number of sellers, and both salesman and trader make a commission.

It's important to know what the big sell-side investment banks are doing, because they sell their information to clients, known as buy-side firms, who can be even bigger institutions. J.P. Morgan Chase might have a billion dollars under its own management, but its clients might include Merrill Lynch Asset Management or Alliance Capital or American Express Financial Services, who among them are holding *$10 billion* under management. The clients might include "pure vanilla" firms, like Fidelity or Vanguard, whose money can be used only to buy stocks, or might include hedge funds, who can short stocks as well as buy them. These clients represent a big part of the market, and any one of them has the wherewithal to move stocks. You can bet the information in the morning call will have an impact on the stock prices of those companies mentioned.

I want to get this information and tell my viewers about it so they have it at the same time that it's distributed to institutional clients, if not before. The fact that I can disseminate that information to a wider audience is one manifestation of the information explosion. The result of that dissemination of information is to level the playing field for individual investors and institutions.

When I call my sources, my first question is, "What's happening?" Maybe there's a story that I glazed over in Bloomberg that they're covering aggressively. Maybe they're talking about what happened in yesterday's Medtronic analyst meeting. Maybe some analyst had a meeting with the company's CEO and came away with a new perspective that contradicts conventional wisdom on the Street.

I ask "What's happening?" because I never know what might turn up. I might have my mind on oil and drilling stocks, following news that supplies have been drawn down and now some of the major firms were raising earnings estimates across the sector. But this trader might say, "Have you seen Gucci? It's up $4 in overseas trading," something I had not focused on. So I'll call up Instinet and see that Gucci is up $4 on the premarket. It turns out that Morgan Stanley is hosting a conference in Europe on the luxury goods sector where CEO Domenico deSole was quoted as saying he saw a strong quarter and people are getting optimistic and buying in anticipation of an earnings report next week. I ask "What's happening?" so that I get a line on as many situations as possible.

It's valuable for me to call trading desks and hedge fund managers, just to broaden my scope. I don't want to miss anything. I don't want to waste energy and time on a press release a company issued about a product that may mean nothing to the company's growth story while luxury-good stocks are what the big money institutional clients are talking about.

Starting at 8:05 a.m., I have between eleven and fifteen live shots in the next two hours, so I'm constantly looking for new and useful information. I'll go down to the floor of the NYSE and take a walk around. I'm looking for activity, for signs of any stocks that might be on the move. If I see a big crowd, I'll ask the traders what they're trading. Some may give me the information readily. Others are more hesitant because they don't necessarily want me to broadcast to the world that there are a lot of buyers or sellers for, say, Compaq. They would rather get their own order in before the word is out and the stock potentially moves away from them—in other words, before it trades higher than what they were planning to pay for it. After all, why would anyone show one's hand before knowing if there is interest in that same piece of business? They have a mandate to get the best price possible for their customers.

These guys are trading for big clients, so they need to get their price in order to do business again. These traders are paid to be anonymous, so it's understandable that they don't want to broadcast their transactions. But I am on the floor, too, and in some cases, I'm seeing exactly the same flow of orders that they do. Only market makers, specialists who bring together buyers and sellers for a particular stock, see the entire picture: they handle all orders, whether zapped to their special computer at their trading post, known as an electronic order book, or orders from the crowd. But I can see as much as the trader next to me. I can see who is buying, who is selling, and, most important, for how much. Those nuggets of news are extremely valuable to individual investors. They get the news from the floor at the same time that professionals receive it, if not earlier.

I finish the morning show at 10:00. I file reports for *Today in L.A.* on NBC and *News Channel* on NBC affiliates across the country. I'm then ready to prepare for *Street Signs,* CNBC's afternoon show. I'm on live from 2:00 p.m. to 3:00 p.m. The large brokerage firms have midday meetings as well as their morning squawk box meeting, so I call my sources to find out what went on in those meetings as well. I'm looking to see if sentiment has changed in any way. Maybe I mentioned in my morning show that Goldman Sachs upgraded Microsoft, so I'll touch base with that analyst in the afternoon to see how it is trading and whether or not he was right. Or maybe my producer has booked the CEO of Morgan Stanley, so I need to ready myself for our chat and come up with a list of timely and intelligent questions about his company as well as the brokerage and asset management sector.

On any given day I may interview live two to six CEOs in a variety of businesses. These CEOs do not know ahead of time what questions will be asked, and I need to stay as current as possible, coming up with questions from e-mail that may have sent in by my viewers, research that I've gleaned from the web, analysts I've just talked to, and from conversations that I have held with holders of those companies' stock. So I start preparing: I pull up the company's financials from the web, I pull up analysts' reports, and I call some money managers to figure out what the buzz is on the stock. I'm trying to get informed opinions from people who have their money on the line on this stock.

I do the same thing to prepare for *Market Wrap,* the daily 5:00 p.m. show that I co-anchor with Tyler Mathisen. Here I might focus on any action in the market's extended hours, such as a mid-quarter update conference call in which Sun Microsystems lowered earnings expectations for the year, causing a late-day sell-off in tech stocks. My weekend show, *Market Week with Maria Bartiromo,* which airs live on Friday evenings, goes even deeper with a longer look at a particular company or sector. I call around to find out what people thought about the day or what they think is going to happen in the next trading session. I'm always looking for little snippets of information that aren't widely disseminated so that I can bring something of value to the viewers.

At 6:05 p.m., there's a hit for CNBC Asia Pacific, then CNBC Europe, then NBC Chicago. Then my live obligations are done (most of the time). On weekends, if I'm not working on future projects, I'm writing my monthly column, "Scene and Heard," for *Individual Investor* magazine. (Incidentally, I had been writing for this magazine for a long time, about seven years, well before I married the magazine's CEO.)

Do I feel overwhelmed with information? Constantly. I've got to sift through the newspapers, the wire services, the sources who are calling me, the phone calls I'm making, and the information that's being generated on the floor just from talking to people. I get a ton of faxes and e-mail. Recently, I've noticed that my e-mailbox fills up so quickly that I have to delete items before I can reply. (Frankly, I think situations like that are why analysts love storage company stocks so much.) I'm always rechecking my favorite websites for the latest updates. When I get a free moment, I flip through *Barron's* and *Investor's Business Daily;* on weekends I go through *Fortune, Business Week,* and *Forbes.* Then there's *Newsweek* and *Time* as well.

Clearly, there is enough information out there to overwhelm even the most seasoned Wall Street professional, let alone a beginner. But at a certain point before each show, I need to decide what is news and what is noise so that I can focus on one and ignore the other.

What do I mean by news and noise? News is important information that may influence your investments. Noise is talk or buzz or some headline that prevents you from seeing a story clearly. News is useful. Noise is a distraction.

Noise is easily distinguished from news in retrospect, but at the time of the event it's hard to tell the difference. Remember when people said that the Monica Lewinsky scandal would destroy Bill Clinton's presidency and bring down the stock markets with it? That was noise, because people soon realized that the scandal had nothing to do with the monetary policy set by the Federal Reserve or the steady economic course taken by then Treasury secretary Robert Rubin. Nonetheless, for a while people were worried.

Or what about when Russia devalued the ruble in 1998? The markets were still jittery after the meltdown of the Asian economies the year before and some investors thought for sure there would be an impact on the U.S. economy. That was noise too. We don't have much of a trade relationship with Russia, so the devaluation of the ruble shouldn't influence our economic fundamentals. And it didn't.

Calling what's noise and news after the fact is easy. The hard part is sifting through the information when it's in front of you and committing to a few sources, that is, gearing up your energy in one place and not wasting your energy in another.

For example, a trade pact with China is news. China is a billion-person economy, the largest potential market in the world. It is newsworthy to see which American companies have a foothold in such a large market. If trade between China and the United States becomes active, that could be a huge opportunity for those companies and the U.S. economy. David Komansky, CEO of Merrill Lynch, recently told me that one of the most newsworthy events for his company and the industry will be an upcoming change in government in China.

Weakness in the Latin American economy is news. The United States has invested more than $120 billion in Mercosur member countries over the past five years. If the economies of those countries sag, then U.S. companies like Ford, Avon, and so many others that have built plants there will get impacted. There were so many newsworthy signs in 2000 that could have raised red flags about the ensuing sell-off in stocks: skyrocketing oil prices; overordering of product ahead of Y2K leading to an inventory glut; and a complete change in the way analysts valued tech stocks, putting earnings secondary.

It's easy for the news to be distorted or hidden by noise. It's easy to lose sight of the real story that is unfolding with regard to your investments when you're bombarded with undifferentiated and often extraneous information.

The Internet can be a great source of news, but it also magnifies the noise. There's been an acceptance of chat rooms airing the opinions of people who may not know anything about a company. That's dangerous. You'll see a story on some website about, say, accounting irregularities at some company or great expectations about its earnings. You don't know how it started, but suddenly people are trading on it. The story accelerates, the stock starts to move, and the buzz gets louder and louder. You might make a decision about your investments without realizing that you're lost in the noise.

Television also ratchets up the confusion. I try hard to deliver value, picking out nuggets of newsworthy information, but still there's a lot out there to digest. CNBC delivers market news fifteen hours a day, and it's not the only station to report regularly from the NYSE. There is a local radio station, Bloomberg, CNN, German television, and Latin American television. On any given day, the major networks might send a camera crew and a reporter down.

One criticism of the information explosion is that there is too much news. Maybe we don't need to know every time Goldman Sachs analyst Rick Sherlund upgrades Microsoft or every time Media Metrix reports that Internet traffic has slowed down. Personally, I disagree. I may not necessarily pay attention to every shred of information, but I want the option of being able to access it. Yes, too much information can be confusing and even dangerous, but I'd rather make the choice of filtering it out myself than having it filtered out for me.

It's never been easy to separate the news from the noise, and, to be honest, these days it's only getting harder. Information comes gushing out— from the government, from companies, and from analysts. You're also influenced by news headlines, market pundits, Internet chat room gossip, and hot tips from your Uncle Joe. One analyst I knows compares researching stocks today to trying to drink from a fire hose: there's so much coming at you so fast that you don't know how to handle it.

I don't think it's humanly possible to read through everything, evaluate every news report, or follow up every lead. No one can interpret and respond to every bit of information that is dumped on us daily. I can't. I don't have the time, and I assume you don't either.

Yet it's vital for all investors to keep abreast of the news that affects their own portfolio. It doesn't matter whether your money is in individual stocks or in mutual funds, whether you're a frequent trader or a buy-and-hold investor, whether you're hoping for a fast payback or are funding your 401(k), or whether you actively manage your money or let someone else make the decisions. You, ultimately, are responsible for your money. If you're trying to grow and capitalize on your nest egg, you need to watch it.

That's why I've written this book: to explain, on the basis of my experience, how to separate the news from the noise.

Information is no longer an investor's key commodity. With information so readily available and basically free, the most valuable commodity for an investor is good judgment: how you interpret the information.

To help you, I've looked to people who have a reputation for being thoughtful interpreters of information. One of my biggest assets as a reporter is my Rolodex. I work very hard to foster relationships with some of the smartest people on Wall Street. I have great access to some of the market celebrities and household names whom individual investors would not ordinarily have a chance to speak to. Similarly, I can call on the behind-the-scenes people you may have never heard of but who, in my opinion, move the markets with their predictions.

In this book I give you that access. I've picked the brains of some of the brightest people on Wall Street: CEOs of the some of the largest and fastest-growing corporations in America who have seen how market trends can affect a company's stock, money managers who have billions of dollars at stake, market analysts, economic analysts, technical analysts, mutual fund experts, and money flow watchers.

You'll get to meet people like Dennis McKechnie, manager of the PIMCO Global Innovation Fund, single-handedly the best-performing technology fund manager of 2000. In a year in which the Nasdaq dropped nearly 40 percent, McKechnie steered his fund to a 41 percent return. You'll meet Jerome Heppelmann, whose three value funds at PBHG racked up returns ranging from 25 to nearly 33 percent in 2000. Both of these portfolio managers and others will explain how they separate news from noise to come up with winning investment strategies.

You'll get to meet the truth-telling analysts who saw behind the smoke and mirrors at companies ranging from Amazon.com to First Union, or ignored the hype in the tech sector, and who were the first to warn investors that Wall Street's drums might be beating the wrong message. You'll learn which factors they used to come up with their controversial calls and which factors you can use to differentiate between news and noise.

Together we'll give you the insider's explanation of how the market and financial news *really* work. We'll tell you exactly which pieces of economic, financial, and company information these market makers and market movers consider news. We'll explain how these experts separate news from noise and how they use the news to make winning investment decisions.

We'll list the top noisemakers too. We'll warn you about the mistakes that are all too easy to make when you're confused by noise and we'll show you how to avoid them. We'll translate Wall Street jargon into plain English. We'll catalog the market's seasonal dips and rises on a calendar so that you won't be riding the market roller coaster blindfolded. One thing I can promise is that you'll never be hoodooed by a triple-witching Friday again.

I have to warn you, though, that the answers don't always come quickly and there's no easy formula to get them. Sometimes you have to dig through a lot of noise to extract the nuggets of news that will make a difference to your portfolio.

But I will tell you what works for me, as I sift the news from the noise every day. I'll tell you how to handle the information overload so that you can get to the goods easily and efficiently. I'll explain how to evaluate the data so you can make them work for you. I'll show you how to get your arms around an unmanageable amount of information and make it manageable.

In short, in this book I'll expand on what I already do in my broadcasts and articles, namely, level the playing field so that individual investors have the same information, understanding, and chances of success as the professionals. Then you too can use the news to make smarter investment decisions and, I hope, profit from them.

1

It's Not Brain Surgery

When you buy a car, you kick the tires. When you buy a house, you look in every nook and cranny. You need do to the same thing with your investments. And there's no reason why you can't.

Learning how the market works isn't brain surgery. I'm living proof of that. I'm hardly a mathematics whiz. In fact, a couple years ago, I ran into my high school math teacher and she said, "I can't believe you cover finance."

I never took any classes in Wall Street 101, either. I learned it from the ground up. Okay, I studied economics in college, where I learned about the relationship between supply and demand and the difference between macroeconomics and microeconomics. Big deal. You don't learn how markets move in school. You learn that by following the markets and watching trends. In my case I learned it on the job.

So how did I end up with this job?

In my sophomore year at New York University (NYU), I took an introductory course in economics. A lot of people are bored to tears by the topic, but I was lucky because I had a professor who made it exciting. I loved it and I was sailing in it, so I decided to make it my major.

Then my mother said, "Why don't you take some journalism classes? I think you'll be good at them." I loved them too. The excitement of covering a story was similar to the excitement of figuring out an equation in economics, maybe even more so because there was a greater sense of urgency. A few more journalism classes and I ended up switching my major to journalism and making economics my minor.

By now I was a junior in college and I had no idea what I was going to do after graduation. That year I took a class in broadcast journalism. It was one of my favorite classes. Every week the class produced a story and each of the students took a different role. One week I was the anchor, one week the guest booker, one week the producer.

I loved being the producer. You formulate the whole show, from soup to nuts. You have to decide what content to run, which video or graphic to use, and how to make each story come alive with sound and interviews. You have to think, Was the video freshly shot today or will it be misleading because it's file video? Do I want one anchor or co-anchors? Who are my guests? Do I want a kicker—a softer story—at the end of the show? How about music or animation? It's a lot of fun.

As a result of taking this class, I applied for admission to NYU's internship program in broadcasting. At the time all I wanted to do was work for NBC, CBS, or ABC. The networks were hot, I thought, and they were where the action was. I was accepted to the internship program, but to my disappointment I was assigned to work for CNN. I didn't even watch cable and felt that working for ABC, CBS, or NBC held more prestige than working for the very young cable channel. I took the job and started work as an intern at CNN Business News in 1988.

I soon realized that CNN was the best possible place for me to have gotten a job. At CNN I was able to do everything. I would get the numbers, that is, fill in stock quotes for the anchors. I would rip scripts—that's what it's called when the scripts are printed out and distributed to the producer, director, and anchors. I would teleprompt, where you manually move the scripts forward on a machine so the anchor can read them on camera. I would follow the wire service stories. I was able to do so much more at CNN than I would have been able to do at the networks, because the networks are unionized and I would not be able to do so many different tasks. So it was so fortunate for me to land at a place where I could gain wider experience and figure out what I was good at.

Eventually CNN offered me a staff position in business news. I worked my way up, first as a writer, then as a producer, and then as an assignment editor, which meant that I came up with story ideas and decided whom I wanted to interview and who would conduct the interview—either reporters or myself.

It was at CNN Business News where I first started noticing the chart trends tracking investor momentum in the stock market, first realized the importance of insider buying and selling—that's when a company's senior management buys or sells some of their holdings in the company's stock, which can be an important indication of their sentiment about the company's future—and first learned the significance of money flows. It was also where I first saw the impact that the price of oil has on the stock market.

The Gulf War began in August 1990, and Operation Desert Storm began the following February. In a nanosecond CNN was the hottest thing on television. You had CNN correspondent Bernard Shaw reporting live from a hotel room in Baghdad while bombs from an American air strike rained down outside his window. The world was watching CNN. It was frightful but . . . (it was thrilling). I felt proud to be a part of the team.

We in CNN Business News were watching the war's impact on the stock market, and that was thrilling too. We looked for the nuggets of news that would explain how the war would affect investments. Oil prices were surging because people were afraid that oil shipments from the Middle East would dry up. It was one of the biggest business stories and it was news. Oil is one of the biggest costs, if not *the* biggest cost, for corporate America. The airline, railroad, and automobile industries are the most obvious businesses fueled by oil; electricity is created from burning oil and gas. The price of oil was also affecting consumer spending. If you're paying more to gas up your car or heat your house, your disposable income drops. You don't have the money for an extra coat, big vacation, or new car. It was the first time in my career that the price of oil became so important to our everyday lives, the economy, and the stock market. It certainly wouldn't be the last.

And one day I woke up and realized that Wall Street and the markets had become not just my vocation but my avocation.

I learned how to follow the markets by following the people who were trading and by interviewing the people whose money was on the line: the chief strategists of large investment banks, the CEOs of various companies, the managers at mutual fund firms and the institutional investors. I called them constantly. I asked them what indicators they watched to make money, and I started watching those things too.

I asked lots of questions. My feeling is, no question is stupid. If the answer wasn't clear, I would keep asking questions until I understood what people were talking about. I learned to always be wary of the guys who talked over my head. I soon discovered that some of them were just trying to sound smarter than they actually are. I consider myself smart and I have good instincts, so if I can't understand what someone is saying, how will anyone else? I certainly can't communicate what someone told me if he or she didn't explain it so that I understand.

It was at CNN Business News that I first began developing great sources on Wall Street. In fact, when I left CNN, one of my colleagues said, "I'm so sorry to see you go because you're taking your Rolodex with you."

I moved to CNBC after I was offered a job on the air, which meant that I could present my news stories myself as well as produce and write them. I'm a very hands-on person and I like it that way. I don't have tons of assistants and writers doing my research and looking for ideas. In many cases, I'm the one on the phone, calling my sources, sniffing out the important information. I figure I know the story better than the person sitting in a newsroom who may not have been talking to people or have been in the field, checking real economic indicators and meeting the CEOs and money managers.

Some people think they need to learn million-dollar theories and use fancy jargon to understand investing. They think there's a special club with a secret handshake that they have to be a member of to understand the significance of earnings expectations and price-to-earnings (P/E) ratios.

I taught myself about the financial markets, and in my experience it really comes down to common sense and doing your homework. That's what will help you separate the news from the noise so that you feel more comfortable researching and evaluating your investments.

I know what you're going to say. You're going to say, "But, Maria, this is your job. It's different for you." I'll admit, it's different because I do this every day. That means that I've got access to contacts who might not be available to ordinary investors. I know where to go to dig up the information I need. I know which financial analysts' opinions are more objective than others.

But much of that information is now available to you.

Today individual investors can access much of the same information that professionals do. As a result, individuals can research, trade, and invest in the same way that money managers and institutional investors do.

Ordinary people keep getting savvier about investing. About a year ago I traveled to Washington to do a story on the Securities and Exchange Commission (SEC). The driver of my taxi back to the airport was wearing dreadlocks and had reggae music blasting, a total contrast to the white-collar market professionals I had just left. We rode along for a few minutes; then he turned down the radio and said, "Maria, can I ask you a question? Do you think oil stocks are going to go up or down?" I was surprised that he knew me but even more surprised that he was worried about oil at the very time it was about to move higher and weigh on stocks. In fact, oil had been at the time one of the best-performing groups in a market that was otherwise trading down considerably. It turned out that he owned some oil stocks, and we ended up having a most informed discussion about the valuations and fundamentals of the oil industry until we got to the airport.

Another time, my husband and I were on vacation in Lake Tahoe. We walked into a restaurant, and the parking valet said, "Maria, what are you doing here? The unemployment numbers are coming out tomorrow. We're watching the tight labor market. Go back to New York!" It was an intelligent comment from an informed individual. The unemployment numbers were coming out the next day and the bond market was moving on expectations of a jump in employment.

The traditional view of the brokerage and investment community is not to credit the individual with any market insight. You've all heard the apocryphal story of how in 1929, Joseph P. Kennedy (JFK's father) realized that the market had gotten out of hand when his shoe-shine boy offered him a stock tip. That helped breed an institutional mentality of "Oh, God, the individual is buying stocks. I'm out of here!"

That mentality has begun to change but it's still entrenched. One money manager said to me, "Maria, there's so much speculation out there." His proof: Every week he took the shuttle flight from New York to Washington, and every week he got his coffee at the same Dunkin' Donuts concession at the airport. One day he noticed that there was a television behind the counter and it was tuned to CNBC. "They're picking stocks," he moaned to me. "This is speculation." I said, "Why assume that these women are speculating? Why assume that they're throwing their money at companies they don't know anything about? Why can't the women at Dunkin' Donuts invest intelligently too?"

The difference today is that there has been an information explosion and there is valuable information out there accessible to the individual. It's a fact. So the mentality that the individual knows nothing about investing just does not stand up anymore.

The landscape of the playing field has shifted. It's up to you to shift your playing style and adapt to the new conditions. It can't hurt—and it might very well help.

Can individuals compete against the professionals? I think the pros still have their place, but the individual sometimes has a leg up.

The reason is that fund managers are under intense pressure to beat the performance of the Standard & Poor's (S&P) 500 Index. They're gauged on a quarterly basis, so every three months their record is compared to the S&P index. Consequently, these fund managers are pressured to buy what's going up.

Now let's say that IBM is down because of worries about Y2K, or Cisco Systems is down because of worries about an economic slowdown. These may well be real worries, but are they short-term or long-term worries? Most mutual fund managers face the prospect of being judged by quarterly reports comparing them to their peers and the benchmark S&P 500 index. If they believe that nothing will move the stock by the end of the quarter—just three months' time—they won't touch it. They need performance, and if the stock doesn't move, they're toast.

The individual, however, has the freedom to take the long view. The individual does not have to feel the pressure of immediate satisfaction or the pressure of experiencing a gain in Cisco or IBM or anything else over a three-month period. So if a stock is reacting to a short-term phenomenon, it can actually end up being an opportunity for an investor with a long-term time line, even though it may take a year, even five years, before the investor gets the satisfaction that he or she may be looking for.

The individual also has the luxury of sifting through information as it becomes available. Markets change. Maybe a company's prospects improved from January to March; maybe it announced a new product line that it will introduce over the next two years or the formation of a strategic partnership that will open up a new market. Now maybe the stock is more attractive. The point is that the individual doesn't have to make snap judgments. He or she has the time to evaluate a company's story and decipher news from noise.

That's where the individual investor with the right research and homework can and should successfully compete against the institutional traders. That one fact—that the individual is not judged on a three-month period—is enough.

You'll note that I differentiate between investors and traders. Repeat after me: Investing is very different from trading. And here's the corollary: Leave short-term trading to the people who are forced to do it.

Professionals still deliver valuable services. They can help you articulate your financial goals and prepare a plan to help you meet them. They can determine the level of financial risk you're comfortable with. They can advise you about special tax concerns that might affect your investing. They can sort through the more than six thousand different mutual funds now offered. More than twenty million Americans rely on a pool of about a half-million investment professionals to help them manage their portfolios.

There's nothing wrong with that. Sometimes there's comfort in knowing that some person is watching my finances every day while I'm concentrating on my day job. But the bar has been raised because the money manager is no longer the *only* person watching my money; I am watching my money as well. I know that in three months I'm going to see a quarterly statement, and I understand the business better than I ever have. So the person watching my money had better be good, because the market for investor dollars is far too competitive for me to settle for mediocrity right now.

Many investors buy mutual funds on the recommendation of their broker or financial adviser. That's fine; there's nothing wrong with a good recommendation. But it takes barely five minutes online or ten minutes in the reference section of your local library to check the Morningstar or Lipper ratings for the fund at www.morningstar.com or www.lipper.com and see how the fund's returns compare to the S&P index. If the S&P index routinely outperforms the fund manager, that fund's investors should know so they can decide whether to switch to an index fund.

Or take the issue of analysts' research. It used to be that analysts were never questioned. Now their picks are scrutinized constantly—and they should be. *Institutional Investor* and the *Wall Street Journal* rank analysts on a yearly basis. Two of my favorite websites are www.bulldogresearch.com and www.validea.com. These websites zero in on analysts' track records, so if I mention on the air that Merrill Lynch analyst Jessica Reif Cohen down-graded Disney, Bulldog Research or Validea will provide a history of her past five years of recommendations to see if her calls actually made money.

Why should you pay an analyst for research that you can look up your-self? Of course, if an analyst has some compelling data that no one else can get, he or she deserves to be celebrated. But those star analysts, like top people in any field, have become few and far between. As a result of the information overload, analysts are just as prone to let the trees obscure the view of the forest as ordinary investors are.

I don't agree with people who feel they don't have an hour in their day and a few hours in their week to sit down and go through their portfolio. After all, aren't we all the CEOs of our own households? I'm very busy too, but it is my money and I find the time to look at my 401(k) receipt, skim the quarterly prospectus from the mutual funds, see what stocks the funds have invested in and make sure I'm comfortable with choices made by my fund managers. (I own only mutual funds, which I purchased about ten years ago and haven't touched. I do not trade in individual stocks because I talk about so many companies that I feel it would be a conflict of inter-est.) While I rarely make changes to my 401(k) account, because it's very long-term oriented and I look at it strictly as retirement income, I love see-ing where my money went over the last quarter. I love to curl up in a chair and scrutinize my company savings report.

I also disagree with people who feel that this information is too sophis-ticated for them. I was not a business nerd and I learned it. Now it's what I live and breathe. I understand that not everyone can be immersed in it like I am. I understand that you're not going to become a great investor overnight. I understand that you may not want to become one. But edu-cating yourself about the stock market is not over your head. To say other-wise is a cop-out.

Besides, you already have some experience. Here's what Arthur R. Hogan III, chief market strategist of Jefferies & Company, says about that: "You know how to go through the process of buying a stock because you already do it when you research a car or a personal computer or a refrigerator or any major con-sumer durable that you want to buy. You read up on it, you talk to your neighbor or coworker, and that gives you the background information to learn enough to make your decision. And the basic routine is the same when you're looking at a stock or evaluating an industry sector.

"You know how to separate the news from the noise in the other purchases of your life. You see some advertisement touting the new Honda Accord because it has seven cup holders or the latest Volkswagen Beetle because it comes in 'cloud.' That's noise. But if you want to buy it because it's the only car that will fit into your garage or because it gets forty miles to the gallon—that's news. What grocery store do you shop at? What's the fat content of the milk you drink? Why did you choose that cell phone over the others? Believe me, you do a lot more research for things that are part of your daily routine than you know, and the same tools are appropriate in analyzing what your investment portfolio should look like."

Be aware of what's happening in your life and in your neighbors' lives. Has there been a lot of building or remodeling going on on your block? Are you and your neighbors buying new cars more frequently or taking vacations more often? Do you compare notes about how much you are paying for gasoline? Those indicators are some of the most obvious signs of what's happening in the economy, and they're right under your nose. They can supply that one crucial nugget of information that you might have ignored because you assumed that the guy in Minneapolis who is watching your investment portfolio knew better. (Of course, now you know that this same guy is making trading decisions based on the need to beat the S&P 500 every three months.) All the activities that are part of our daily life can be applied to deciphering what's news and what's noise. Trust your instincts.

Markets change all the time. Even if you want to go the full-service route and pay someone to pick your portfolio, you need to understand where your money is so you can at least form an opinion on it.

Just because your money is in a mutual fund doesn't mean you can forget about it. The mutual fund company won't tell you what stocks it's buying now, but at the end of every quarter, it has to report the stocks it's invested in. After looking through the quarterly lists of various funds, you might discover that 60 percent of your money is in Microsoft or 20 percent of your money is in Wal-Mart. You don't have to make changes, but it's helpful to know exactly where your money is so that you can keep up with the news flow and arm yourself with the information you need.

Investors have won independence, but with independence comes responsibility. I don't think it's responsible to hand your money off to someone else and not know what that person is doing for it. I don't think full service without any thought process is responsible. Having said that, I don't think trading online without having done your homework is responsible either.

I remember back during the excitement over the dotcom phenomenon in 1999 and 2000, the biggest group of investors in Internet stocks were Internet users. Individuals were going online, exploring sites, and then deciding to invest in the companies that owned those sites purely because of the sites' popularity, their "stickiness," or their ultracool graphics and whizbang features. There was little or no examination of the companies' fundamentals. This sort of investment behavior was highly criticized by many professionals, and in retrospect clearly the professionals were right. Throughout 2000's volatility we all learned that many traders invested in stocks that they knew little about. Today we see how irresponsible that was.

I think an individual has a responsibility to feel comfortable with what he or she is investing in. That comfort level can only come from doing your homework. Only once you've done your homework will you be able to understand how the stock market works and learn to distinguish between news and noise.

Getting Your Arms around Information

Learning to handle the information explosion is not an easy task. The fax, the phone, the e-mail, the meetings—oh my, is it the weekend yet?

As a business journalist, I have to follow a lot of industries and subjects. I constantly have to be ready to discuss the semiconductor sector or the oil industry or any other group.

One week in December 2000, I was anchoring *Squawk Box,* CNBC's morning show, and was told our guests included the CEO of Vertex Pharmaceuticals, the CEO of OSI Networks, and an analyst following the utilities sector. That's just one show. Later that same day, on CNBC's *Street Signs,* I interviewed the CEO of Cendant Corporation, a personal computer (PC) analyst to discuss companies like Dell and Compaq, and an overall market watcher who discussed broader market trends. Later that day at 5:00 p.m., I sat down with the CEO of ExxonMobil. And I haven't even told you about the biggest interview of all on *Market Week,* which I'll get to later. This is what I do every day for every show, and I have to be thoroughly prepared for each one.

On one show one week I might focus on business-to-business (B2B) Internet commerce, an area I know pretty well. But another week I might focus on the leisure sector. Now this is not a sector that I look at every day.

I don't know the major players any more than you may know the companies or industries you're thinking of investing in. But I've got two analysts lined up to interview about hotels, gaming, and cruise stocks. So I ask myself, How do I prepare for this interview? How do I approach learning about the companies that are in this sector?

Each week on *Market Week* I interview the CEO of a company that is going to be in the news. (We focus on upcoming catalysts on *Market Week*.) One week it could be the head of Oracle, another week the head of Merck, another week the head of Southwest Airlines. How should I attack each of those interviews? What questions would elicit useful information and real news for my viewers? How do I come up with those questions?

This is what someone goes through when he or she is deciding to invest in a certain sector or a specific company. So I'll tell you how I went about preparing for an interview with the CEO of ExxonMobil.

First I went online and pulled up a profile of the company. (You can get this through any investment portal, such as CNBC.com or Yahoo Finance. I describe my favorite websites in more detail in the appendix.) I took a look at the company's income statement and compared earnings growth over the past five years. Then I pulled up a chart of the stock and looked at what the stock had done over the past year, the past three years, the past five years, and the past ten years. I immediately discovered an interesting fact. I realized that while ExxonMobil was going to be the most profitable company in the world that year, as of July 2000 the chart line was virtually horizontal. The stock was up only 8 percent, which made it an S&P 500 laggard.

Next I gathered up all the analysts' reports from the research firms that cover ExxonMobil to try to figure out what was going on. I read through them looking for hot buttons for the interview.

Here's one area in which being a professional makes it easier for me to get proprietary research that isn't readily available to individual investors. There's no set fee for analysts' reports; they're part of the "value-added" package the investment banks provide their institutional clients to justify the commissions they charge. The average institutional customer pays between $1 million and $2 million a year in commissions to the sell-side firms. In return, the customer gets trades executed, has the opportunity to buy shares in IPOs or secondary offerings, and receives investment ideas and research reports, as well as other perks, such as private meetings with the CEO of companies it has a big stake in. One trader pegged the value of his firm's research at $10 a page, but there's no official price tag to be put on research.

However, this information isn't inaccessible to individual investors. You might have to work a little harder to get it, but it's available in a variety of places. For example, I often mention the latest analysts' reports in my morning call for *Squawk Box*. After I report on them, they can be accessed on CNBC.com. You can also access a synopsis of the reports from news links on your investment portal. If you have an account at one of the brokerage firms covering the stock, you can get that firm's take on it. And many other firms publish their reports or in-depth analyst interviews on their Internet sites for free, such as US Bancorp Piper Jaffray's www.gotoanalysts.com, Wit Soundview Capital's www.witsoundview.com, and Robertson Stephens's www.rsco.com. (Just keep in mind that analysts' reports are not always the unbiased, evenhanded research conclusions that you might like. I explain why and discuss the significance of analysts' reports more fully in Chapter 9.)

Back to ExxonMobil: For starters, gasoline prices were at ten-year highs, and that's something that the world cares about. As a driver I'm at the gas station once a week filling my tank, and every time I fill my tank it costs about $35. So that's Big Issue Number One.

Number Two: Exxon and Mobil merged in 1998 in a $75 billion deal. That's a big, big deal. How is the integration of the two companies going? Exxon is already one of the largest companies in the world. The merger with Mobil makes it enormous. Does that take away the company's ability to be nimble? Is it *too* big? I looked back to the company's press releases when it announced the deal—a cinch to call up from the company's own website. They talked about cost savings of $3.8 billion. Seven months later, are those cost savings projections on track? How's the marriage going? What's the company culture like?

I then scrutinized the management team, as part of my routine due diligence. How long had CEO Lee Raymond been in charge? How has the stock performed under him over that time frame? What's his salary? And what kind of stock options does he have? How much does he make compared to what shareholders have made? Is there a direct incentive for him if this company does well?

Those questions led directly to the $64,000 question: What's wrong with the stock? Oil prices were high, which was bad for consumers but great for Exxon. Eighteen months earlier, when oil was $10 a barrel, OPEC (the Organization of Petroleum Exporting Companies) promised that it would lower production to boost the prices. It also promised that it wouldn't let the price exceed the target price of the upper twenties. Well, a year and a half later, crude oil was going for $33 a barrel. So I wanted to know if Exxon had any idea of what OPEC was going to do? Would it keep quotas in force or raise production to lower prices? How would Exxon react? And what effect would that have on the stock? Would that keep the stock in the dumps for the rest of the year or would it suddenly look like an undiscovered value?

I figured that these questions covered the important issues, but just to make sure I called the top institutional holders, industry analysts, and money managers to find out what was on their minds. They filled in the blanks and that's how I came up with my final list of questions.

At the time of the interview, ExxonMobil had a market capitalization of over $315 billion. That's intimidating. But by the time I finalized my list of questions, it was no longer intimidating. I felt I could get my arms around the company, and I came away from the interview feeling that I had a very good take on the company.

My point is, the oil business is not second nature to me. But I figured out how to get my arms around the story because I had a basic plan, a framework into which to fit the information. That's the first and most useful tool in separating news from noise.

What do I mean by framework? It's how you view the world. You're constantly sifting news from noise in your daily life; now you just need to apply that discipline to an investment philosophy. It doesn't matter whether you are a growth investor, a value investor, a momentum investor or an investor who uses a blindfold and a dartboard (although I certainly hope you're not the latter). Your fundamental framework will provide a radar screen that will enable you to distinguish potential red flags from things you don't need to worry about.

It's astonishing how many individual investors disregard it. Here's Robert A. Loest, senior portfolio manager for IPS Millennium Funds: "Probably the most fundamental problem I run into when talking to groups of individual investors is that they never put in place the rules of the game. They never decide what they're going to look at from a top-down fashion and what they're not going to look at. So they never know what to ignore and what not to ignore. So they get overwhelmed. Duh."

Loest builds his framework on value creation. "You have to ask from the standpoint of an industry sector and an individual company: are they doing something that makes people's lives easier and better and is worth the cost and trouble to implement? We think value is created when companies drive down the cost of what used to be a critical limited resource, like food or power or information or bandwidth. Historically, companies that have driven down those costs are where the value has gone. That shows me that I don't need to pay attention to a whole range of sectors of the economy like retail stocks, restaurant stocks, automobile stocks or railroads. They have already done the things that added all the value; they have expanded all they can.

"If an industry sector is growing at 2 percent a year, you can just ignore it. That philosophy helps you read a lot less of the newspaper. From an investment standpoint, there's a lot of news in the newspaper that has to do with areas of the Old Economy where there's not a lot of growth, or areas where the products have been commoditized and management has no control over growth, like PCs or automobiles or lumber. So if there's a big article on the tire industry, you can ignore it.

"I talk to lots of investment clubs. I remember asking one club for its stock portfolio. So help me, they had alphabetized their stocks. That means that they look at every single stock in the world to decide whether they ought to buy it. I told them the first thing they should do is group those stocks into investment sectors and pick the sectors that make the most sense to them. That way, at least they know what sectors they're interested in and where they're placing their bets. They can see if they're overweighting any sector of the economy, and they can begin viewing the economy in larger terms.

"Don't ask yourself, 'Is this stock going to grow fast?' Instead, ask yourself, 'Is this sector going to grow rapidly?' Let's say you're considering buying stock in Krispy Kreme doughnuts. Why? Because the CEO said they were going to grow earnings at 15 percent a year. That's nice, but unless the police forces double in size all across this country, you can bet the company won't grow 15 percent a year because the sector is growing only a couple of percentage points a year. Asking yourself this sort of question will help you from getting sidetracked by company statements saying they can grow 20 percent a year even if the sector is growing only 2 percent. [As it turns out, Krispy Kreme tripled its IPO price in less than nine months, and remains one of the top-performing IPOs on record.]

"If you don't have some understanding of where a sector's value is and how it's created, you don't know where to look to invest—and what to ignore. If you have a clear idea, it's easier to look at certain segments of the economy and say, 'They don't know how to create value, so I'll look elsewhere.'"

That's Loest's framework. Other investors use other frameworks. It doesn't really matter which type you choose, so long as you're comfortable with it. In other words, it should be something you understand and with a level of risk that allows you to sleep at night.

Once you have the framework of your investing philosophy in place, you can choose to follow the stock on a daily basis or much less frequently, depending on your time and level of interest. The main thing is that you have a framework in which to evaluate new information about the stock. Like polarized sunglasses, it will help you see things more clearly.

The Three Steps I Take in Deciding Whether It's News or Noise

I can't help you figure out your investment philosophy; that's not my area of expertise. But I *can* help you handle information overload. When I get new information about a company that I'm researching, I follow three steps in deciding whether it's news or noise.

First, I Focus

Let's assume you've invested in a biotechnology company. You've already done your basic homework on a company. You know that earnings have grown consistently at 30 percent for the past five years, the company has a great lineup of existing products, and its pipeline is full of promising future products. You know that the majority of the analysts have rated the company a strong buy. You've seen interviews with the CEO and were impressed by his or her intelligence, strategy, and candor. I'm always impressed with CEOs who tell it straight. In good times or bad, if they communicate well and discuss issues frankly, investors will usually listen and support them. In short, you have confidence in the company and feel really comfortable owning this stock.

Now let's say that the company gets hit in a big sell-off of biotechnology stocks. Is this sell-off news or noise?

I constantly look for indications of whether the competitive landscape has shifted. One of the instigators of the technology slump of autumn 2000 was that Apple Computer and Intel both preannounced that their earnings would fall below expectations. Both companies blamed weakening demand for the PC in Europe. At the time we did not know that the U.S. economy was slowing down too and how much it would affect earnings across the entire tech sector.

Have these issues affected the company that you're interested in? How much revenue does the company derive from Europe or Asia? Maybe the company deems Europe or Asia an unimportant market. Has the growth of the company slowed? Has anything else changed to alter your initial expectations? Your company could have gotten caught in the tech sell-off unnecessarily. A clear focus on the company behind the stock could have kept you from getting lost in the noise and possibly spotlighted one significant piece of news: namely, that the stock price was down 20 percent, so you might be able to pick it up at a bargain.

Focus can help you steer more clearly through confusing hype. There's been a lot of excitement about applying the cost- and time-saving efficiencies of business-to-consumer (B2C) e-commerce to the automotive industry. In 1999, the two largest U.S. automotive corporations, Ford and General Motors (GM), put together a B2C exchange to sell auto parts together online. It sounded exciting and there was a lot of movement in the stocks of those companies. Was it news or noise?

The answer: It was noise. Maybe this exchange is going to be fruitful for the consumer who wants to buy auto parts online, but if it's not something that Ford is doing itself or GM is doing itself, then it's probably not going to have an impact on the individual companies. The most important gauge of a company's growth is earnings. That has not changed in a lifetime. The investor has to ask: How important is this exchange to *earnings?* How much earnings growth is going to be derived at Ford from this B2C exchange? If you can't answer these questions, then you've got a red flag signaling noise.

As it turned out, there already was something going on at Ford that was newsworthy and influential enough to influence shareholder value. Ford had initiated its own online effort and was aggressively using the Internet to cut costs and sell its products. Doing your homework would have revealed that Ford was the better investment opportunity—at that time.

Later that year the competitive landscape presented a different picture. A sharp slowdown in economic growth and a resulting hit to auto sales was compounded by Ford's recall of Bridgestone/Firestone tires, sending Ford's stock down 20 percent in 2000. Meanwhile, GM's prospects were looking brighter in advance of its spin-off of Hughes Electronics.

Even without the tire recall, Ford would have suffered from an economy that went from 5.6 percent growth quarter over quarter to no growth in less than a year. This is why you need to measure your own investment ideas against the broader context of the performance of the industry group and the economy. When investing in economically sensitive companies, you need to look at the biggest possible picture.

Focus means paying attention to the news and ignoring the noise. When I broadcast from the floor of the NYSE, I'm frequently reporting in the middle of action. There are traders buying and selling all around me, so there's a lot of noise coming in one ear. I have an earpiece in my other ear with a direct feed to the studio and control room where the audio guy may be asking me to count to ten so that he knows my microphone is okay. Meanwhile, I'm trying to think about the notes I've prepared from my research earlier that morning so that I know what I want to say and how I want to present it.

So, I focus. I zero in on exactly what I need to do now, namely, deliver the news. I ignore the noise of the traders, I give my audio guy his ten-count without thinking and I get to work. I have been called a multitasker, and I find it's not that difficult to do with a little focus.

Focus is an especially useful tool when companies are reporting earnings. (I'll explain in more depth how to evaluate an earnings report in Chapter 8.) A company's earnings may look weak on initial notice and the noise about weak earnings may mask what's really going on. A closer read of the earnings release may reveal that its earnings were affected by charges that the company had to write down. Those charges may have been due to acquisitions or other onetime events that might, in fact, be beneficial to the company in the future. Conversely, the company's earnings may look strong, but the stock slumps. A closer examination of its earnings report could show some concern about where the revenue will come from in the future. Sorting through an earnings release may provide the focus that will prevent you from making the wrong decision about the company.

Focus helps you see the big picture. A lot of analysts and portfolio managers use the analogy of putting together a jigsaw puzzle without the box cover that has the original picture on it. Each new nugget of information, each additional data point is a piece of the puzzle. As you start to fill in the puzzle, you get a sense of the big picture. You can see the important parts of the puzzle and, even more important, you can see where the holes are.

As you focus in on those holes you've discovered in your jigsaw puzzle picture, you will have generated a list of significant issues for the company or sector, which act as the springboard for the next step.

Next, I Ask Questions

Ask lots of questions about the company or the sector. I group my questions into two categories: headline questions and analysis questions. The first are the basic questions, the kind of topics that may seem obvious but are fundamental to the operations of the company or sector. Build out the answers to the headline questions with analysis questions. The analysis questions go into more depth and may be specific to the company or sector.

Any question, even one on a topic that doesn't apply, is a good question. For instance, government intervention in the PC sector is just not a big issue. But in asking that question—and learning the answer—you'll increase your overall knowledge of the sector. Then you can bat the question out of the way.

I tend to ask a lot of questions, but initially you don't have to go into the same detail. Don't overthink this, because otherwise you'll start to panic about where to find information about customers and suppliers. Just try to get a good sense of where the money is coming from and where it's going. Who's buying the product, who's supplying the company with that product, how is it sold, and how well is it selling? In other words, how do things work?

It's like evaluating the likelihood of making money from your lemonade stand. How much does it cost to buy the lemons and sugar? How much can you sell a glass of lemonade for? Are there a lot of potential lemonade-drinking customers in your neighborhood? Is there some little kid who will try to cut your prices and destroy your business? I know this sounds simplistic, but believe me, evaluating a company's business prospects is really not as complicated as you might think.

My Favorite Questions

Here are my favorite headline questions and subsequent analysis questions. (I explain how to find the answers throughout the rest of the book.) Keep in mind that some of these questions may not be relevant at all. You just want to give yourself a checklist, so you can check it off and say, "Yup, I've looked under that rock."

❏ *Headline Question.* What has been the growth rate of this company?

❏ *Analysis Questions.* How have earnings grown over the last three and five years or, if the company is young, over its entire history? What has driven that growth? How have revenues grown? Which unit, division, or product contributes the most to earnings and revenue growth? For example, what percentage of IBM's revenues comes from PCs rather than mainframes?

❏ *Headline Question.* Is there reason to believe that the current growth rate will be sustained or accelerated in the future?

❏ *Analysis Questions.* Will demand for the current product or products accelerate? Or is there a new product that will keep that growth level up?

❏ *Headline Questions.* What about the rest of the industry? What is its overall growth potential? What were the most recent annual industry sales? Where does your company fit in terms of market share?

❏ *Analysis Questions.* Who are the company's competitors? Have their growth rates been picking up compared to the company you're interested in? Who are the company's complementors, the other businesses from whom customers buy complementory products (e.g., cars need gasoline and parts, and gasoline needs cars; computers need software and parts, and software needs computers).

Most of the time the interests of the company and its complementors are aligned. However, new technologies and new approaches can change the relative influence of the complementors or cause a break in the alignment. For example, for years the relationship between Microsoft and PC makers was indivisible. Then Linux software began making inroads and most of the major PC manufacturers now offer a choice of software operating platforms.

What is the company's percentage of market share compared to its competitors? If you have a company like Intel, which commands about 80 percent of the semiconductor market for PCs, who has the other 20 percent and is that company increasing its foothold? You want to get a sense of where this company fits into the broader picture.

❏ *Headline Question.* Who are the main customers? Are they consumers or other corporations?

❏ *Analysis Questions.* Are those customers buying more or less of the product? Let's investigate that a little. If the consumer is the main customer, what is the consumer economy like? Does the consumer have a lot of disposable income, or is he or she slowing down spending? Similarly, what forces might affect corporate spending? At the end of 1999, many corporations postponed major computer hardware and software purchases because of fears of Y2K problems. In the second half of 2000, the worry was that networking equipment makers and semiconductor manufacturers would be affected if telecom companies cut back their spending levels. If Nokia slows production, Cisco gets zapped. If consumers don't buy as many PCs, Intel and AMD won't sell as many microprocessors and Microsoft won't ship as many boxes of Windows. If the end users, meaning you and me, stop buying from Nokia, it will slow its ordering of parts by Nortel. Nortel may slow its buying of circuits by Applied Micro Circuits.

Throughout most of 2000, the slowdown in technology had much to do with the slowdown in information technology spending by big corporations. Shortly before the turn of the millennium, many corporations had ramped up their spending as they bought new equipment and upgraded their systems in preparation for Y2K. Once they had up-to-date computers, software, servers, and Internet platforms, there was no need to buy more.

Furthermore, the death of the dotcoms added to the inventory buildup. One by one, each sector took a hit in the tech sell-off of 2000 and 2001. Still, many people thought the storage and server companies would be immune. Then in February 2001, Merrill Lynch analyst Tom Kraemer downgraded Sun Microsystems, saying that the inventory backlog had reached a three-year high, exacerbated by the increasing availability of used equipment from dead dotcoms. Kraemer predicted that it would take at least three quarters to burn through all of Sun's excess servers and that price cuts would be necessary to move inventory out of the warehouse.

❏ *Headline Question.* Who are the suppliers?

❏ *Analysis Questions.* The supplier is just as important to a company's health as the customer. How much does it cost the supplier to manufacture the parts? How easy is it to ship them to its customers? When a major earthquake struck Taiwan, home to the world's major manufacturers of motherboards for laptop computers, companies like Dell and Gateway were forced to cut back production. The resulting drop in sales showed up in disappointing quarterly earnings.

❏ *Headline Questions.* What does the company spend most of its money on? Where are its biggest expenses?

❏ *Analysis Question.* Railroads and airlines, for example, spend huge amounts of money on oil; if oil prices skyrocket, how will that affect the bottom line? Satellite companies pay big bucks to construct and launch their communications satellites; if a launch goes awry, the company is out of pocket in a big way.

❏ *Headline Questions.* Is there a seasonality to the business? Is there a certain time of year when new products traditionally are introduced or when there's a predictable increase in business?

❏ *Analysis Questions.* The retailing sector has a real seasonality. Two-thirds of all retail sales occur during the two-month period before and including the Christmas holiday. That's a major "what if." As in, What if the weather is so warm that people don't buy big-ticket winter coats? What if bonuses plummet so people don't have as much disposable income?

❏ *Headline Question.* Who is running the show?

❏ *Analysis Questions.* How has the stock done under him or her? How old is the CEO? Is there a chance he or she may retire soon? What kind of succession plan is in place? How is turnover at the company? Is there new talent coming in? And, more critical, is important talent leaving?

❏ *Headline Question.* What is the operating environment for the industry sector?

❏ *Analysis Questions.* Is this an industry that is subject to government regulations or the political environment? The tobacco industry was hit with a

$400 billion liability in the United States; if this is not reversed, tobacco companies will be paying this fine for years to come. How will that affect their earnings? Does this liability change with a new political administration? The automotive companies are waiting to see whether California's recent regulations mandating a growing percentage of "green" cars that emit fewer pollutants will spread to other states. In 2000, utilities in California were on the verge of bankruptcy because state regulators did not allow them to pass high energy costs on to customers. These companies' fortunes in effect depended on a decision by the California Utilities Commission.

Don't ignore the negative questions. When considering investing in a company, you must remind yourself of the bear slant. Ask yourself, What is wrong or could go wrong with this picture? Is the company prepared to take appropriate action?

Once you've gone through the pertinent fundamentals, you can examine the company's stock. Focusing solely on the stock and evaluating it through market volume and price studies is what's called technical analysis.

❑ *Headline Question.* How has the stock acted?

❑ *Analysis Questions.* Pull up the stock chart from one of the online finance portals to see the short- and long-term perspectives. Where is it year-to-date? What has it done over the past six months? Over the longer term? Maybe it's been up 200 percent over the past five years, but over the last six months it's been down 50 percent. This might tell you to have your antenna up for a problem that may be developing right now. Often the trading of the stock will tell you what's to come.

Have you seen dollars moving into or out of the stock? I'll explain later how to gauge how what Wall Street likes to call the smart money—big institutions and mutual fund portfolio managers—feels about the stock. Are they buying or selling? That will indicate market sentiment about this stock.

What is Wall Street saying about the stock? Call up the analyst coverage to see the analyst ratings: What's the number of strong buys, of buys, of holds? When was the last rating change and by which analyst? Have they been right? Or have the analysts been just mouthpieces for company executives? For reasons I'll explain in Chapter 9, you always want to take what analysts say with more than a few grains of salt, but you want to know what the consensus on the Street is about this particular company. Why might Wall Street have a "buy" rating on the stock when it's already up so much? Why might it be recommending a "sell" when it seems to be doing well?

And, of course, check out the same criteria for the company's competitors. You always want to compare companies not only fundamentally but also technically, that is, against the performance of their sector.

Finally, I Put the Answers in Context

Look for answers to your headline and analysis questions. However, as you look for answers, there's one important caveat to keep in mind, and that's the third step in this process: put it in context.

Knowing the context of the answers—recognizing whether the data points will clarify or cloud your investment picture—helps you evaluate information so that you can decide whether it is news or noise. It enables you to channel the information flow, prioritize the important pieces of information, and discard the nonessential items that are a waste of time. It acts as a filter for news sources, screening out agendas and biases so that you make an objective judgment.

Context is especially important when you evaluate popular news for investment ideas. It's what legendary portfolio manager Peter Lynch made millions on.

His stipulation to invest in what you know is as credible as ever. It's no secret why the Snapple initial public offering (IPO) was such a great performer; kids loved the drink and the purchaser of the household would have known that. Three years ago my nephew was going crazy over Pokémon. So I wasn't surprised that Kid Entertainment, the company that distributes Pokémon, soared. Similarly, five years ago a friend came back from Asia and reported that everyone was chatting on Nokia mobile phones. Two years later the wave hit the United States, and Nokia stock skyrocketed. Today the trend of handheld devices is much more prevalent in Asia than in the U.S.

Of course, many of these trends were temporary, and clearly you should not rely on only these data when making an investment decision. I mention them because they are important phenomena that may tip off an investor that a broader trend is occurring that may be worth investigating.

Putting information in context can also clue you in as to when to sell. A friend had owned Microsoft for years and had profited handsomely from it. Then one day he went to his local Sam's Club, a discount warehouse for Wal-Mart, in search of a computer learning game for his three-year-old daughter. Much to his surprise, he saw that a bunch of the computer learning games were based not on Microsoft's operating system but on Linux. Up until that point Linux had been considered an upstart rival but not a serious competitor. My friend figured, though, that if Linux was so popular that it was being used as a platform for kids' computer learning games that were being sold through Wal-Mart's discount warehouse, then Microsoft was losing market share. At the same time, Microsoft was on trial for monopolistic practices, so my friend knew that it would be difficult for the company to regain its former market share. He sold his Microsoft holdings in the fall of 1999; the stock price declined nearly 40 percent in the next year.

This sort of information isn't always going to work, but more often than not, where there's smoke, there's fire. And knowing the context helps you evaluate the news that's coming in so that you can more accurately predict how dangerous the fire will be.

One of the greatest benefits of the information explosion is that the answers to your questions are more readily available to you than ever before. They're available in print and on television and on the Internet. For example, you may not have the opportunity to pick the brain of the CEO of a company, but you do have access to his knowledge either by watching an interview on television, reading a profile in a magazine or newspaper, or researching the subject online. Maybe you'll even log on to his quarterly conference call to analysts, available on the company's website.

There's a surprising amount of useful investment information in the popular press, not just in the personal finance pages. News is like a needle in a haystack; it's sitting right in front of you but it may be hidden by noise.

When *Time* and *Newsweek* run a cover story about the search for an AIDS vaccine or the latest breakthrough in biotechnology, they're writing about one of the most important sectors of the economy. You might learn something new about the specific companies involved in these developments or about the prospects for the sector as a whole. *Newsweek*'s slant might be America's need for these drugs, but your investment slant is in deciding to investigate some of these companies, which happen to be publicly traded. It's no coincidence then that biotech stocks were among the best performers of 2000, a year when most stocks lost value.

Energy was one of the major stories of 2000. A telltale sign of the growing energy shortage was the brownouts in California. The fact that electricity was in such short supply was great news for companies like Calpine, Duke Energy, Entergy, and Enron. The fact that oil prices were surging was great for integrated oil drilling and refining companies. On the downside, airlines were hit with mammoth cost overruns. And higher prices at the gas pump cut into consumers' disposable income so they might not have as much money to buy clothes or remodel their houses, which, in turn, would affect retail stocks and companies like Home Depot and Lowe's.

Television news is one of the major contributors to the information explosion. As such, it's come under a lot of criticism for, among other things, encouraging a day-trading mentality. I recognize that criticism, but I do not entirely agree with it. I do not get the feeling from my viewers that they throw money at companies without understanding their businesses.

I meet and talk to viewers all the time. My doorman recently asked me about a garbage-hauling company. At the time I didn't know much about it. He asked me if I could find out what investment professionals were saying about it, because he had bought some shares and was planning to attend the upcoming shareholders meeting. In talking with him I discovered that he was very familiar with the company and already knew all the right data points: he knew that earnings had been growing consistently for the past five years; he knew the management team and the results of their decisions; he even knew that there had been insider buying at the company recently. And he was only one of many doormen in my building who regularly watch stocks.

In fact, all my doormen are active investors. They ask me questions from time to time. Does that worry me? Not at all. These men are intelligent, informed individuals and they're trying to discover their own winners. My feeling has always been: Go for it. Understand the risk and the responsibility that you take on, do your homework, and make your own decisions.

Every day during the "Taking Stock" segment on CNBC in which we interview a money manager and take calls from viewers, I'm pleasantly surprised at the level of detail and understanding that viewers have when asking about a particular company. I feel that my viewers are using the tools that are available to access information about the market.

Of course, there are cases in which people have leveraged their holdings and bought on margin, and that is disastrous. But I do not think that is the overriding trend among the one hundred million people who invest in equities. In fact, I think that kind of irresponsible and dangerous behavior, and the knee-jerk reactions of day-traders, is exactly the opposite of the thoughtful, disciplined research that I hope to encourage with this book. (Incidentally, the blow-up of dotcoms and the resulting loss in market value triggered margin calls, and investors who had bought stocks with borrowed dollars were forced to sell them to pay back what they owed. Today, much of the margin debt has been squeezed out of the market, which makes for a fundamentally healthier market.)

That said, what's news to some on television will be noise to others, and there can be a lot of noise. But while the information that's disseminated may add extraneous pieces to the jigsaw puzzle, it might also supply that crucial piece that completes the picture.

What can an investor learn from watching financial news? You can accumulate as many data points as possible. You can hear both sides of the situation, from the bear who's selling it to the bull who's buying it. You are getting the top stories of the day, whether it's a stock market rally or a stock market sell-off, with real-time data. When a company reports earnings, you get comments from the company executives and commentary from analysts and fund managers.

You can watch an interview with the CEO of a company you might want to invest in and watch that CEO's response to the questions. Did the CEO answer the questions? Did he avoid the questions? Does his story make sense to you? Similarly, individual investors may not be able to get access to analysts' reports, but they can hear the condensed version straight from the horse's mouth during a television interview.

Responsible news networks will always give you two sides of the story. You may be very bullish on a company, but have you heard from the bears? Maybe a stock has been acting well and business is booming, according to the CEO, but the bearish analyst notes that this company doesn't have any follow-up products ready to come out of the pipeline. If you need a reminder of why you should always search out the bearish argument, no matter how muted, remember 2000, when most analysts, who were bullish on many Internet and telecom companies, did not downgrade their ratings on those companies until the stocks went from triple digits to single digits.

Finally, in some cases, you're getting news that might not otherwise be publicly disseminated. I've tripped over a nugget of information like that every now and then. For example, one day, as part of my morning routine for *Squawk Box,* I was skimming Credit Suisse First Boston's "Tech Daily" fax. It mentioned that the highly regarded head of technology sales at i2 Technologies had resigned a week earlier, but Credit Suisse First Boston didn't think it would have a big impact on the business, despite the fact that this unit contributed 40 percent of annual sales.

I looked at it and said, "Wait a second. The head of a division that makes up 40 percent of a company's sales just left?" I went on the major wire services and pulled up Bridge and AP and Dow Jones. There was no mention, no press release, no company acknowledgment that the head of tech sales had resigned.

The stock had been trading up the previous couple of days. But that day, after CSFB's report and my on-air mention, the stock opened down 20 percent. An irate company manager called immediately and asked why I did that story. I asked, "Doesn't this unit account for 40 percent of sales?" Yes. "Did you release this information?" No. "Did you put out a press release?" No. The company claimed the guy's departure wouldn't affect the bottom line, but it was important enough for CSFB to put out a report on it to its clients and I judged it important enough to let other investors know too. Anything that affects a division that accounts for 40 percent of sales to the overall company is newsworthy.

Business television is just one tool in your information research kit. However, watching television is a passive act. You need to couple it with active investigation using other tools to gather enough data points to fill out the picture. Always remember: It's your money. Look under the rocks.

The noise is there, but so is the news. Focusing, asking questions, and putting the answers in context help investors get a handle on the enormous amount of information out there, how to use the right news.

To do that, it's useful to understand what makes markets move.

What Moves Markets

Working at the NYSE is one of the most exciting things I've ever done. A thick sheet of glass separates the CNBC broadcast booth from the balcony railing overlooking the Garage, a large trading floor annexed to the Main Room of the NYSE. On a typical morning, I can hear the hum from the trading floor coming through the glass. During frenetic moments, the hum ratchets up into a roar and the glass vibrates from the noise.

The opening bell clangs at 9:30 a.m., but on busy mornings you'll see knots of brokers already clustered around the posts where the stock for which they have orders is being traded. These posts are enormous kiosks topped by big banks of computer screens showing the latest price of each stock traded at the post. Each company's stock trades at only one post on the floor of the exchange, so you can see where the action is simply by following the crowds.

I'm frequently asked, "Who are all these people anyway?" Well, they're brokers trading for their firms and clerks assisting those brokers; specialists making markets in the stocks they cover; specialists' clerks entering those trades into their computers; and people called "reporters," who work for the NYSE and record large trades into a handheld device, which zaps the news up to the ticker, where it is broadcast to the entire floor. Some of the guys—it's still mostly men, although there's an increasing number of women—are muttering the bid and ask prices into their headsets, covering their mouths with their hands so that no one can overhear or read their lips. Others have their cell phones clapped to their ears or are pawing through their pockets to check their pagers. Some brokers have handheld electronic communicators slung over their shoulders and holstered at their hip, on which they scribble the flow information—how much is for sale, how much is to buy, what other firms are in the crowd and what their orders are—and have it transmitted instantaneously. Brokers on the rim of the huddle are up on their tiptoes, peering over the guys in front of them, trying to shoulder into the action.

Who are they talking to on their headsets and cell phones? Who's receiving the telegrams from the electronic communicators? They're communicating with their booth. Each brokerage house rents a booth along the perimeter of the trading floor. Real estate is hard to come by at the NYSE; a typical broker booth is sixteen inches long, only big enough for a phone and a computer screen. Some of the bigger brokerage firms pay for what are known as superbooths, miniature offices bristling with fax machines, banks of phones, and all sorts of electronic equipment.

As is always the case in real estate, location is everything. The trading floor of the NYSE is actually made up of four huge rooms: the Main Room, the Garage, the Blue Room (guess what color it's painted?), and a new high-tech trading space in the building next door. The brokerage firms want their booths located close to the posts where they do a lot of trading. Time is money, so they don't want a broker to waste precious seconds carrying an order from, say, their booth in the Main Room to the trading post in the Garage, about 90 seconds' brisk walk away. In that time, another buyer may have entered the crowd and as a result the price is now more expensive.

Even the firms that rent space for a superbooth in one room often have smaller sixteen-inch booths sprinkled throughout the other rooms. Back at the brokerage firm's headquarters on Park Avenue or in the World Financial Center or Minneapolis or anywhere else the brokers have printouts of the layout of the floor of the NYSE. They know the location of every post where every stock is traded. If the firm just got a big order from a client at Fidelity Funds or Alliance Capital—funds with a significant amount of dollars behind them—to start selling Chevron, it would put the call through to whichever of the firm's booths is closest to the Chevron post.

The broker walking into the crowd knows his order, but he may not know the full extent of the amount of stock his firm wants to sell.

Information like that can really move a stock. And if the firm wants to sell at the highest price possible, clearly it doesn't want its broker to show his cards because that will move the price lower. That's why brokerage firms play both ends against the middle by hiring freelancers.

Sometimes the brokerage firm will hire a "two-dollar broker." These are independent brokers who will trade for any institution that signs them up; they're called two-dollar brokers because years ago, when they first became popular, institutions paid $2 for their services.

Why hire a two-dollar broker? Maybe he has a very good placement on the floor. Maybe he has time that the firm's own brokers don't. If Merrill Lynch Asset Management wants to load up on AOL Time Warner, it will want a broker in that AOL crowd all the time, every hour of the day, angling to get the best price. It might give a big order—two million shares to buy—and say, "Get me in slowly." The broker will stand in the AOL crowd, along with all the other traders working for other clients—hedge funds, institutions, brokerage firms, mutual fund companies, certain wealthy individuals—and wait for his entry point. He won't show the entire two-million-share order. Instead, he'll put in orders of twenty-five-thousand-share or fifty-thousand-share blocks at a time.

Maybe a big seller comes into the crowd with plans to sell one million shares at $50. The average institutional order is anywhere from one hundred thousand shares to one million or more. Before doing anything, he asks the specialist what the market for that stock is: how much stock is there to buy and how much is there to sell and at what price. Basically, he is waiting to see how the stock trades to see if his initial plan to get $50 per share still makes sense. He's waiting for a better price, so he waits all day and sees how the stock trades. If he feels there's a big buyer looming, he may be more aggressive, selling less at $50 with hopes that that buyer will bite at $51 or even $52. But maybe he realizes that there are three sellers in the crowd, and who knows how much they have to sell? Maybe he'll manage to sell one-quarter of his million-share order at $50, but two days later the stock might be down to $45 due to those other sellers in the crowd. The two-dollar broker needs to do the best thing for his client and he wants to be able to call CSFB, who may be buying the stock for Merrill Lynch Asset Management, and say, "I sold a quarter of your XYZ stock at $50. I know it's down to $45, but I'm still working the order. I think I may be able to get more sold at a higher price."

Or Merrill Lynch might hire a direct-access broker. These are brokers who compete with large brokerage firms' in-house brokers. They stand at one stock post all day, every day, for as long as the firm needs them to. They're called "direct access" because they have a handheld computer strapped to their hip that instantaneously zaps information to their client so the client always knows who's in the crowd, how much stock is for sale, at what price, and by whom. Direct-access brokers are more expensive than two-dollar brokers, and for good reason. That broker may go for weeks before doing anything. She's only testing out the waters, seeing who's buying and selling the stock in order to get a sense of its movement; then she reports her findings back to the firm.

That's why there are so many crowds around the posts. Each trader is trying to get the best possible price for his trade. The only way to get that price is to be part of the crowd.

You can feel the energy pulsing off the floor. Floor brokers are striding from the trading posts back to the brokerage booths lining the walls, their heads down while they scrawl the latest transaction on the order form. Clerks in light blue jackets are eeling through the crowded aisles, delivering the latest orders to brokers, or taking them back to the brokerage booths. The traffic in the aisles is as crowded as Times Square at rush hour, except that no one stands still—at least, not for long. It's estimated that a broker walks an average of twelve miles a day as he or she crisscrosses the floor, and I believe it.

Everyone's scribbling prices on slips of paper as they scurry about— pink slips for the latest stock quotes, white slips for orders. By midmorning, the floor of the exchange will be confettied with discarded orders and quotes, gum wrappers, even empty coffee cups dumped by people too busy to get to a garbage can.

Random phrases punctuate the background noise: "'Scuse me, 'scuse me." "Hey, Frank, I've got fifteen thou at two teenies." "Addy, lemme know when they tighten it up." "Yeah, Peter, talk to me." "Johnny, what're you selling?" "Fifty thou at $18." "'Scuse me, 'scuse me." "Jeez, you guys are killing me!" Underneath, you hear the constant staccato of receivers being slapped back into the hooks of the telephones pegged to every spare piece of wall space.

What's going on down there?

Basically, an enormous auction.

Let's say you want to buy or sell a block—one hundred shares—of IBM. You telephone or e-mail your order into your broker or brokerage house, who passes it along to the brokerage booth at the NYSE. When an order is received at a brokerage booth, it gets passed to a floor broker, who takes it to the trading post for that particular stock. (Small orders get combined into larger ones.)

The actual transactions at the post are handled by a specialist, who stands outside the kiosk. The specialist acts a broker to the brokers. He watches two separate order flows, one from the gesticulating brokers in front of him and one from a computerized trading system, called an electronic book or the NYSE's Superdot System. If a trader back at the UBS Warburg offices on Sixth Avenue in Manhattan has an order for a particular stock, he may not want to waste time having someone physically walk the order over from UBS Warburg's booth to the stock's trading post. He may want that order to get to the specialist as soon as possible, so he'll put it right through to the specialist's electronic book.

The specialist keeps a list of unfulfilled orders in the electronic book, and it's his job to facilitate the transaction from the electronic buy and sell orders and from the brokers in front of him. It's also his responsibility to make an orderly market for a stock. If the spread between the bid and the ask (the gap between the highest price offered by a buyer and the lowest price asked by a seller) becomes too wide, the specialist turns into a dealer himself, buying and selling the stock on his own account. This narrows the spread and stimulates trading.

Just to make matters more complicated, floor brokers aren't restricted to using a specialist. Often floor brokers are standing right next to one another on different sides of a trade. So, in addition to the specialist's trying to make an orderly market, the brokers might start negotiating among themselves, bluffing one another to the best price like players in a high-stakes poker game. Meanwhile, their clients are sitting on the sidelines on the other end of the telephone or the electronic hookup, waiting to find out what price was paid for the stock.

No matter how the trade is accomplished, it still has to be noted by the specialist and recorded by a clerk, who shadows the transactions from inside the kiosk. The computer screens instantly display the stocks being traded, the last sale price, and the order size to everyone standing near the post, while the information is simultaneously transmitted to giant boards above the trading floor and to the trading desks of brokerage houses around the country. Confirmation of the trade is made when the floor broker sends the transaction details back to the branch office where the order originated. Total time elapsed: about five seconds.

Some of the oldest, largest, best-known companies in the world are traded by people on the NYSE. Thousands more are traded by computer and telephone over the electronic Nasdaq network, and still more of the newest and smallest companies list their stocks in the over-the-counter market.

I'm right in the middle of the action, and I mean right in the thick of it, because when I'm reporting from the floor of the NYSE, I stand in one of the busiest avenues of traffic. I'm sandwiched among the posts for IBM, Morgan Stanley Dean Witter, Schering Plough, Viacom, Lucent, and Halliburton. I'm constantly being jostled and elbowed by floor brokers as they rush from their booths to the trading posts and back again. Sometimes it's so noisy that I have to shout into the microphone to make sure I can be heard. Sometimes it's even hard to stay on my feet. It sounds a little nutty, but frankly, I love it.

When I'm reporting from the floor, I'm delivering news in its purest, most basic, most immediate form. Here's one of my favorite stories: It was the day after IBM reported its third-quarter earnings for 2000 (October 18, 2000). Its earnings were in line with the Street's estimates, but IBM management had made cautious comments about the upcoming quarter due to the weakening euro. IBM had closed the day before at $113 and was already down $15 in the premarket, where it had traded through Instinet, an electronic communicating network. IBM is clearly a market leader, so I knew the market was going to be down big on this news.

I stand right in front of IBM's post, so I had a bird's-eye view of the action. The opening bell had just rung and the Dow Jones Industrial Average was down 200 points. IBM hadn't opened yet, but because IBM is a Dow component, I knew that once it opened the market was going to fall much further. The crowd around the post was packed, mostly with sellers. The specialist told me he was about to open, probably at $93.50.

Then the cameras were rolling and I was on live, reporting that IBM was about to open down 20 points from yesterday's close. The next thing I knew, one of the brokers reached over to the phone bank right next to me, got on the phone to his trading booth, then yelled, "Hold it up! I've got half a million more shares for sale!"

The tension was so thick you could practically cut it. First of all, the guys in the crowd were promised a price at which to sell their stock. If they're told the stock's selling at $93.5, they want to get $93.5 a share. But if someone has half a million shares coming in, that will push the price lower. Because that broker yelled, "Hold it up!" and the trader held up the opening, the stock opened at $90.25. And the Dow was down 436 points within a nanosecond.

It's days like that when I recognize how fortunate I am to be working for CNBC and reporting from the floor of the NYSE. I have covered the stock market during some of the most exciting days in the history of trading, and I'm right at the nucleus of the action.

The value of my being there is not just that I can pass on the comments that the company made about the fourth quarter or explain why the CEO's prognosis is disheartening. My value is finding out that five hundred thousand shares of IBM are for sale. Who's buying, who's selling, and for how much? Is there an imbalance in the trading? Are there too many buyers or too many sellers, forcing the market maker to delay opening the action? As widespread as the impact of the information explosion is, the individual does not see the electronic book or all the activity in one particular stock. It's my job to report who is in the crowd and what they're doing to the stock. That is news, and it is that type of news that you can use to make profitable investment decisions.

Often upstairs traders—that's the term for brokers who are not on the floor but are on trading desks back "upstairs" throughout Wall Street—tell me about their orders. They may whisper to me, "I have a million-share order to sell XYZ" or "I have a million-share order to buy XYZ." That information is important and extremely confidential. I walk a fine line in this sort of instance. I don't want to isolate such a trader by going on the air and saying what his order is. Furthermore, his client has a right to have a broker execute an order with complete anonymity and confidentiality. Still, my allegiance is to my viewer, so somehow I need to get out the information that there is a big order looming to buy or sell XYZ.

What do I do? I believe there is room for finesse. Here's an example: In the summer of 2000 one upstairs trader I speak with regularly told me that he had a big order to buy AOL. I checked out his tip. I went over to the AOL post every day to see the amount of buy orders that were in the crowd. I noticed that there was, in fact, a broker with stock to buy every day. So I put two and two together and figured that this was probably the order that my upstairs trader had been telling me about. That way, I was able to report that there was an order to buy in size in AOL.

Similarly, I remember that about a year ago General Electric (GE), the parent company of CNBC, had been unusually weak. I started investigating, asking different upstairs traders, "Who's in GE?" I also asked some of the traders at the GE post. What I found was that there was a big seller unloading much of his stake in GE but that he was almost done selling. That was news. That was one of the nuggets of information that an investor should know. I reported that and soon learned that the stock completely reversed and started trading up after weeks of pressure. The seller was out of the way.

When I first started broadcasting from the floor, people thought I was getting news from the traders. Here's the ironic part: In some cases I'm telling them the news. The brokers I'm interacting with on the floor are moving the market, but they don't necessarily know the news that's impelling their trade orders. They may not know that XYZ Corporation just reported blow-out earnings, that the company exceeded revenue expectations by 40 percent, and that the CEO just hired a new lieutenant from his competitor who's going to add significantly to the management bench strength. They may not know that QRS Company has been losing market share, that its top competitor has just introduced a better product than theirs, and that a key manager just jumped ship.

I look on the news wires and see that a regional bank has warned that earnings would fall below expectations, so all the regional bank stocks are declining as a result. The traders may not know that and they don't care; they only know that they have a big order to buy or sell and that a market maker is putting an indication on XYZ Bank, for example, saying the stock is going to open down 5 points. They only care about who's buying, who's selling, how much, and at what price.

These guys are the physical manifestation of what moves the market. But the forces that really move the markets are going on behind the scenes. Knowing what these forces are, what they're based on, and how they interact with each other is crucial in filtering market news from market noise.

What makes a stock rise or slide? How do you know if it's worth owning and when to buy or dump it? The answers lie in three interrelated factors, all of which play equal roles: fundamentals, expectations, and sentiment.

What Wall Street Means by "Market Fundamentals"

The gyrations of the stock market in the past couple of years may lead you to conclude that the public equity markets are a form of legalized gambling. Or that there's no sense to them at all. I know it may occasionally seem that way, but I don't believe that's actually the case. Here's Jonathan Cohen, who runs the research department at Wit Soundview Capital. As the company's resident Internet maven, he has seen plenty of ups and downs, but even he believes there's some method to the madness. Says Jonathan, "Even though the markets occasionally behave like a roulette table and there seems to be a lot of emotion and irrationality, at the end of the day, there will always be a fundamentally tight relationship between stock market performance and economic fundamentals."

The term *economic fundamentals* means different things to different people. What I'm going to talk about in this chapter is the fundamentals that move markets—the fundamentals that are most important to Wall Street.

When Wall Street talks about a company's fundamentals, it's primarily talking about its earnings and revenues. That's the nuts and bolts. Ignore (for now) references to book value, ROI, ROE, EBIDTA, P/E ratios, and the rest of the alphabet soup. Revenues are how a company makes money and earnings are what's left after it spends it. You can't get more funda-mental than that.

A company's money flows, of course, both in and out. "In" is revenue for service companies and sales for manufacturing companies; it's also known as "the top line" because that's where it appears on a company's balance sheet. "Out" is a smorgasbord of operating expenses ranging from selling, general, and administrative (SG&A) costs—those costs that en-compass salaries, advertising and marketing expenses, office expenses, insurance, rent, and the bill for that executive golfing retreat in sunny Arizona last February—to research and development (R&D) to extraordi-nary items such as restructuring or acquisition charges.

You can get a complete picture of a company's financial history very eas-ily. All you need are the most recent versions of these documents:

- the annual report
- the annual 10-K statement
- the quarterly 10-Q statement

Annual reports are some of my favorite examples of combinations of news and noise. The front part usually features glossy photographs of a cheerfully grinning management team and some snazzy graphics. If the past year was a good one, there will be lots of self-congratulatory chest-pounding interspersed with phrases like "far-sighted vision" and "bold new initiative." If it was a bad year, you'll see a lot of references to "challenges," "configuring for the future," and "an investment year." That's if you even bother to read this part. My own opinion is that you can ignore it; it's mostly noise. I do like to read the letter to shareholders, though. It gives a window into man-agement's personality.

I normally take most reports or releases issued by companies with a grain of salt. Most of the time it's the company's take on things, and you need an outsider's view. The annual report is just one piece of the puzzle.

The news is all in the financial statements. There are three main financial statements in an annual report: the income statement, or statement of earnings; the balance sheet; and the statement of cash flow. As I discuss in the next section, the income statement shows how much money the com-pany made over the past year and its profit margin. The balance sheet reveals how much cash, inventory, and debt the company has. The cash flow statement is probably the most complex, but it also contains the juiciest information: how much money the company is really making, based on the cost of daily operations; the return on its investments; and the amount of money it has borrowed. These are all very important to understand.

These financial statements also appear in a company's 10-Q and 10-K reports, which are forms required by the SEC of every company with listed securities. The 10-Q reports the company's quarterly performance. The 10-K covers a company's financials and includes information you won't find in most annual reports, such as insider stock holdings and brief biographies of the management team. The 10-K is issued once a year, while the 10-Qs are issued three times a year, at the end of each quarter. When the market goes into its periodic spasm over earnings reports, it's responding to or anticipating the release of the companies' 10-Qs.

You can obtain these documents by calling the company's investor relations department and requesting an "investor information packet." These packets are free. You can also access them online from the company's website or from the SEC's website at www.sec.gov. Many of the web financial portals also have links to these documents.

The Financial Facts of Life

Three statements reveal the financial facts of life about a company: its income statement (or statement of earnings), its balance sheet, and its cash flow statement. The income statement reveals the profitability of a company over a specific period and usually contrasts this performance with the results of the previous two years, so you can put the latest numbers in perspective. The balance sheet is a snapshot of the company's finances at a particular moment in time. The cash flow statement is like the company's checkbook; by looking at cash flow statements, you can determine where the company's money is coming from, where it is going, and, most important, how much money the company owes. As you can see, the information is pretty straightforward; once you take a look at it, you'll realize it's nothing to be intimidated by.

I think all of the information in these statements is newsworthy, but there are a few points that really stand out. A quick glance at these will immediately tell you whether or not the company is in good financial health.

The Balance Sheet

The first statement you should look at is the balance sheet. It gives you a sense of how much cash the company has on hand and how much money it owes. Take a look at Wal-Mart's balance sheet, shown on pages 55–56 as an example.

Assets. Assets are everything a company owns.

Cash and cash equivalents. What kind of cash does the company have on hand? Does it have enough to give it the financial freedom to make an acquisition, grow the business, invest in other companies, and make shareholder-enhancing moves, such as increasing the dividend or buying back the stock? Wal-Mart's cash levels at the end of 2000 were $2.05 billion. Comparing that to its 1999 level of cash, you see that Wal-Mart is socking away more and more cash. This is a good sign of prosperity.

Receivables or accounts receivable. This is the money that is owed to Wal-Mart; it counts as an asset because it is money coming to the company. It's like a big I.O.U. If you want to dig a little deeper into the finances of this sector, look up what's called the "days receivable." That's the number of days it takes for the accounts receivable to get paid. In other words, if their customers buy their products with a credit card, how long does it take before Wal-Mart gets the money from the credit card company? In Wal-Mart's case, it's three days. In comparison, Walgreen's days receivable in 2000 was ten, and they are a best-in-class retailer, according to Deborah Weinswig, retail analyst for Bear Stearns.

Goodwill. Goodwill is an intangible item, so why is it worth $9 billion? In 1999, Wal-Mart acquired a British supermarket chain. They paid $15 billion for its assets even though its book value—the dictionary definition of what a company is worth (I'll get to that in a minute)—was $6 billion. Wal-Mart paid a $9 billion premium for the value of the chain's brand name. That's an intangible asset, but an asset nonetheless, so it's classified as goodwill.

Total assets. This number comprises everything the company owns: cash and cash equivalents, receivables, goodwill, property, equipment— you name it. Look for spikes from the year before and then look for the reason. Wal-Mart's total assets jumped $7.5 billion. There's a corresponding spike in property, plant, and equipment, which is consonant with its acquisition of the British supermarket chain the year before.

Liabilities. Liabilities means what the company owes. To get the entire figure, add the total current liabilities ($28.9 billion), the long-term debt ($12.5 billion) and the long-term obligations under capital leases ($3.1 billion). The total: $44.5 billion. That may sound like a big number, but to see what it really means, you need to break it down and look at it in perspective.

Current liabilities. This figure is the amount of debt that the company needs to pay this year. Between commercial paper, accounts payable (money owed to the suppliers), and other current liabilities, Wal-Mart has $28.9 billion in short-term debt. To put this in perspective, compare it to Wal-Mart's assets. Are they valuable enough to cover the short-term debt? No problem.

Long-term debt. The long-term debt for 2000 is $12.5 billion, but what's really important is that Wal-Mart reduced this debt by $1.1 billion from the previous year. Debt reduction is another sign of prosperity. When cash increases relative to debt, it's an improving balance sheet. When it's the other way around, it's a deteriorating balance sheet.

Long-term obligations under capital leases. This number refers to the rent Wal-Mart pays for its stores. This number is growing because the company is expanding the number of its stores.

What's important in calculating a company's financial health is comparing its long-term obligations, that is, long-term debt and long-term obligations under capital leases, to the total shareholders' equity.

WAL-MART STORES, INC.
CONDENSED CONSOLIDATED BALANCE SHEETS
(Unaudited)
SUBJECT TO RECLASSIFICATION
(Amounts in millions)

| | Twelve Months Ended | |
	January 31, 2001	January 31, 2000
ASSETS		
Current assets		
Cash and cash equivalents	$ 2,054	$ 1,856
Receivables	1,768	1,341
Inventories	21,442	19,793
Prepaid expenses and other	1,291	1,366
Total current assets	26,555	24,356
Property, plant and equipment	47,813	41,063
Accumulated depreciation	(10,196)	(8,224)
Net property, plant and equipment	37,617	32,839
Net property under capital leases	3,317	3,130
Net goodwill and other acquired intangible needs	9,059	9,392
Other assets and deferred charges	1,347	632
Total assets	$ 77,895	$ 70,349
LIABILITIES & SHAREHOLDERS' EQUITY		
Current liabilities		
Commercial paper	$ 2,286	$ 3,323
Accounts payable	15,092	13,105
Accrued liabilities	6,355	6,161
Other current liabilities	5,216	3,214
Total current liabilities	28,949	25,803
Long-term debt	12,501	13,672
Long-term obligations under capital leases	3,154	3,002

(continued)

WAL-MART STORES, INC.
CONDENSED CONSOLIDATED BALANCE SHEETS
(Unaudited)
SUBJECT TO RECLASSIFICATION
(Amounts in millions)

| | Twelve Months Ended | |
	January 31, 2001	January 31, 2000
Deferred income taxes and other	1,043	759
Minority interest	1,140	1,279
Shareholders' equity		
Common stock & paid in capital	1,858	1,160
Retained earnings	30,169	25,129
Other accumulated comprehensive income	(919)	(455)
Total shareholders' equity	31,108	25,834
Total liabilities and shareholders' equity	$ 77,895	$ 70,349

Total shareholders' equity. This figure is what's often called a company's "book value," or in other words, what the company is worth on paper. Wal-Mart's book value is $31.1 billion, double the amount of its debt. That's another sign of a prosperous company. But it's only one part of the equation.

The Income Statement

The income statement reveals whether the company is earning enough money to cover its expenses. Let's use Wal-Mart's income statement as an example.

Net sales. Also known as revenues or "the top line," this figure is the amount of money that Wal-Mart generated from selling its products. It's up significantly from the year before—a good sign, but not the only factor you should consider.

WAL-MART STORES, INC. AND SUBSIDIARIES
CONSOLIDATED STATEMENTS OF INCOME
(Unaudited)

(Amounts in millions except per share data)

| | Twelve Months Ended January 31, | | | |
	2001	% to Sales	2000	% to Sales
Net sales	$ 191, 329		$ 165,013	
Other income-net	1,966	1.03%	1,796	1.09%
	193,295	101.03%	166,809	101.09%
Cost of sales	150,255	78.53%	129,664	78.58%
Operating, selling, and general and administrative expenses	31,550	16.49%	27,040	16.39%
Interest costs:				
Debt	1,095	0.57%	756	0.46%
Capital Issues	279	0.15%	266	0.16%
	183,179	95.74%	157,726	95.58%
Income before income taxes, minority interest, equity in unconsolidated subsidiaries and cumulative effect of accounting change	10,116	5.29%	9,083	5.50%
Provision for income taxes	3,692	1.93%	3,338	2.02%
Income before minority interest, equity in unconsolidated subsidiaries and cumulative effect of accounting change	6,424	3.36%	5,745	3.48%
Minority interest and equity in unconsolidated subsidiaries	(129)	(0.07%)	(170)	(0.10%)

(*continued*)

WAL-MART STORES, INC. AND SUBSIDIARIES
CONSOLIDATED STATEMENTS OF INCOME
(Unaudited)

(Amounts in millions except per share data)

	Twelve Months Ended January 31,			
	2001	% to Sales	2000	% to Sales
Income before cumulative effect of accounting change	6,295	3.29%	5,575	3.38%
Cumulative effect of accounting change, net of tax benefit of $119	—	0.00%	(198)	(0.12%)
Net income	$6,295	3.29%	$5,377	3.26%
Net income per share: Basic earnings per share Income before cumulative effect of accounting change	$1.41		$1.25	
Cumulative effect of accounting change, net of tax	$0.00		($0.04)	
Net income	$1.41		$1.21	
Diluted earnings per share Income before cumulative effect of accounting change	$1.40		$1.25	
Cumulative effect of accounting change, net of tax	$0.00		($0.04)	
Net income	$1.40		$1.20	
Average number of common shares:				
Basic	4,465		4,451	
Dilutive	4,484		4,474	
Lifo credit/(charge)	$176		$96	

Cost of sales. This is the amount that Wal-Mart paid for the products it puts on its shelves. Subtract the cost of sales from the net sales, and you'll see that Wal-Mart bought its products for $150 billion and sold them to you for $191 billion, a nice profit of $41 billion. Out of that figure, you also have to subtract the following two items:

Operating, selling, and general administrative expenses. The SG&A, as it's known, is the basic cost of running the business. The figure covers everything from employees' salaries to office rent to health insurance.

Interest costs. This figure is the amount that Wal-Mart has to pay each year on its underlying debt and capital leases.

Income before income taxes, etc. The amount of earnings before income taxes is very important. When you divide the earnings before income taxes by the net sales, you get 5.29. That ratio shows what Wal-Mart is earning on its revenues. The higher the percentage, the better, because it shows how well Wal-Mart is leveraging its infrastructure. Wal-Mart's 5.29 percent is a moderate number, higher than K-Mart but lower than Target, but, according to Bear Stearns retail analyst Deborah Weinswig, that's because Wal-Mart is willing to trade margins for market share. By offering the lowest price possible on its goods, Wal-Mart simply rolls over the competition.

Net income. Wal-Mart's net income was $6.29 billion. Again, this figure doesn't mean much unless you compare it to something else, namely, their interest costs. Wal-Mart is generating so much revenue that they can cover their expenses five times based on what they're earning.

The Cash Flow Statement

The cash flow statement is like a company's checkbook. It reveals exactly when and what money is going out, and when and what money is coming in. Obviously, a positive cash flow is a lot healthier than a negative one. Again, let's look at Wal-Mart's cash flow statement.

WAL-MART STORES, INC.
CONDENSED CONSOLIDATED STATEMENTS OF CASH FLOWS
TWELVE MONTHS ENDED
(Unaudited)
SUBJECT TO RECLASSIFICATION
(Amounts in millions)

	January 31, 2001	January 31, 2000
Cash flows from operating activities:		
Net income	$ 6,295	$ 5,377
Adjustments to reconcile net income to net cash provided by operating activities:		
Depreciation and amortization	2,868	2,375
Increase in inventories	(1,795)	(2,088)
Increase in accounts payable	2,061	1,849
Other	301	681
Net cash provided by operating divisions	9,730	8,194
Cash flows from investing activities		
Payments for property plant and equipment	(8,042)	(6,183)
Investment in International operations	(627)	(10,419)
Other investing activities	(45)	(244)
Net cash used in investing activities	(8,714)	(16,846)
Cash flows from financing activities:		
Increase/(decrease) in commercial paper	(2,022)	4,316
Dividends paid	(1,070)	(890)
Payment of long-term debt	(1,519)	(863)
Proceeds from issuance of long-term debt	3,778	6,000
Purchase of Company stock	(193)	(101)
Proceeds from issuance of common stock	582	—
Other financing activities	(374)	167
Net cash provided by (used in) financing activities	(818)	$ 8,629
Net increase/(decrease) in cash and cash equivalents	198	(23)
Cash and cash equivalents at the beginning of year	1,856	1,879
Cash and cash equivalents at end of year	$ 2,054	$ 1,856

Increase in inventories. As is often said in the computer industry, inventory has the shelf life of lettuce. No company wants to have a lot of inventory hanging around, depreciating. Wal-Mart actually paid less for its inventory in 2000 than in the previous year. In fact, according to Weinswig, while sales increased 16 percent, inventories increased only 8 percent. Usually you see the two figures grow in lockstep: as the company sells more, it's also stocking more products in its warehouses. However, Wal-Mart implemented a much more efficient ordering and tracking system. The result: a big reduction in inventory—and a higher amount of net cash provided by operating divisions.

Net cash used in investing activities. Even though this is a negative figure, it's not money that the company lost on stock market investments. Instead, it refers to capital expenditures such as purchasing property and equipment and paying for new stores. Yes, Wal-Mart took a loss of $8.7 billion, but it's not so much a loss as an investment in the company.

Cash flows from financing activities. In this section, you can see all the debt the company owes as well as whatever money it made from issuing stock or bonds. The result is:

Cash and cash equivalents at the end of year. This figure corresponds exactly to the first number we discussed in the balance sheet.

What's Wrong with Amazon.com?

Why did Lehman Brothers credit analyst turned money manager Ravi Suria sound the alarm about Amazon.com in June 2000? After many challenges regarding his analysis of Amazon, Suria left Lehman to work for a hedge fund. He looked at the company's balance sheet. What concerned him was that the company's total assets barely exceeded the amount of its long-term debt and its debt was nearly five times the amount of the stockholders' equity. That signaled a problem with working capital, the cash that the company has to work with.

Amazon.com's balance sheet at the end of the third quarter 2000 is shown on page 62. By the end of the fourth quarter, Amazon's current assets had increased 7 percent to $1.36 billion. However, its current liabilities had increased 75 percent to $975 million. This resulted in a sharp drop in working capital to $386 million and Suria said it raises even more questions about the company's liquidity and its ability to continue as a growing business concern. Others disagree with Suria's scrutiny but it is worth taking a look.

AMAZON.COM, INC.
BALANCE SHEETS
(In thousands, except per share data)

	September 30, 2000	December 31, 1999
	(Unaudited)	
ASSETS		
Current assets:		
Cash and cash equivalents	$ 647,048	$ 133,309
Marketable securities	252,976	572,879
Inventories	163,880	220,646
Prepaid expenses and other current assets	99,181	85,344
Total current assets	$1,163,085	1,012,178
Fixed assets, net	352,290	317,613
Goodwill, net	383,996	534,699
Other intangibles, net	136,474	195,445
Investments in equity-method investees . . .	91,131	226,727
Other investments	73,345	144,735
Other assets	54,306	40,154
Total assets	$2,254,627	$2,471,551
LIABILITIES AND STOCKHOLDERS' EQUITY (DEFICIT)		
Current liabilities:		
Accounts payable	$ 304,709	$ 463,026
Accrued expenses and other current liabilities	160,073	181,909
Unearned revenue	142,046	54,790

	September 30, 2000	December 31, 1999
	(Unaudited)	
Interest payable	35,056	24,888
Current portion of long-term debt and other	17,213	14,322
Total current liabilities	659,097	738,935
Long-term debt	2,082,697	1,466,338
Commitments and contingencies		
Stockholders' equity (deficit):		
Preferred stock, $0.01 par value:		
Authorized shares—500,000		
Issued and outstanding shares—none	—	—
Common stock, $0.01 par value:		
Authorized shares—5,000,000		
Issued and outstanding shares—356,102 and 345,155 shares at September 30, 2000 and December 31, 1999, respectively	3,561	3,452
Additional paid-in capital	1,342,574	1,194,369
Stock-based compensation	(19,504)	(47,806)
Accumulated other comprehensive loss...............................	(65,637)	(1,709)
Accumulated deficit	(1,748,161)	(882,028)
Total stockholders' equity (deficit) ..	(487,167)	266,278
Total liabilities and stockholders' equity (deficit)	$ 2,254,627	$ 2,471,551

Factors That Affect a Company's Earnings

After reading a company's financial statements, you'll know such useful information as how quickly sales are growing, how the company is financing its growth, whether it has taken on too much debt, how much profit it makes on its products and services, and exactly which products and services contribute the bulk of the profits. This useful information will give you a full picture of a company's business prospects and the likely performance of its stock.

Say you're evaluating a company like Dell Computer Corp. Dell made its reputation in the early 1990s from manufacturing PCs to order and selling them directly to customers, bypassing the middleman. Since then, price competition has narrowed the profit margin on PCs. Dell has since expanded into other products, such as servers, workstations and storage units, and other services that have a higher profit margin. These other units now contribute nearly half of the company's total profit. However, because Dell still derives 51 percent of its profits from PCs, its stock suffers whenever PC purchasing is down.

Because Dell is one of the largest PC manufacturers in the world, when Dell stock drops, it sets off a landslide among the stocks of lesser-known companies affiliated with it. Electronics contract manufacturers like Jabil Circuit, Solectron, and SCI Systems supply components to Dell. Not surprisingly, on October 5, 2000, after Dell warned of lower sales, *TheStreet.com* ran a story with the following headline: "Jabil Circuit, SCI Systems Head Lower in Sympathy with Dell."

I remember the first sign of the troubles that triggered the tech sell-off of 2000. On July 5, right after the holiday weekend, analyst Jonathan Joseph of Salomon Smith Barney called the peak in the semiconductor sector and downgraded four major companies. He downgraded those companies because of a slowdown in cell phone use, which affected the number of chips those companies sold to cell phone manufacturers. At the time, the semiconductor index, or SOX, was trading at a level of 1,180. The weakness in the cell phone market was later compounded by a weakness in the PC market, which hit the rest of the semiconductor group that hadn't already been downgraded. From July through the rest of the year, like one domino after another, each sector within technology took a hit, because everything within technology is related. By the end of December, the SOX index was trading at 704.

Conversely, when a major customer reports increased demand for its products, its suppliers often experience a spike in their own stock prices. Announcements that a company has inked a deal with an important new customer, signed a significant marketing pact, or formed a joint venture with a strategic partner can also bounce the market. Even a company's decision to buy back shares can have an impact on its stock.

This type of news comes out on an ongoing basis in different sectors. Like a fire under a pot of water, it keeps the market simmering and occasionally boiling on a daily basis. But its true impact is best measured at the end of each quarter.

What does Wall Street look for in these quarterly reports, and what is it about them that moves the markets? The answer is a variety of factors that affect earnings. These include earnings growth, sales growth, and actual cash flow from operations. All of these add up to the big picture of a company's stock: its price-to-earnings ratio, or P/E.

Earnings Growth

After you subtract the "out" from the "in" on a company's balance sheet, what's left is a company's earnings. Earnings equal, quite simply, profits, and profits are the most reliable mover of stocks. A lot of other things have moved stocks during the 1990s bull market, but without earnings growth you can't really bank on sustained upward movement in the stock.

"In the long term, good earnings are the driving force of most up-trends in the stock market," says Steve Shobin, portfolio manager at Americap Advisers, with $200 million under management. **"Good earnings ultimately prevail."**

What do market experts mean when they talk about good earnings?

You might think that Wall Street refers to good earnings as a description of what happened to a company over the past quarter or past year. That's true to a certain extent. The fact is, however, that the earnings statement is nothing more than a history report. Although good report cards are appreciated, Wall Street is *more* interested in using the past as prologue. In that respect "good earnings" means strong profits coupled with projections of good *ongoing* earnings growth.

That's why a company can report a rise in earnings, but Wall Street will still punch the air out of the stock. For example, Walt Disney Company delivered better than expected earnings during the fiscal fourth quarter of 2000, but analysts were concerned about a softening advertising market and lower ratings for its profitable *Who Wants to Be a Millionaire?* show.

Consequently, even though the company beat the consensus forecast earnings of 7 cents a share for the quarter by 4 cents, Merrill Lynch's media and entertainment analyst Jessica Reif Cohen downgraded the company's stock and the market knocked 15 percent off the share price.

"I care more about how fast earnings are growing relative to the rate at which they had been growing," says Arnie Berman, technology strategist for Wit Soundview Capital. "A company whose growth rate is accelerating or stubbornly refusing to slow, those stocks boggle the imagination. You have no idea just how large they might be."

Not all companies have earnings to report. Many Internet companies were infamous for growing revenues without posting a profit. Amazon.com is probably the best-known example. Credit analyst Ravi Suria of Lehman Brothers was among the first analysts to question Amazon's future prospects. As he pointed out in a report in June 2000, when Amazon stock was selling in the $40s, the e-commerce pioneer with one of the best-established brands in the B2C space suffered from a basic inability to make money. "From 1997 through the latest quarter, the company has received $2.8 billion in funding, while its revenues have been $2.9 billion—a whopping 95 cents for every dollar of merchandise sold." The weak balance sheet, poor working capital management, and massive negative operating cash flow add up, Suria concluded, "to the financial characteristics that have driven innumerable retailers to disaster throughout history."

Yet for a few years, investors ignored earnings growth. Putting a dotcom at the end of a company's name acted as a siren call to the analyst community, the press, and much of the broad investing public. They threw their venerable Graham and Dodd treatises on fundamental valuation out the window. We don't care about earnings growth, they said; we care about revenue. No, we don't care about revenue; we care about expected revenue and expected usage. We don't care that the company is losing money and expects to keep bleeding for years; we only care that it's part of the hot new trend. It was the new "eyeballs-to-price" and "traffic-to-price" ratio that Wall Street analysts had invented and were crazy for.

"There was a certain rationality to the approach," explains Berman. "What made it rational was the emergence of web-based computing as the most important thing to happen to technology since the invention of the PC. The way you made the most money was by accepting risk, by owning companies that had minimal revenue bases but great markets associated with the build-out of the Internet. People thought that a lot of these companies might not make it but some would be the next Cisco or Microsoft."

From November 1999 through early March 2000, the Nasdaq jumped from 3,000 to nearly 5,000 points. Skepticism was penalized; "stickiness," "eyeballs," "monthly unique users," and "mindshare" took precedence over actual earnings. But at a certain point, investors realized that these spurious measurements were just so much noise. The result of that realization was the technology sell-off of 2000.

The sell-off may have been triggered by the bursting of the dotcom bubble, but it did not stop with the dotcoms. It went on to affect virtually every sector of the economy. Media companies went down because dotcoms stopped advertising. Banks and brokerage firms went down because their venture capital arms had seen the value of their dotcom investments plummet. Even the automakers were adversely affected because of the economic slowdown that ensued.

"One thing investors should never use is any metric that has been invented for the sake of that industry," cautions Ravi Suria. "At the end of the day, a dollar made is a dollar made. It doesn't matter whether it's made from selling hot dogs or books on the web. That's why accounting rules for business are standard. 'Eyeballs' don't translate to any of the numbers. 'Subscriber growth' is meaningless if the company isn't making money from it. Unless you can explicitly figure out how to grab a metric and translate it into revenue, cash flow or earnings, it's not worth using."

In short, jargon is noise. The essential nuggets of news are earnings and earnings growth.

Sales Growth

A key aspect of earnings growth is the growth of sales or revenues. After all, you can't have earnings without sales.

For some market experts, sales growth is more important than earnings growth. "How do I decide whether a company is creating value?" asks Robert Loest. "I look at sales growth, not earnings growth.

"Right now, B2B e-commerce companies don't have any earnings, but they are growing sales at 300 percent a year. They enable customers and suppliers and other business stakeholders to do things more efficiently and more easily than they could before, so instead of a purchase order costing $100, a B2B company like Ariba or Siebel can cut those costs to maybe $6. They are clearly creating value.

"The more complicated something is to do, the slower the growth is to decline. B2B e-commerce is a complicated software technology. It takes a long time to install and implement and an even longer time to get a company's clients to install and implement it. So this growth can last a long time.

"Similarly, how do I determine when the company has expanded as far in its space as it can? I watch sales and look at the market share. If sales growth declines dramatically and the company still has a small market share, then it may be that something has gone wrong. But if they have a large market share, approaching 50 percent or more, then probably what's happening is that they've exhausted that component of their growth. Remember that the two components for growth for growth companies are the expansion rate within their sector and the expansion rate of that sector. So you have two numbers: top-line sales growth and market share.

"Microsoft expanded as the use of personal computers expanded. The growth rate among people learning to use computers was high, so Microsoft had a long way to go to spread its market share within its sector. Microsoft expended an enormous amount of value in a segment of the economy that's obviously large. But over the past year, we've seen a dramatic slowing in the rate of people buying PCs; pretty much everyone who's going to buy a PC has already bought one. The market has become saturated. Plus Microsoft has 90 percent of that market, so it has expanded as far within its market sector as it can go. That component of growth is zero. The only growth that's left is among people who have yet to buy PCs, but until Asia and Europe pick up that slack, that won't grow quickly."

Sounds compelling, right?

Not for everyone.

Paul Meeks, senior portfolio manager of Merrill Lynch's technology and Internet funds, looks for a combination of growth in revenue and growth in earnings per share: "You want to see a nice margin structure each and every time that the company reports. You don't want to see a company that's growing sales quickly but has profitless prosperity. Many of the Internet companies were so intent on the land grab, on taking market share in an emerging industry, that they were losing money on every sale. You can only grow your earnings per share as fast as the revenues if you have a profitable business model. So I look for companies with a growth of profitable revenues, not growing revenues for revenue's sake."

Cash Flow

Sales growth can be a mesmerizing figure, but if operational costs are already high and are getting higher, profitability will be jeopardized, rendering the company's sales growth less significant. "If I sell you one banana and I lose cash on it, I am most likely to lose money if I sell you five," points out Ravi Suria. "But if I make a cent on every banana I sell you, I can afford to sell more bananas and at some point, I'll make enough money to build a grocery store and sell lots of bananas. At a very simple level, if the business does not throw off cash, the more money it spends on capital expenditures, the more it will suck up. That's what cash flow is all about."

Cash flow is a measure of the movement of money through a business; it's the amount of money a company takes in as a result of doing business. A cash flow statement is actually three statements in one: cash generated (or spent on) operating activities, or the company's businesses; investing activities, such as expenditures on "hard assets" like property and equipment; and financing activities, such as inflows like common-share offerings and outflows like repayment of debt.

The number of times a company comes to market to raise money is very newsworthy, particularly if it does so via a bond offering. With a common stock offering the money goes to the company, but with a bond offering, borrowing and paying back the loan with interest is involved. Companies that sell bonds need to pay interest. So there are several questions investors need to ask: How much in interest payments will this company need to pay back and when is it due? Is the company raising more money to expand its business or does it need more money to pay back previous borrowings? In other words, is it raising money just to stay alive?

Management guru Peter Drucker likes to say, "If a start-up promises profits in the first five years, do not invest in it because it has no growth. But if the start-up has not generated cash flow in the first eighteen months, do not invest in it because it has no sustainability."

Here's why: All companies take in cash, but some have to spend more than others to get it. Positive cash flow means that in the course of running its business, the company has managed to generate cash rather than consume it. That's important because a company that can crank out free cash from operations has the necessary funds available for internal expansion, acquisitions, dividend payments, stock buybacks, and all those other activities of a healthy, growing company. The amount of cash a company has on hand tells you how much wiggle room the management has to do those things. A company that has negative cash flow has to borrow money in order to maintain and grow its business, and may be shackled to heavy interest payments.

You might think that every profitable business generates positive cash flow; ironically, that's not always the case. A company may have difficulty collecting payments from its customers while having to pay its suppliers right on time. It may have gotten stuck with a large amount of inventory. It may have revenues of $100 million but has to spend $80 million each year to keep its plant and equipment up-to-date, so the first year it doesn't fork out that $80 million, it will lose business to more efficient competitors.

Many people use the cash flow numbers to evaluate stocks. For example, a $40 stock with $4 per share in annual cash flow has a 10 to 1 ratio, which is standard. That ratio corresponds to a 10 percent return on cash, which has pretty much been the standard long-term reward for investing in the stock market. A $40 stock with an $8 per share cash flow gives a 20 percent return on cash, which investors love because it is better than the average.

One increasingly common measure of cash flow is EBIDTA (earnings before interest, depreciation, taxes, and amortization), which some companies use as a proxy for cash flow. EBIDTA is a useful application in specific industries and companies in a specific part of their growth phase. For example, it's useful for the cable industry because cable companies don't have inventory, receivables, or payables.

But, cautions Ravi Suria, while EBIDTA is a reasonable approximation of cash flow, it's not entirely correct. EBIDTA doesn't measure the amount of money that needs to be invested in working capital, which is the amount of money necessary to run a business. If you are in an industry that has inventory, receivables, and payables, your EBIDTA can be artificially distorted. Once a cable company starts doing programming, for example, it has to consider receivables and payables. "When Warner Cable was growing, then EBIDTA was a correct measurement," he says. "But now that it's Time Warner and encompasses so many different businesses, you can't measure it on the same basis."

How important is cash flow in the overall picture of a company's financial health? As Ravi Suria says, "You can make your income statement look better than it is, but cash flow statements never lie."

P/E Ratios

When Wall Street evaluates a company's stock, the important number is not the price per share but how the per share cost of the stock measures up within the context of the company's earnings or earnings growth. That number is called the P/E ratio.

Also known as "the multiple," the P/E ratio is the price of a stock divided by its earnings per share. One of the yardsticks for valuing stocks that Wall Street has been using forever, the P/E ratio is the most common measurement used to express the relative value of publicly traded stocks. Basically, it's the price tag that the market puts on a stock. In other words, the cost per share is essentially noise; the P/E ratio is the news.

The P/E ratio gives investors an idea of how much they are paying for a company's earnings power. The average S&P 500 stock is selling at about thirty times earnings. The higher the P/E ratio, the more investors are paying and therefore the more earnings growth they are expecting.

The P/E ratio may either use the reported earnings from the past year (called a trailing P/E ratio) or be based on an analyst's forecast of the next year's earnings (called a forward P/E ratio). The trailing P/E is listed along with a stock's price and trading activity in the daily newspapers. For example, a stock selling for $20 a share that earned $1 a share last year has a trailing P/E ratio of 20. If the same stock has projected earnings of $2 next year, it will have a forward P/E ratio of 10.

A forward P/E ratio essentially gives you an idea of how highly the market values that company. If the market values it below what it values an average company in its sector, that could be an opportunity. Similarly, if a company's P/E ratio is at a lofty level compared with its competition, it could mean that the stock is overvalued and is risking a fall.

The P/E ratio is a vital measurement because it's consistent for all companies across all industries. (There is, however, one notable exception: many Internet companies were infamous for growing revenues without posting a profit. Since you couldn't have a P/E ratio without the E, Wall Street had to invent a new yardstick—and the rest, as they say, is history.) It's especially useful as a consistent comparison of companies within a particular sector. If, for example, ExxonMobil is selling at $100 a share with earnings of $5 a share for the past twelve months, it has a trailing P/E ratio of 20. Now let's say that its competitor, Chevron, also has a share price of

$100 but has reported earnings of $10 a share. That should raise a red flag. Why is Chevron selling at a lower multiple than its rival? Is it a better bargain or is there a reason for the disparity? That's the sort of thing the investment community looks out for.

However, the P/E ratio need not—and often does not—correspond between all stocks. Some stocks may be considered underpriced at fifty times earnings, whereas others may be grossly overpriced when their P/E ratio rises to 10.

This is because the market's price tag is a compilation of the past, the present and the future, all of which vary from company to company and sector to sector. A trailing P/E ratio represents the company's present circumstances as reflected in its stock price, divided by its past history (the trailing twelve months' earnings per share). But Wall Street's future projections, or growth rate, have a great effect on its forward P/E ratio.

And those future projections are, to a great degree, governed by the nebulous but no less powerful force of market expectations, which I discuss in detail in Chapter 5.

But first, here's how the pros evaluate the fundamentals of the most popular industry sectors.

Gauging a Sector's Fundamentals

Although all companies ultimately share the same economic fundamentals, different industries are gauged in different ways. Technology companies, for example, are applauded for dominant market share, but retail companies in the same position are in danger of oversaturating the market.

To the extent that investors can discern the quality of the fundamentals for different industries and different companies, they will be better able to determine what's news and what's noise. Here is what market pros say about how they evaluate the economic health of some of the most popular industry sectors, what the warning signs are, and where they find their best information. I've added my 2 cents too.

Automotive Stocks

Gauging This Sector's Economic Health

NICK LOBACCARO, *senior auto analyst, Lehman Brothers:* "At one level, the auto sector is a proxy for the strength of the consumer economy. So regardless of corporate action, expectations of the economy move the stocks. The stocks react best when the economy is in a Goldilocks environment, when it's not too hot and not too cold. Historically, the best performance has been when we're transitioning from a weak economy to a strong economy.

"The primary drivers for individual companies are the level of profitability and what the company is doing to unlock value. Companies like General Motors and Ford are always limited as far as the P/E ratio the market is willing to give (they have almost never broken out of a range of seven to nine times earnings), but they own businesses within the corporation that command higher multiples. GM owns a lot of Hughes Electronics. Ford owned The Associates, which was taken over by Citigroup. Both GM and Ford recently separated out their auto parts subsidiaries to become less vertically integrated. Ford has had at times as much as $25 billion of cash in its bank account but it wasn't reflected in its stock price. The stock price is a function of how aggressively the companies manage to unlock the value in their portfolio of assets—whether they hold valuable assets that don't get reflected in the multiple or assets they can spin off to shareholders.

"The key factors in evaluating automotive companies: Look for earnings. Look at how well received new products are when they come out. Right now, we have a strong preference for Ford. They have a strong product portfolio and they have a strategy to grow in high-margin segments and they will be able to achieve that with their acquisitions of upscale lines like Jaguar, Lincoln, Volvo, and Land Rover."

Red Flags

LOBACCARO: "Disappointing earnings; poor positioning in terms of product pipeline, branding and the demographics of the customers."

Information Sources

LOBACCARO: "Given that the product pipeline is the biggest contribution to the bottom line, you can't ignore trade magazines like *Car & Driver*. If something good is going to happen to a company, you can usually read about it there first. The *Detroit Press* and www.autos.com are also good resources.

"Try to go to the National Auto Show to get a gut feel for the success of the new models. That's an opportunity to beat the institutional investors, who tend to wait to announce their ratings until after earnings are being generated. People who study the auto industry for their job get desensitized to new vehicles, so putting on a consumer hat instead of an analyst hat gives you a better perspective."

Maria's 2 Cents

From my standpoint, the economy is one of the biggest factors, if not the single most important one, when looking at auto stocks. We saw that pretty clearly in early 2001, when the economic slowdown was so marked that DaimlerChrysler shut down some production lines and GM and Ford saw their markets plummet. There used to be a saying that as GM goes, so goes the economy. I would say instead, as the economy goes, so go the Big Three automakers.

Moves in market share are also worth watching. For a long time, U.S. auto makers were in a sweet spot as the sole producers of highly popular, high-margin sport utility vehicles. Today, Japanese and European manufacturers are getting into the light-truck market and have taken market share away from U.S. auto makers in that area.

Bank Stocks

Gauging This Sector's Economic Health

TOM BROWN, *partner in Second Curve Capital, a financial services hedge fund:*
"Banks are gauged on the P/E multiples of their estimated earnings. The price-to-book ratio has become less relevant, dividend yield is less relevant, and banks don't have cash flow in the conventional manufacturing company sense. The range of those P/E multiples has widened over the past five or six years. Today some banks trade at thirty-five times next year's estimated earnings, while some trade at six. It's a range of multiples that has never been seen before. Still, P/E multiples are the best relative valuation tool and the best predictor.

"Today in the financial services sector, the gap between strategy and execution is so large that it's much less important what the strategy is than the ability to execute. If you're a customer of a bank, can you get good service? It sounds easy but it's not. "

Red Flags

BROWN: "The biggest swing factor for a bank is its loan quality. On the commercial side, loans go on what's called nonperforming status before they're resolved, which usually ends up in a write-down. So the percentage of nonperforming status commercial loans is a red flag.

"On the consumer side, when a consumer stops paying off the loan, the loan goes on what's called delinquent status. Delinquent loans get written off after 180 days. So delinquency rates are another red flag.

"Both of these numbers are published when banks announce their quarterly earnings. The 10-Q statements also give some indication of near-term future outlook. So it's important to review press releases and 10-Q reports. "

Information Sources

BROWN: "www.bankstocks.com, which provides free research on the financial services industry. "

Maria's 2 Cents

Don't forget the venture capital arms of banks. Over the last ten years, major banks have seen real profit growth from investing in securities. In 2000 and 2001, however, ownership of the high-flying telecom, technology, and, in particular, Internet stocks that once boosted their earnings have since hurt them. Chase Capital Partnership, for example, was a major investor in this area, with holdings in Broadcom, Cisco, CMGI, Exodus, Qualcomm, and Salon.com, among many others. (It's not difficult to go to J.P. Morgan Chase's website, click onto the Chase Partners' portfolio, and take a look at which stocks they're betting on.)

Holdings like that can cause a lot of volatility in the bank's earnings, but CEO William Harrison told me that he prefers it that way. "If you go back to 1984, our returns on an annual basis have been over 20 percent a year," say Harrison. "2000 was the first year that we had not experienced that. We think the valuation creation from the fund is there and we like that business as a component of our overall portfolio. It does create some volatility in earnings from quarter to quarter, but we think the long-term value creation is very significant. "

Brokerage and Asset Management Stocks

Gauging This Sector's Economic Health

HENRY MCVEY, *research analyst for the asset management and brokerage indus-try, Morgan Stanley Dean Witter:* "There are three macro themes which will shape this sector over the next three to five years:

1. "Distribution companies and financial services companies are gain-ing power over the traditional manufacturers. Companies that con-trol the customer relationship, like Charles Schwab and Price Waterhouse, will outperform their peers.

2. "I believe that the financial services industry is increasingly a global business, and the U.S. investment banks are dominating the compet-itive landscape in Europe and Asia. After the 1998 collapse of the emerging markets, Citigroup was one of the biggest beneficiaries of the healing of the global economy. It would be impossible for domestic firms like Paine Webber to deliver the earnings that Citi-group did, because Citigroup derives about 30 percent of its rev-enues from outside the U.S. That gave them a huge advantage over U.S. competitors.

3. "The impact of technology has resulted in a seismic shift in the competitive landscape. With the introduction of online trading, Schwab went from being a discount brokerage firm to a leading online brokerage almost overnight. Merrill Lynch went from being a leading retail brokerage to a firm that needed to dramatically revamp its offerings. Merrill Lynch has obviously rebounded and their offerings now match Schwab's, but those types of shifts can cre-ate huge changes."

AMY BUTTE, *managing director for brokerage, asset management, and financial technology, Bear Stearns:* "I divide the group into three subsets: capital markets, asset-based businesses, and e-finance. With capital markets firms like Merrill Lynch, Goldman Sachs, and Morgan Stanley, earnings growth is the most important thing to think about. What is the amount of risk these firms are taking on? What is the return on equity? Is one firm allocating capital more efficiently with less risk? Let's say Firm A takes $100 of its capital and, depending on the leverage (i.e., equity versus debt financing), they put a high-quality bond on their balance sheet. Let's say the return is something in the 15 percent range. Then let's say Firm B has the same amount of capital to buy a bond to put on its balance sheet, but that bond is high-yield paper with a higher risk. Firm B's return should be double that of Firm A, but how much risk did Firm B take on? Over time, you'll have defaults. So you look for a combination of what type of securities these firms are buying and selling, how much capital they choose to allocate, and, most important, how much risk they assume.

"Bank of America is a good example of a company with a lot of risk right now. Here's a company that is trying to build its market share by allocating more capital to riskier types of clients. Is Bank of America willing to work with an issuer that a leading bank won't work with just to take one more risk for the possibility of a greater return? If Bank of America buys those bonds and its customers don't want them, they end up on Bank of America's balance sheet.

"Liquidity ratios are also important to watch. This is the same thing that credit rating agencies do. What is the ratio of long-term funding to fixed assets? The higher the ratio, the more secure the likelihood that the firm can fund the balance sheet at any one time. Back in the age of leveraged buy-outs, there was always the threat that the brokerage firm could not meet its funding obligations as a result of one bad trade.

"You'll also want to ask if this is a story about growth or cost-cutting, which would have an impact on the stock's multiple. Are earnings growing purely from operations, or did earnings grow because management laid off employees and cut costs from the business?

"In e-finance and asset-based businesses, such as Charles Schwab, Franklin Resource, Ameritrade, or T. Rowe Price, the main driver is the growth in underlying assets, so the issue is one of fund performance. I look at organic growth versus growth that comes with market appreciation. For example, Schwab might say their total assets grew from $950 billion to $1 trillion. Another figure they would give would be net new assets—how many assets did they bring in from new customers minus any assets they lost from old customers? That's organic growth, and for Schwab, that figure has been about $10 billion to $12 billion a month.

"You also want to look at the ability to translate that growth into earnings, so the expense side of the equation is important. For example, both Schwab and e-Trade spend the same amount of money on advertising, but because of Schwab's scale, that advertising expenditure represents less than 10 percent of net revenues, while at e-Trade it can represent more than 50 percent of net revenues. So for an investor, it is important to differentiate the best place you choose to use as a broker versus the best brokerage stock to own."

Red Flags

MCVEY: "My key drivers are interest rates, global trends, and consolidation.

"Rising interest rates are typically a negative for financials. Higher funding costs typically lead to higher credit losses and sluggish fixed income and equity issuance.

"Because the financial services industry is a global business, companies that have global exposure are at greater risk, as well as being in a position to reap greater rewards. After 1998 investors lost confidence in emerging markets. A firm like Franklin Resources, which had been one of the golden boys, suffered a material change in their competitive position.

"Consolidation announcements like Credit Suisse First Boston buying Donaldson Lufkin Jenrette, or J.P. Morgan buying Chase drove the asset management sector to record highs. The same thing happened in 1998 when Citibank merged with Travelers and First Union bought Core States. The stocks typically experience a huge rally, but then the market turns against them because all the good news has been discounted in the stock and it's now up to the executives to execute on the game plan that they laid out during the deal announcement. And often reality is a lot tougher than their promises. The long-term story may be sound, but the near-term performance hurdles are huge."

Information Sources

MCVEY: "The Securities Industry Association (www.sia.com) does an excellent job for the overall sector. Strategic Insight is a value-added news agency for asset management. The *Wall Street Journal* is a must-read for this business. Even if it's just a five-minute scan, reading the headlines on the front page and spending a couple of minutes on the C section can dramatically increase your knowledge base.

"One of the best things a retail investor can do is use the product. Experiment with Merrill Lynch's retail offering and compare it to Schwab's or T. Rowe Price's. Consumers are a great indicator of future value, so if you find the product to be convenient, attractively priced and value-enhancing, that typically will help to drive revenue growth at the related company."

BUTTE: "Look at trade magazines, such as *Investment Dealers Digest* and *Institutional Investor.* These are good for issues and trends taking place in the industry."

Maria's 2 Cents

The deal calendar and the sheer performance of the stock market are key when assessing brokerage stocks. The real bread and butter at brokerages comes from deals, in the form of IPOs or secondary offerings. It's a good idea to watch how business is going overall. The new issue calendar offers a back door into the business of brokerages and investment banks. For example, in January 2000, a total of fifty IPOs were done, according to Thomson Financial, compared to just ten in January 2001.

If we see a volatile market and stocks are selling off, this is going to affect trading activities. We may even see an increase in the number of people taking money out of their mutual funds.

Energy Stocks

Gauging This Sector's Economic Health

DENNEY CANCELMO, *vice president of sales trading, Simmons & Company:* "With energy, you have to have a fundamentally sound balance of supply and demand. That sounds overly simplistic but with energy it's quite true. You have to have a commodity price that allows energy companies to make money. To get to that commodity price, you have to have significant demand and a supply that does not include a large amount of overcapacity. As in any type of cyclical commodity-oriented investment you have to be careful of times of oversupply.

"How a company makes money goes to the capacity of the specific area of the industry sector. The question for a major integrated or independent exploration and production company such as ExxonMobil or Chevron is what kind of production capacity they have. In the past several years, these companies have added to their reserves and production mainly by acquisition and consolidation. But the fact is, the ability of these companies to add to their product has fallen off, because they're not spending money. So I look at their budgets and what they're putting into explo-ration and production, and what they say they're going to produce and what they actually produce.

"What you're looking for in oil service stocks depends on what part of the cycle they're in. Their revenues are derived from rig counts, and how these rigs are turning determines how companies like Halliburton, Schlumberger, and Baker Hughes earn money. When they get to a certain level of utilization of their rigs, day rates start to expand to a level where it becomes profitable or economically feasible to build new rigs. But because it costs so much to build a new rig and the rig adds capacity to the system, which puts a cap on day rates, at that point, earnings flatten out.

"For refining stocks, look at inventory levels. As inventory levels get low, the margins they get from cracking a barrel of oil into motor gasoline, diesel fuel, heat-ing fuel and residual fuel are generally higher. A new refinery hasn't been built in this country in two decades. That's the problem with heating oil prices in the North-east—not the lack of crude oil but the lack of infrastructure to refine it.

"With convergence stocks like Calpine, Enron, Dynegy, and Williams, you look at their ability to generate power. Look at their trading ability—how do they hedge their production and how good are they at wheeling this electricity from one area to the next and making money on it? What is their actual megawatt per hour output in certain areas?

"One interesting situation is what's been going on in California. The move toward deregulation has given these companies the ability to create excess genera-tion and profit from it. But the second the regulation board talks about capping what the wholesalers can charge, you'll see these stocks tick down."

Red Flags

CANCELMO: "With exploration and production companies, the Street is very focused on production volumes. Production is their product; without it, they don't have anything to sell. The drivers for refiners have historically been inventory levels of crude oil and its products. For convergence companies, continuing volatility will be the big driver."

Information Sources

CANCELMO: "The American Petroleum Institute releases a global inventory of oil stocks every Tuesday afternoon at 5 p.m.; it's reported in most financial newspapers the next day. The Department of Energy (www.doe.gov) releases its numbers on Wednesday morning at 9 a.m., and those numbers are generally viewed as more reliable.

"For oil service stocks and energy service stocks, the Baker Hughes rig count is released every Friday at noon. Look for longer-term trends, not just the week-to-week numbers, which are affected by seasonality and weather. Offshore Data Services also shows the number of rigs contracted; as the percentage of rigs contracted goes up, the price for rigs goes higher. And if there are more rigs working, then servicing companies do better, too. You can also find the number of rig permits at the Minerals and Mining Management website at www.mms.gov."

Maria's 2 Cents

One of the key points about oil and energy prices is the impact that this group has on the entire market. The higher the price of oil, the more a negative factor it can be not just on the obvious groups such as automotive, airlines, transportation, and utilities but on almost all industries. One of the resons that California's state electricity suppliers, Pacific Gas & Electric and Edison International, are in trouble is that they are paying premium prices for oil but state mandate forbids them from passing the costs on to their customers. As a result, they are facing the threat of bankruptcy. However, energy traders, such as Enron and Williams, benefit from this type of volatile market because they make their money supplying electricity to the companies that need it.

Internet Stocks

Gauging This Sector's Economic Health

JONATHAN COHEN, *managing director, Wit Soundview Capital:* "The quality of the business model should be the number one point: Is this a company that can make money, that can generate real profitability over the long term? Does it have a sustainable competitive advantage through strategic partnerships, technology, the ability of its management, and a customer base that's large and growing and sustainable? What is the quality of its relationships with its vendors and suppliers?

"The quality of the company's balance sheet is also very important. At this moment in time, many consumer Internet companies are out of favor. As a result, it's become more difficult for companies in that sector to raise capital, which means that investors need to pay close attention to the quality of a company's balance sheet and its ability to sustain itself during a period of time when capital is scarce.

"I look at competitive positioning in the market, growth rates of the business at issue, and the effect on profitability of a particular piece of information. If a company announces that they have a strategic partnership with AOL, that was news that a year or so ago would have doubled the price of the company's stock. But a lot of those deals that were done with AOL or Yahoo proved to be bad deals for the companies that did them. At the end of the day, the companies weren't able to capitalize on the value of the AOL or Yahoo platform that generated a positive return on the capital they invested in the deal itself.

"It's easy for perception and reality to become divorced when you're talking about a new medium, a new technology, or a new industry. Netscape circa 1995 was widely considered to be not only the preeminent Internet company but the company that would forever own the Internet. It was perceived to have cracked the code for the structure of Internet communication and was in such a preeminent position that it could never be replaced. The reality was that they had done some nice work with browser software, but their product was a commodity. It wasn't too difficult to develop or produce, and the barriers to entry were not as compelling as was believed at the time. Microsoft's entry into the market was not the source of too much initial concern, but it turned out to be an enormous detriment to Netscape's ability to grow and maintain market share. Netscape is now part of America Online."

Red Flags

COHEN: "A company that's losing market share, that's seeing diminishment in growth rate, declining margins, new competitors entering its market, higher than normal rates of turnover in senior management, and insiders selling stock. The valuations are higher, so the sensitivity to the issue of insider selling is naturally greater."

Information Sources

COHEN: "www.witsoundview.com has research reports available for all of the technology it covers. The brokerage firms that make information available to individual investors represent an enormously valuable tool.

"www.sec.gov, the website for the Securities and Exchange Commission, contains all the publicly available disclosure information from publicly traded firms. That includes quarterly reports, annual reports, proxy statements, and documents filed when a company is getting ready to go public."

Maria's 2 Cents

Here's another red flag: What about debt and profitability? Does the company keep hitting its profitability targets? Does it keep coming back to the markets to raise money?

Here's another source of information on this sector: I look at Media Metrix (www.mediametrix.com), which gauges traffic on the Internet and ranks the most popular websites.

Media and Entertainment Stocks

Gauging This Sector's Economic Health

JESSICA REIF COHEN, *media and entertainment analyst, Merrill Lynch:* "The overall health of the advertising market and the overall health of the economy are the two biggest factors affecting this sector. A ticket to Disney World or Universal Studios costs a lot of money, so consumer confidence is a critical factor in theme park visitations. And the overall health of the economy has a major impact on advertising.

"I balance that against television ratings for broadcast networks and how the movie box office is doing. By that, I mean not just the revenue but the cost of the movies, which is released once a year by the Motion Picture Association of America.

"The companies that can perform these days are companies that are involved in mergers. Viacom merged with CBS so there's the potential to take out huge costs and move into new businesses. 'Nick Junior' ratings are up 200 percent. CBS has new programming, which it promotes across Viacom. And because CBS can't air all the sports coverage it bought the rights to, our guess is that those games will show up on other incremental networks. In the case of Fox and NewsCorp, Fox News ratings are up 250 percent and FX ratings have gone through the roof. Fox has an enormous backlog of TV syndication, which will start to ramp up in September 2002 and will stay at a high level for the next five years. That's money in the bank.

"Cable companies are more recession resistant, so I look at the underlying cash flow growth and new service rollouts—how fast are they adding new cable modem subscribers, how strong are their balance sheets. Many cable companies are turning cash flow positive; these were highly leveraged companies, so that's a big change. "

Red Flags

COHEN: "I look at the overall health of the economy. If the trend is down, then get out of the way of companies that have advertising- or consumer-related businesses. Stocks don't go up when earnings go down. Many of these stocks go down six to nine months before the economy goes down, then they tend to overcorrect and get beaten up. I also look at the regulatory environment; looser regulations lead to consolidation and rate rollbacks. "

Information Sources

COHEN: "I read *Variety* and the trade magazines, such as *Hollywood Reporter* and *Electronic Media.* Also keep aware of the overall health of the advertising market by reading related articles in business newspapers and magazines. "

Maria's 2 Cents

Always consider how an advertising slowdown might impact these companies. One of the ripples of the dotcom crash of 2000 was that dotcom companies suddenly stopped advertising. Dotcoms represented 3 percent of all advertising for major media companies in the United States from 1999 to 2000. It wasn't until six months later that most analysts decided to lower estimates for the media companies, but in retrospect we all could have seen this coming. As soon as dotcoms crashed, clearly the next step was drastically reducing their advertising spending.

Pharmaceutical Stocks

Gauging This Sector's Economic Health

JOSEPH RICARDO, *pharmaceuticals analyst, Bear Stearns:* "Analyzing pharmaceutical companies is a relatively simple exercise: Prescriptions make sales make earnings make stock prices. Food and Drug Administration [FDA] approval and patent expirations have a bearing, but you have to evaluate the individual companies on their own terms.

"Back in 1989 and 1990, Pfizer had a $5 billion market value. The market was saying that the company was only worth $5 billion because it sold defective heart valves, and some patients in whom they were implanted died. At that point, Pfizer had a wonderful pipeline of drugs. The market totally discounted it because they were overly concerned about the heart valve. So whoever bought Pfizer in 1989 and 1990 bought one of the greatest pipelines in the pharmaceutical industry at a major discount. In the next ten years, Pfizer increased in value thirty times.

"That's Part A of the equation. Part B is that if you miss Part A, wait until the product gets to market. In 1995, Warner-Lambert had a $6 billion market value. By January 1997, when Lipitor hit the market, it had a $10 billion market value. Eventually, Lipitor sales went from zero to $3.5 billion and Warner-Lambert was bought for $100 billion by Pfizer.

"I pay a lot of attention to what's going on in the political and regulatory environment. When managed care was instituted, people said it would be the worst thing for the pharmaceutical business. The stocks went down for two years. But the fact is, managed care turned out to be the biggest bonanza in history. You didn't have to take $100 out of your pocket to pay for drugs; you got a little card and that card allowed you to buy a drug for $15, so you bought more drugs."

Red Flags

RICARDO: "Fifty years of history says that when S&P earnings accelerate, drug stocks underperform. People look for relative earnings strength and they believe there's better relative earnings strength in other industries. When S&P earnings decelerate, they buy things that are predictable and visible, so they buy drugs."

RAY GILMARTIN, *CEO, Merck:* "I pay a lot of attention to what's going on in the political and regulatory environment. That's a very important part of how we think about the company and what kind of actions we take."

Information Sources

The FDA's website, www.fda.gov, lists the latest information about product approvals for drugs, medical devices, and food additives, as well as safety alerts and recalls and clinical trials. These last are especially important so that you can see which company's drugs or devices are in which phase of approval. If the product has reached Phase III, it's close to coming to market.

Maria's 2 Cents

Here's another red flag: What about patent expirations? Wouldn't patent expirations on hot-selling drugs open the door to the possibility of generic drugmakers producing the same drug for a fraction of the cost? This is going to become an increasing concern as most major pharmaceutical companies are expecting patents to expire beginning at the end of 2002.

And another alert: Typically, when money comes out of technology stocks, it goes into pharmaceuticals. Compared with the volatility of the technology sector, pharmaceuticals are seen as a safe haven in an uncertain economic environment, because they have consistent revenue growth. So you want to keep a watch on the sentiment of the whole market, because there is definitely a rotation that goes on.

Retail Stocks

Gauging This Sector's Economic Health

DANA TELSEY, *retail analyst, Bear Stearns:* "When looking at the retail sector, you want to look at the macro side first: how is consumer confidence, what's the unemployment situation, what are interest rates. Those are the key elements in the big picture to see if the pace of consumer spending will remain healthy.

"On the micro side, I look at store saturation. I believe there are only four hundred good malls and eight hundred good strip centers. Even with companies like Talbot's and the Bombay Company, whenever they get past four hundred stores, you can't get the same sales productivity in each store. In strip centers, take a look at Pier 1 and office superstores; when they pass eight hundred stores, they're past their prime.

"There are three elements that make a retail company successful: concept, execution, and management. The concept is successful when you have a store that customers go to on a repeat basis. If you don't get repeat business, then why have a store? Execution typically means having the right systems in place, so you don't have too much inventory, which leads to markdowns, or too little inventory, which leads to missed sales. With management, I want to know whether they've been there a long time, so they've had experience with the up-and-down cycles of the retail roller coaster, and whether they own a lot of stock.

"Newness is the driver of retail sales gains—new concepts, new ideas. Look at the Internet, at international retailers like Zara and H&M coming to the United States. You always have to be on the watch."

Red Flags

TELSEY: "When the number of stores gets to that four hundred or eight hundred level. When you see more markdowns or more promotions. When the economy begins changing and you see higher unemployment, rising interest rates, and lower consumer confidence."

Information Sources

TELSEY: "I read the trade magazines like *Women's Wear Daily* and *Chain Store Age*. I walk the stores. Is Tiffany going to have a bad Christmas? I go into a Tiffany store and look at the lines at the counter. I look for markdowns or sales signs. I'll go to a mall and count the shopping bags. If you see a predominance of one store's shopping bags, you know this store must be working."

Maria's 2 Cents

Keep your eyes open in your own neighborhood for too many mark-downs. Do you see a lot of sale signs? Are the sales so great that they're luring consumers in but also hurting margins on low-priced items? Like the auto sector, retail is all about the economy.

Technology Stocks

Gauging This Sector's Economic Health

PAUL MEEKS, *senior portfolio manager of technology and Internet funds, Merrill Lynch:* "On a qualitative basis, I look for leadership companies—companies that have leadership with technology, leadership with market share, and leadership with their business model. The companies must have a competitive advantage that is sustainable. As for market share, I want to make sure the company is addressing a market that is large and growing. It doesn't matter if you go from zero to 100 percent market share in a market that is small.

"A quality management team is especially important with tech stocks. Things move so fast that the company may have to change its business plan many, many times, so you need more superior management than otherwise.

"I look at the track record. Has the company had a consistently strong financial performance? That's only achieved by good execution, which gives you an idea of the management team. You want to see minimal management turnover, so that you can attribute that track record to them. And you want to see management teams that are properly incentived for delivering the mail financially. I don't mind seeing my management have options as part of their total compensation, so they will be totally interested in having the stock go up."

Red Flags

DAN NILES, *senior PC and semiconductor analyst, Lehman Brothers:* "I compare revenues to gross margins. One common trick that will generate revenues is for a company to cut prices so much that gross margins go down. Or it will cut core expenses, like people or R&D, so the revenue line looks good and so does the earnings per share, but if you look at the quality of the results, it's not so hot.

"I also look at the balance sheet. The income statement may look fine but the accounts receivable [AR] have gone through the roof. Skyrocketing AR is a sign that the company thought demand would be better than it actually was. It's the same with inventory. In technology, inventory has the shelf life of lettuce—the older it gets, the less valuable it is. So if a company has too much inventory, maybe sales weren't as good as expected, which means they may have to be more aggressive with pricing, which will drive down the gross margins and the profitability.

"I walk the stores a lot. I go to my local Circuit City or CompUSA and ask the salespeople what's selling and which products aren't doing well. I remember vividly in the first part of 1998, I walked into Circuit City and noticed boxes of Compaq computers stacked on the floor. When I asked a salesperson why there were so many boxes of PCs, he said, 'Because the warehouse in the back is all full.' I went to a few other stores in the area and got the same answer. I remember thinking, 'Oh, my God, we have a big inventory problem coming in the March quarter." I called up one of the big distributors and they confirmed that there was a lot of inventory in the channel. Based on that, we downgraded Compaq and Intel and said the PC market might have a lot of problems because of inventory issues."

JONATHAN JOSEPH, *semiconductor analyst, Salomon Smith Barney:* "Several bottom-up indicators are important to watch:

"Capital spending growth. In 2000 the typical semiconductor company was spending 65 percent more money than the year before on expansion, new fab plants, new equipment, etc. In fact, the top twelve makers were growing capital spending by 82 percent. We thought that correlated with the peak capital growth spending of 1995, 1988, and 1984, which were previous peaks. It was a sign to us that too much capacity was coming online.

"The availability of certain commodity semiconductors. This is such a sensitive supply issue. It's key to recognize when supplies are beginning to loosen, because it means you'll begin to see a change.

"Changes in specific end markets. In July 2000 we were beginning to hear about weakness in cellular phone demand, so we downgraded semiconductor stocks which had exposure to the cell phone market. As things unfolded, it became apparent that the PC market was weakening too. That's important because the PC manufacturers consume about 50 percent of all semiconductor chips. So in September 2000, we downgraded Intel and Micron."

Information Sources

MEEKS: "I subscribe, either in hard copy or via the web, to some of the big trade periodicals: *Electronic Buyers' News, Electronic Engineering Times, The Industry Standard, The Red Herring.* Some of these are software based, some talk about Internet stuff, some talk about semiconductor stuff. You can get a good grasp of industry themes with these periodicals, as well as an indication of what's hot and what's not in a certain industry. Weeks and weeks later it will show up in the *Wall Street Journal* when you could have gotten it here first. If the *Wall Street Journal* and *BusinessWeek* are your only sources, you're probably doing yourself a disservice.

"Dataquest, IDC and Forrester Research all cover the technology sector and post press releases on the Web."

ARNIE BERMAN, *technology strategist, Wit Soundview Capital:* "CNET (www.cnet.com), because I have an obsessive focus on technology. There's a lot of breaking news there and it has just a tad more credence than it would if I heard it in a chat room."

KEVIN MCCARTHY, *co-director, technology research, Credit Suisse First Boston:* "CNET, Techweb (www.techweb.com), and the Register (www.theregister.com). You can't take everything for gospel, but it's a matter of sniffing out different ideas."

Maria's 2 Cents

Remember the interrelationship among different companies in the tech sector. When PC companies or cellular phone manufacturers get hit by reduced sales, at some point, depending on the severity of the slowdown, it will likely impact throughout the entire sector, from semiconductor and microprocessor manufacturers to the component suppliers. We saw this domino effect during the 2000 sell-off. Having said that, I always like to remember what GE chairman Jack Welch likes to say: you always want to be either number one or number two in the business; if not, get out of the business. Market share is key in all areas of business.

Telecommunications Stocks

Gauging This Sector's Economic Health

PAUL MEEKS, *senior portfolio manager of technology and Internet funds, Merrill Lynch:* "Delve into the business mix of the telco. Right now, you're seeing a change in priority from voice technology to data technology. That's why companies that used to sell primarily consumer long-distance access are having problems—the voice part is going the way of the dinosaur. Long-distance could ultimately be available for free over the Internet. Make sure you understand what part of the percentage of revenues and operating income come from potential problem areas, i.e., voice versus goodies which have a future, such as data, Internet, and wireless.

"That situation will also be transferred to telecom equipment companies. You want to be with New Era vendors who supply optical networking equipment to telecom providers, not legacy equipment. That's one of the problems Lucent has had—they sell a lot of legacy product, which is very slow growing.

"It's very important to have an R&D team on top of product cycles. Technology used to be years in development; now it's months. The company has to run on the treadmill faster than before, so it has to have funding for R&D that keeps up with rapid changes in the space.

"You have to hope that management executes very well too. Right now, OC48 technology is mainstream, but over time OC192 technology will be important. If a company is dominating OC48 and cannot meet the aggressive ramp that customers demand for OC192, then Nortel becomes Lucent."

Red Flags

MEEKS: "Major telecommunications providers that are known for their updated technology, like Qwest and Williams, do well-publicized trials of the latest technology. You can see who are the latest and greatest upstarts that are getting high-profile trials. Whenever you see an incumbent not invited to a trial or thrown out of a trial, that's a heads-up. These trials are closely followed by Wall Street analysts, so you'll see qualitative results long before you see the impact to the financial statement."

RAVI SURIA, *credit analyst, Lehman Brothers:* "Debt leverage can be a real pitfall. Debt leverage for the group has grown significantly in the past four years, doubling to $210 billion from $93 billion, due partly to acquisitions and partly to new issuance.

"One reason for the increased debt burden: capital expenditures related to the 3G wireless infrastructure upgrade. The capex program is perhaps the largest capital spending endeavor on infrastructure that is being done in a free-market, unregulated competitive environment. The cost of the auctions of the U.S. spectrum is estimated at $56 billion, plus another $30 billion for build-out over the next couple of years. The total spend on a global basis is estimated at at least $250 billion before 3G is up and running."

Information Sources

MEEKS: "Companies generally talk about their research in their quarterly conference calls. Typically, there will be website presentations available to everyone. In addition, technology websites such as ZDNet (www.zdnet.com) and CNET (www.cnet.com) regularly discuss the latest news in this sector."

Maria's 2 Cents

Don't be fooled into thinking that the hope of the next-generation product means the actual execution of it. Most people expected European wireless companies to launch 3G products in 2001, but Qualcomm CEO Irwin Jacobs told me that we shouldn't expect to see 3G technology until 2004 and 2005. One of my biggest issues with telecom companies is the amount of money that they've raised through public offerings and whether that money was raised through bonds or common stock offerings. During the late 1990s, many of the small telecom companies had such heavy interest payments on their bonds that they had to borrow more money just to stay alive. We often criticize the amount of borrowing in the 1980s, which was the heyday of junk bonds. According to Ravi Suria, the amount of borrowing among the telecom companies in the last two years of the 1990s was double the *entire* amount borrowed during the eighties. Obviously, that economic model couldn't sustain itself, and that's why there have been so many bankruptcies in this sector in 2001.

With telecom equipment companies, be careful of overreaction from problems in the technology sector and vice versa. These sectors have a way of raising the tide throughout the market and, conversely, bringing down all the boats.

How to Gauge Expectations—and Measure the Results

"It's one thing for you and me and the average investor to know the DNA and the fundamentals of a company. It's another thing to figure out whether Wall Street agrees," says Steve Shobin, portfolio manager at Americap Advisers. "If we say yea and Wall Street says nay, guess who's going to win?"

From a Wall Street perspective, earnings are significant but even more important is this caveat: earnings drive expectations. Expectations are the estimates for future growth that analysts and investors come up with based on a combination of past earnings growth and future prospects. The fate of most stock prices rests squarely on the market's perception of the outlook for future earnings. Earnings drive expectations, and expectations of future performance drive equity value.

"The absolute dollar number of revenues or earnings per share is interesting, but what moves the markets is the delivery versus the expectation," says Paul Meeks, senior portfolio manager of Merrill Lynch's technology and Internet funds. "The key is delivering results that are better than or as good as Wall Street's expectations."

How big a role do expectations play on Wall Street? Let me give you an example. On the morning of August 3, 2000, I heard from some analysts that Motorola was calling its suppliers and telling them that it was going to ship eighty million to eighty-five million handsets that year. Now, at an analyst meeting six months earlier, Motorola had commented that it would like to see one hundred million units shipped. As a result of Motorola's making a comment at an analyst meeting that it *would like* to see one hundred million units shipped, people raised the bar and started thinking that the company *would* ship 100 million. So when the company started calling its suppliers and telling them that it was going to ship *only* (my italics) eighty million to eighty-five million handsets, people surmised that the information was a preannouncement of bad news that demand for Motorola's handsets was softening. Lehman Brothers in its morning call termed the lowered guidance a negative. Expectations needed to come down.

The result: The stock opened down more than 10 percent. Furthermore, people figured that Motorola's news meant weakening demand for the entire cell phone sector, so stocks in other mobile phone companies dived, as did the stock in companies that supply microprocessors for mobile phones. The ripples spread and the Nasdaq opened lower.

Meanwhile, I called Motorola to get its take on the news. The company's spokesperson told me he was stunned by the market's reaction. He told me that first of all, the eighty-five million figure was not new information, and, second, Motorola had never said it was *planning* to ship one hundred million units anyway. According to him, Motorola merely said that at some point it *would like* to ship one hundred million units. But someone, somewhere, misinterpreted that to mean that Motorola *intended* to ship one hundred million units, so when the company said that it would be shipping eighty-five million, a confirmation of its earlier announcement, the response was, "Uh-oh, they missed expectations," resulting in a 10 percent drop in the value of the stock.

As it turned out, both the stock—and the Nasdaq—recovered. In fact, both closed up for the session.

At the end of the day, the news about Motorola's expectations could be seen as a flurry of noise. But people traded on them and they moved the market significantly. Therefore I count expectations as news.

Furthermore, there was a nugget of news that fostered the expectations. At the time of the analyst meeting, the Motorola executive felt confident enough to make a passing comment that he would like to see the company ship one hundred million units. That comment raised the bar for expectations. Maybe investors should not have taken a passing comment for an official statement of fact; on the other hand, the comment was made by a company executive. Whether the comment was official or unofficial is irrelevant. He made it, analysts heard it, and therefore it became an expectation.

When the company later announced that it would ship eighty-five million units, it was clear that company was less optimistic than it had been six months earlier. Yes, there was a knee-jerk reaction and possibly that reaction seemed overblown at the time. But an investor could have raised a red flag and said, "Wait a minute, eighty-five million is not in step with what was mentioned at an analyst meeting. Is there a problem here?"

There was. Where there's smoke, there's usually a fire. Sure enough, one quarter later, Motorola reported that the handset market had indeed slowed. Other handset manufacturers were also experiencing trouble. So one could have extracted real newsworthy information from the noise of the expectation. (Incidently, six months later, in February 2001, Motorola did officially preannounce weaker growth, sending its stock down to a near-fifty-two-week low.)

Another case in point is Bank of America. It was the first week of 2001 and I was in my office at the NYSE preparing for the day ahead. Virtually every trader I had spoken to that morning brought up the possibility of an earnings miss at Bank of America. One trader reported rumors that Bank of America was going to see credit quality issues in its next report. Another said that California's utility crisis was affecting Bank of America because the company had lent money to the California utilities which were now on the verge of bankruptcy. Yet another trader speculated that Bank of America was going to report derivatives losses.

The opening of Bank of America's stock that day was one of the more exciting openings I've seen. I was standing on the floor of the NYSE facing the Bank of America post, so I could see that the crowd was getting thicker and the tension was building. The stock had gone out the day before at $51.50. At about 9:20 a.m., the specialist put up an indication of opening between $47 and $49. Then more sell orders came in. Suddenly, just before opening, the NYSE put a halt on the stock, with the explanation "news pending."

Now, when the NYSE issues a news-pending halt, that means that news will be released imminently that is expected to materially impact the stock. The news could come from the company itself, another company if it's a tender offer, or from the SEC. All transactions in the company's stock are frozen until the news is out and widely disseminated. Under NYSE rules, after the specialist gets the news, he must put up another indication and then open the stock within ten minutes of that indication.

The "news pending" was a press release that said something to this effect: "We are seeing no big losses from trading and derivatives, we are comfortable with our credit guidance for 2001, and any speculation is erroneous." I thought, How strange that this is the company's news. When the NYSE halts trading on stock-pending news, it's rarely a defense of a company's position. But Bank of America was so concerned about the rumors that it felt compelled to respond to the scuttlebutt and that response was the "news" that the NYSE halted the stock for.

Initially, the press release helped the stock. It opened down only about $2, much better than a lot of people had speculated that morning. At the end of a day on which the Dow was down 250 points, the stock was down $4. The situation was fluid; it was a reaction to speculation and expectations. Yet at the end of the day, I don't think investors were really sure that the company had told the whole story.

That evening on *Market Week,* I interviewed Tom Brown of Second Curve Capital. Tom made his name on Wall Street criticizing First Union and Bank of America for making ill-advised acquisitions. Through much of the 1990s, he said that these stocks were going to go much lower and investors should stay away from them, calls that cost him his job at one company and caused him to be flagrantly rebuked at another, when his own firm bought heavily into the bank he had turned negative on. Now he was vindicated. I'll describe his experience with First Union in Chapter 9. Here's what happened with Bank of America.

Brown was an analyst working at Tiger Management, one of whose biggest holdings was Bank of America. Bank of America was on an acquisitions binge, and when it announced plans to buy NationsBank in April 1998, Brown strongly advised against it. But Bank of America's CEO, Hugh McColl Jr., was a good friend of Richard H. Jenrette of Donaldson Lufkin Jenrette (since bought by Credit Suisse First Boston), who sat on Tiger's board. Julian Robertson, the head of Tiger, returned from a lunch with Dick Jenrette and Hugh McColl, feeling even more bullish about his colleagues' company. Brown's advice was ignored. Not only that, Tiger doubled its stake in Bank of America to $1 billion, making it the largest bank holding at the firm. Brown soon left to start his own hedge fund and since then he has maintained his sell recommendation on Bank of America. Was he too harsh? The answer came in 2000: most bank stocks climbed, but Bank of America tanked, plunging from $61 to $38.

Here's Brown's comment on *Market Week* that night: "The issue is real serious in that they have a poor management team and an even worse board of directors. I'd need to see some serious housecleaning before getting excited about long-term prospects." In short, it seemed that expectations finally met reality. (As for Tiger Management, its expectations met harsh reality in March 2000 when, after sustaining heavy losses, it was forced to liquidate its holdings and go out of business.)

Wall Street's expectations for a stock's performance are often reflected in whisper numbers. As a company approaches the time when it reports quarterly earnings, the analyst community engages in a game in which the analysts try to predict the exact dollar figure that's going to be announced. As more and more analysts place their bets, companies like First Call (www.firstcall.com) and I/B/E/S International (www.ibes.com) collect them, take the average, and come up with what's known as a "consensus estimate." In the quiet period of two weeks leading up to the actual earnings announcement, the company isn't allowed to let out so much as a peep about the accuracy of the consensus. But everyone else in the financial community is free to speculate, and the resulting rumors are known as whisper numbers. You can check the latest whisper numbers at www.whispernumber.com.

Today, whispers have far less impact because of the Fair Disclosure Regulation enacted in 2000 by then SEC chair Arthur Levitt. Regulation FD, as it is sometimes called, ensures that every investor gets the same information at the same time, and this has completely changed the playing field from where I sit. I will speak to CEOs and company executives during a private interview or at a cocktail party, and they are very, very reluctant to say anything that could get them into trouble with the SEC.

Analysts' positions have also become closely scrutinized. With Regulation FD in full force, company executives are prohibited from giving any one analyst more information than the rest of the market. Analysts used to think, "I have a close relationship with the CEO, so I know what's going to happen." They can't do that anymore. They can no longer be a mouthpiece for what the executive tells them. They now need to do their own independent research to have a leg up on the competition. The SEC has also begun to question analysts and require them to report conflicts of interest when they recommend a stock.

Still, whisper numbers are important, says CSFB analyst Kevin McCarthy, because they set expectations. But they can also raise expectations to unrealistic heights. That can lead to the paradoxical situation when the company's earnings beat the consensus but not the whisper, and the stock gets punished as a result. "If the whisper is 55 cents and the original consensus number was 50 and the company comes in at 55, that's good," McCarthy explains. "But if it comes in at 52, the stock will be down. The company beat the consensus but it didn't beat the whisper."

The idea that a company's stock should get pummeled because it made one penny less than what the analyst community thought it might is, of course, ridiculous. The whisper number is noise. What's news is the company's earnings growth compared with the earnings of its competitors and the growth of the sector. Whisper numbers are no reason to throw out fundamental earnings analysis. They're just another example of how expectations rule the market.

Expectations are both a reflection of and a driver of market sentiment. Sentiment is essentially the psychology of the market. It's the aggregate of investors' "gut feelings." It may seem too nebulous to be news, but the effects are anything but noise. That's why economists watch consumer confidence so closely. If the consumer is confident, he or she will spend money. It's like the wealth effect: when the stock market is doing well, people feel richer so they will spend more, even if it's all on paper.

Sentiment can blind even the most seasoned investor's eyes. "For a long time, there was an expectation that the growth rate in the Internet sector would be so strong that investors could afford to ignore some of the fundamental components that govern success or failure in any business," comments Jonathan Cohen, who runs the research department at Wit Soundview Capital. However, that sentiment has since shifted, he notes. "I think that trend is now well and truly over. Investors are now focused appropriately on the essential building blocks."

During the dotcom sell-off in March and April 2000, market sentiment turned negative, shifting away from volatile Internet companies with their exhilarating highs and gut-wrenching lows to predictable companies that were growing more slowly but also more consistently. The interesting thing was that the individual investor did not leave the stock market. We have had some ugly days for sure, but investors haven't given up on equities.

Money still flows into the market; it just rotates into and out of different sectors. While investors were selling technology stocks, they were buying "safer" energy, pharmaceutical, and financial stocks. The psychology of the market had changed.

The Tools to Measure Expectations and Sentiment

In the last couple of years, the market has been easily swayed by emotion and, say many market watchers, has become increasingly volatile as a result. Even though expectations and sentiment seem unquantifiable, they can actually be measured by hard data and with accurate research tools. Here are the indicators that I watch the most closely.

Money Flows

Money flows indicate how much money is going into and out of certain sectors of the market, as well as the market as a whole. It is hard evidence of expectations and market sentiment.

Finding out about money flows isn't difficult. TrimTabs.com Investment Research (www.trimtabs.com) tracks daily flows of about 850 stock and bond funds in approximately ninety mutual fund families that comprise about 20 percent of all equity fund assets. While specific information about specific sectors is limited to subscribers, anyone can click on to their weekly liquidity updates and twice-weekly mutual funds flow reports. AMG Data Services (www.amgdata.com) makes its news reports available to non-subscribers. The Investment Company Institute (www.ici.org) lists monthly mutual fund assets, money flows, sales, and analyses, also for free. Connecticut-based investment company Birinyi and Associates tracks money flows by individual sectors and specific stocks. This is very important to see the rotation that goes on as money comes out of certain sectors and flows into others.

Jeff Rubin, director of research at Birinyi and Associates, has a specific formula for rating stocks on the basis of money flows: **"Money flows are a key lead indicator for future prices. The market tends to anticipate good or negative news, which is reflected in the money flows. When looking at flows, we look at non-block and block trades separately. Non-block trades represent the retail investors with trades** of less than ten thousand shares. Block trades represent institutional money with trades of more than ten thousand shares. Generally, we like to see an agreement in both the non-block and the block, not placing emphasis on one more than the other.

"We classify stocks on a scale of one to five. A one is the lowest classification and is given to stocks with continuous selling; any opportunities in prices are opportunities for more selling. A two rating goes to stocks that are appreciating, but it's usually only a rally and not the beginning of a sustained positive move. A five is given to stocks with ongoing persistent accumulation. Issues that are not quite as positive but still quite attractive are coded a four. These are stocks where the buying may not be as strong and continuous as a five, but flows and price are generally coincident, where buyers do not buy on weakness and sellers do not sell into strength."

The value that Birinyi and Associates bring is that they look at specific stocks, as well as specific sectors. TrimTabs.com measures money in and out of the broader market. Birinyi's work can give you specific details and zero in on particular stocks poised to move.

Watching the money flows will tell you what is happening to the market. "All there is in the stock market is shares of stock and money," explains Charles Biderman, CEO of TrimTabs. If $12 billion flowed into mutual funds specializing in aggressively growing telecommunications stocks last week, then you know that sector is going to move. It may not move immediately but it will eventually because when you have money flowing into a certain sector, it provides a cushion for that sector. Maybe the fund manager won't buy stocks at that moment, but he's got the money to. It's supply and demand.

Let's say that you invested $5,000 in your growth and income fund through your Vanguard online account last Tuesday. You were maybe one out of ten million people putting money into that fund that week. TrimTabs and AMG Data Services track how much money went into Vanguard's growth and income fund, as well as how much money was transferred from its value funds into its aggressive growth fund. You can also watch the holdings of that fund to see which ones move specifically. Tracing that money is like taking the pulse of the market.

Early in 2000 Biderman kept telling me that while money was coming out of some mutual funds, bond funds kept seeing inflows. No surprise then that the year 2000 was one of the better performing years for bonds of all types.

Here's why Charles Biderman thinks money flows are important: "Liquidity is the key to understanding why and how markets move. It's a consistently reliable indicator on which to base the timing of trading and investment decisions. Price is a function of liquidity. If one knows where liquidity is heading, one will know where stock prices are headed.

"Between the end of 1994 and the end of 1999, the number of shares in stock in the U.S. stock market kept declining. Companies were buying back more shares, whether in the open market through stock repurchase programs or cash takeovers of public companies, than were being issued through new offerings or insider selling. At the same time, income growth in the U.S. was rapidly accelerating and cash available for investment in the market was growing dramatically.

"Money flows start with income gains. Since 1997, we've been writing that productivity gains of the New Economy were not accurately captured by the conventional statistical bureaucracy in Washington. Not just withholding tax collections have been growing dramatically but the category that the Treasury has for all other income taxes paid that are not withholding—underreported withholding, 1099 income, capital gains—had been growing at double-digit rates as well. When you have double-digit gains in income, obviously a lot of money will go into the market. Consequently, P/E ratios, price-to-book ratios, and all those other valuation models were thrown out the window simply because there was so much cash and a shrinking number of shares, a lot of money chasing too few shares.

"The conventional paradigm is that the overall market cap is a function of value in some shape, manner, or form. Traditionally, the current market price was a function of discounted future expectations and cash flow. We say that's not true. It's a function of the number of shares and the money available.

"You had a combination of more money looking to buy fewer shares, so the market tripled in value between the end of 1994 and the end of 1999."

Biderman believes that all you really need to look at is supply of stock and demand of dollars. At the height of the dotcom mania, all you needed to do was look at the money flows to see that the technology stocks and the dotcoms were extremely popular. On any given week and during any given month during that period, you had literally billions of dollars moving into aggressive growth funds.

It's easy to have 20/20 vision when you're looking back, but the fact is that as a result of studying money flows, Charles Biderman suspected that the end of the five-year bull market was in the offing, and he actually called it in his December 21, 1999, weekly report. "Shrinkage in the number of available shares was being reversed: companies were issuing new shares and, starting in November 1999, insider selling just soared," he recalls.

The market continued to go up for a couple more months because income growth was so strong and there was simply so much more money. In the first four months of 2000, equity mutual fund inflows averaged just over $40 billion in January, $54 billion in February, $34 billion in March, and $34 billion in April, Biderman recalls. "That was an all-time record pace. The record year prior to that was 1997—and the whole year saw inflows of $227 billion, or just under $20 billion a month."

But Biderman was looking at margin debt and he concluded that the levels weren't healthy. Even though the inflows were there, people were borrowing too much money and he had to question whether some of the inflow was being borrowed through margin debt. Between the end of October and the end of March, over $100 billion was borrowed to buy shares. In November alone, margin debt spiked over $24 billion, compared to the prior record of $16.4 billion the previous April. The year-to-date margin debt rose 46.3 percent compared with the year-to-date market capital gain of 18.5 percent. "The last time margin debt rose that much faster than the overall market was in 1993—right before the market dropped for the year as a whole," Biderman wrote.

He was also concerned about options expirations, that is, the deadlines by which company insiders had to sell their stock options. News about selling by corporate executives (insider selling) is public information, available on the website www.insidertrader.com. It's also a good idea to check www.unlockdates.com, to find out how many shares of a company will be unlocked, opening up a window for senior management to sell some of their holdings. December is normally a month that is slow for selling stock options; it's a time when tax avoidance is more typical than aggressive dumping. Yet a headline in Biderman's February 3, 2000, bulletin proclaimed, "Insider Selling an Unreal $30 Billion in December." Finally, another negative news nugget for him was the flurry of takeovers and consolidations, many of which were financed by company stock. In a cash takeover, the company pays shareholders for their stock in cash, money that they can pour back into the market. But a stock takeover just cancels everything out.

So Biderman made his prediction, and he was right. Within three months, the Nasdaq unloaded a third of its value. By the end of April

Yahoo was down 32 percent, Amazon was down 40 percent, Commerce One was down 60 percent. Other companies fared even worse. That was the first part of the sell-off that lasted the rest of the year and beyond.

This is a perfect example of combining important pieces of information that don't fall under the classic definition of news but were definitely newsworthy.

In addition to using money flows to predict major market trends, there are also seasonal liquidity patterns that help investors in determining the direction of liquidity and therefore stocks. "Tax collections are highest between December and early May, and mutual fund flows are the highest between January and May," according to Biderman. "They're not high in December because mutual funds have to distribute their capital gains in December. Investors have to pay taxes on that gain even if they have only owned the fund for one day, so investors don't want to buy into the fund and pay the capital gains tax twice. Virtually all of the tax payments are made before Christmas, so flows boom after Christmas."

October tends to be a weak month. Before the market was heavily invested by mutual funds, stocks that had been down for the year got weaker in December as investors sold their losers so that they could have a deduction in the capital gains tax they had to pay on their winners. However, mutual funds are now a bigger factor in the market. Fidelity and some mutual fund families' fiscal year ends in October. Other fund families end their fiscal year in November. So tax-selling season has shifted to October and November.

Seasonal factors are an underlying trend to bigger market forces, Biderman cautions. Just because they exist doesn't mean that other factors can't trump them. But wherever the market forces go, the money flows will always provide a clear indication of their direction.

Volume

Where the money flows, the trading volume follows. Volume is the total number of stock shares, bonds, or commodities futures contracts traded in a particular period. The volume figures are reported daily by the exchanges, both for individual issues and for the total amount of trading executed on the exchange.

Volume is important because it shows how much interest there is in a particular stock or sector. If there's no volume, there's no liquidity. You want to see heavy volume, because that shows there's a lot of investor participation, enabling you to get in and out of stocks easily.

If you're following a specific stock, knowing the average daily volume gives you a baseline of knowledge about its trading pattern. If nothing else, it lets you know how easily you'll be able to get in and out of the stock, because it indicates whether buyers and sellers are available on the other side. Changes in volume can signal news in the stock or the sector that you should follow up. If the average volume is forty-four million shares but the volume on a particular day is double that, that could indicate something is going on that you should know about—an earnings announcement, a change in sentiment, an impending stock split, a new product introduction.

I'll never forget the day in September 2000 when Intel traded 308.7 million shares, a monster amount of volume. Ten years ago, that was a day's work for *all* the stocks at one of the major exchanges. Volume days like that are worth watching. It's common sense—if so many investors have their fortunes tied to this one stock, clearly the health of that company is going to have an impact on more than just that stock. It may have an affect on that sector or even the overall economy.

Momentum

Just as earnings drive expectations, volume drives momentum. Momentum refers to a herd mentality. In other words, are the masses piling into a certain stock or sector? If so, there's real momentum there.

Momentum investing is based purely on the price movement of a stock. If the stock has been trading well for a certain amount of time, that's a positive sign. Conversely, if it's trading down every day despite a rallying market, there's probably something wrong with it. At any rate, there's not enough money supporting it. I'm not a fan of buying and selling on momentum because it's tantamount to day-trading, which I think is not appropriate for the typical investor. But knowing a stock's momentum is another way to take its pulse; any change in the usual pattern indicates something to look into.

"Momentum implies performance," explains Steve Shobin, portfolio manager at Americap Advisers. "The quality of the performance is a measure of confidence. Strong momentum implies not only confidence about the fundamentals but the willingness to manifest and leverage that confidence by buying or selling the stock. ""

Technical Analysis

Using information about volume and momentum is a hallmark of the investment style called technical analysis. ""Technical analysis basically examines the performance of the market and the psychology of investors in an attempt to gauge how confident they are about the fundamentals of a company,"" explains Shobin. ""It's the study of supply and demand. The technician attempts to figure out who is the more urgent player: the buyer or the seller. By urgency, we mean their confidence level: who's more confident, the buyer or the seller?""

Most technical analysis is done for the short or intermediate term. It's especially useful in identifying what's known as a technical rally, a short-term rise in securities prices within a general declining trend. These rallies may result because investors are bargain hunting or because analysts have noticed a particular support level at which securities usually bounce.

A quick timeout for a few definitions from *Barron's Dictionary of Finance and Investment Terms:* A support level is defined as "the price level at which a security tends to stop falling because there is more demand than supply. Technical analysts identify support levels as prices at which a particular security or market has bottomed in the past. When a stock is falling towards its support level, these analysts say it is 'testing its support,' meaning that the stock should rebound as soon as it hits the support price. If the stock continues to drop through the support level, the outlook is considered very bearish. The opposite of a support level is a resistance level." For a long time, people said that Compaq faced resistance at $30 a share. For some reason, every time it rallied close to that level, it would then back away. Shobin says that once a stock breaks a longtime resistance level, it suggests it can keep going.

Although technical analysis is often used by short-term investors, it's really much more than a timing tool, insists Shobin. ""It's more of a measure, a gauge of how confident the Street is about fundamentals. Momentum is bipolar—it can be up or it can be down. When a stock gaps to the downside as the result of unfavorable earnings estimates, the implication is a bearish sea change in the confidence level of Wall Street in the fundamentals of that company.

"I evaluate stocks, not companies," Shobin says. "The profile of a stock is different from the profile of a company. That's one of the reasons that people don't perform in the market as well as they possibly could. They're not bilingual. They know the language of companies but they don't know the language of stocks. And I might add that they do call it the stock market, not the company market.

"The language of stocks is basically that when we analyze a stock, we look at the industry group in which it exists. It's better to buy a weak company in a strong group than a strong company in a weak group. A weak group acts like a weight on the shoulders of even the strongest company, pushing it down to the very ground, whereas a strong group acts like a buoy, elevating even the weakest of companies. It's truly a herd mentality; you don't have to be a genius. When the semiconductor sector was going up, all the semiconductor stocks were going up. Same with B2C Internet companies, then B2Bs, then EMS (electronics manufacturing service) companies and fiber optics. We saw the same thing when these sectors went down—one by one, each sector fell from favor.

"Then I look at the relative strength of the stock itself vis-à-vis the S&P 500. The ability to outperform a broad index is a measure of investor confidence in the stock. I like to buy stocks in strong groups that are exhibiting superior relative strength.

"I use the financial index as a barometer for the overall market. I'm always aware of what the financial stocks are doing. Their performance is very, very important because the performance of financials is indicative of the trends of interest rates and inflation and the market generally does best when financials are strong.

"I think performance is the most important way of understanding or interpreting the confidence level of investors—the actual performance of the market and the performance of the stock. How is the stock acting in relation to its industry group and the overall market? Is it able to go to certain levels that were impenetrable before? How does it respond to news—does it go up quickly one day and down the next? Does it hold up well when the market is down? All these factors are a measure of how confident investors are about the fundamentals. If the stock was $110 and is now $115, that means buyers are more urgent than sellers. And if we can add indications of relative strength in a strong industry group, then the probability of profitability has risen."

Technical analysts use price charts to identify and project price trends in a market, security, or commodity future. Individuals can access these charts as well through most financial websites. Just click on the ticker symbol of a stock and pull up the company's stock price graph. Check on its performance for the past week, the past month, the past quarter, and longer periods. You want to look for sustained moves up in a company's graph. It may be fluctuating around the trend line, but the trend line should be going up, and going up steeply. That tells you right there whether to pay attention to a company.

"You have a huge amount of news embodied in the company's stock price chart," says Robert Loest, senior portfolio manager for IPS Funds. "That enables you to ignore the rest of the noise. Looking at the stock price is the first thing an investor ought to do when he or she hears a hot tip. If the long-term trend line is up strongly, then you should pay attention to it. If it's not, then you can ignore everything else. There are more than enough companies in the world with good price charts so that you don't have to waste your time on something dubious."

In the short term, using technical analysis to evaluate the stock's and the sector's response to earnings announcements can give you a sense of market sentiment. "How a stock responds to news is pivotal," explains Shobin. "A good stock will respond within a couple of days. You like to see rising volume when the stock responds to good news and you like to see a strong close.

"Talbot's is a stock that bucked the downward trend of the retail sector in 2000 and was able to do okay," recalls Shobin. "Back in early August 2000, it had a number of gaps on the upside in response to its earning announcement. [An upside gap means that the low for the current day is higher than the high for the previous day. A downside gap means that the high for the current day is lower than the low for the previous day. So if yesterday's low for GE was 50 and the high for today was 48, there would be a downside gap of 2 points.] That said, hey, even though the sector is stumbling in the dark, this stock is worth looking at because it responded so dynamically to good news. That reflected a growing Wall Street conviction and optimism about the fundamentals of the company."

Talbot's went from $54 a share to $62 within two days of reporting its 2000 third-quarter earnings. "An investor could say, 'Geez, it's had an almost 15 percent move, it will be hard to buy.' But I look at this move as critical evidence that Wall Street's confidence in the fundamentals of the company had surged and it was willing to invest in it. An investor doesn't have to respond right away; you don't have to buy at bottom tick to make money in the market. While it's sometimes frustrating to miss a few points, I think one can gain conviction about the importance of the development by looking at how the stock responds to news. Good trends persist. If they didn't, we wouldn't have had an Intel or a Wal-Mart or a Cisco."

Technical analysis can also help explain what it means when a company reports good earnings but its stock goes down. That's because while a history of good earnings will ultimately prevail, one quarter's report is a single data point and it's important to watch the Street's response to that data point.

"At first blush, the inability to embrace good earnings is a negative," Shobin comments. "Micron Technology reported better than expected third-quarter earnings in 2000 but its stock could not bounce. That was telltale; it said something was amiss here. Then other semiconductor stocks couldn't bounce and started reporting less than hoped for earnings, which reinforced the feeling that something really was awry.

"The caveat is that sometimes there's a delayed response. In a real bull market, however, the response shouldn't be too delayed—the stock should go up in a few days. I look very closely at the sector group for edification and confirmation.

"In the case of the semiconductor group, Micron had a big gap on the downside in early September, maybe 6 or 7 points, resulting from a prominent analyst expressing skepticism. [Jonathan Joseph of Salomon Smith Barney had downgraded the group a couple of weeks earlier.] At the very same time, Intel was also gapping down, the result of a hint of earnings and sales problems. The fact that Intel gapped at the same time as Micron suggested that something was awry not only with these stocks but with the sector in general, because these are bellwether stocks for that sector. On the night of September 19, Micron announced earnings and the stock could not respond. That was a confirmation of the prior gap. You had a trend of negative things happening. What the stock price charts showed was not only the inability to respond to good news but the prior trend of what was happening to other stocks in the industry group." The group continued to sell off in the ensuing months.

Loest uses stock price charts when he teaches a securities seminar to individual investors. "I show them a page with the graphs of five companies—Bethlehem Steel, Clayton Homes, International Paper, Eastman Kodak, and Dillard's Department Stores—where there's a lot of variation on the trend over five or ten years but the trend is essentially sideways or down. You'd be amazed at how many people in these seminars are interested in buying these stocks. 'Why in God's name do you want to own this company?' I ask them. 'Well, it's cheap.' 'Well, it's cheap for a good reason—it's a bad investment.'

"Then I show them the second page with charts of high-growth-rate, high-tech companies like JDS Uniphase, EMC, and AES. The variation in the stock price is far less, so long-term investors in these companies are getting higher returns and taking less risk. It's that simple."

I sometimes see technical rallies happening on the floor of the NYSE. Let's say IBM has been testing its support level but then goes up every day for two weeks straight, at a time when the rest of the market is choppy. Technical analysts like to see a stock act well, and when they see IBM bucking a down market, they tend to believe the stock will go higher yet.

You'll see a trader in the crowd at the IBM post buying the stock at $101, then $102 and $103. That indicates that there's a large buyer looming somewhere in the background who just wants to own IBM and will pay higher prices for it even as it trades up. The price momentum and the technical analysis are on IBM's side.

People don't think that technicians are breaking any news, but I think technical trading is important because it's a subset of money flows. I call technical charts the message of the market. They quantify what the market is telling you.

However, be advised that you can't buy on technical analysis alone. If the fundamentals do not support a rally in IBM, it will fade. Technicians say that technical rallies without supporting fundamentals will not last long and prices soon resume their usual declining pattern. That's why technical analysis tools, such as momentum and charting, must be used along with fundamental analysis.

"To look only at a stock chart can be misleading," cautions CSFB's chief strategist Tom Galvin. "Some stocks have been going up for five years and if you'd said their charts showed too sharp an ascent three years ago, you would have gotten out before they quadrupled in price. And some stocks trade along at the bottom and people buy them because they think they're low risk, then get caught in the value trap. What changes those charts is a change in the fundamental pattern of the specific company or its industry."

Money flows, volume, momentum, and technical analysis—each of these data points is another piece in the jigsaw puzzle. As with any puzzle, you can rarely see the entire picture by picking up just one piece. You need to examine all the pieces, screen them according to your benchmarks, and fit them into your investing framework.

There's only one hitch: Even though these tools explain major market forces and how to evaluate them, they don't provide all the pieces in the puzzle. You can't look at a data point in a vacuum. To complete the picture, you need to know how to use the news that directly affects a specific stock.

Chapter 6

The Changing Nature of Market-Moving News

It used to be that you woke up in the morning, picked up the *Wall Street Journal,* and read news that had broken the day before. By the time you called your broker, the stock had already moved. The individual investor could only surf the reaction, not be part of it.

Television news wasn't much different. When I started as a production assistant at CNN Business News, we often read a story in the *Wall Street Journal* at 7:00 a.m., spent the day trying to add new information to it, and then went on the air with it at 7:00 that evening. By that time, it was already over twenty-four hours old.

That's no longer the case.

Everything involving financial news has changed: the speed at which it's delivered, the methods and media by which it's delivered, the breadth of its coverage and even the nature of the news (and, of course, the audience—but you already know that).

Today corporate and financial news is delivered as fast as you can log on to the Internet or turn on your television. Companies call us up and tell us that they're going to release news and would like to come on the air to release it. Or they hold a conference call, as Microsoft did to explain how it would respond to the decision in the federal antitrust case, and simultaneously broadcast it over the Internet, allowing anyone in who wants to log on. When companies release their earnings, they broadcast a conference call with their management team and Wall Street analysts on the Internet, enabling any individual to listen in on the analysts' questions and the executives' answers.

Every time the Federal Reserve's Board of Governors holds its quarterly meetings, CNBC stations a reporter with a cell phone at the Federal Reserve Building in Washington. He's hooked up to my set on the air. At 2:15 p.m., as soon as the Fed announces its decision, he jumps in live to report whether interest rates will go up, go down or stay the same. We learn the news as soon as anyone in Washington learns it, and our viewers hear it at the same time that everyone on Wall Street hears it.

I can tell you firsthand that at CNBC we have thrown all of the old television rules out the window. It used to be that you needed good video and pictures to make a story into a broadcast story, as opposed to a newspaper one. Today, information is what's hot, even if the information is just about numbers. When the Fed speaks and our Washington reporter is on the phone, we run the story live, no matter how boring the picture may look. The graphs, charts, and live ticker are what people most care about, not some pretty background shot.

As the financial news flow has increased, the trading environment has undergone a sea change. The world has more access to more news than it ever had before. With information flowing more freely, the markets respond more rapidly.

News is broadcast as it's happening, and investors can actually watch the information move the markets as its implications sink in. I will never forget the day in October 2000 when the Dow Jones Industrial Average went down 436 points, mainly due to a sell-off in IBM. As I described earlier, the stock had already sold off in the premarket and people expected it to open much lower. The market specialist told me he expected to open at $93.50. Then, just as he was about to open, a trader yelled, "Hold it up!" The trader had another five hundred thousand shares to unload, putting more pressure on the stock price. The specialist held up the opening for a full five minutes, then opened IBM at $90.25. IBM is a component of the Dow; within minutes, the Dow went from being down 119 points to being down 436. It's that kind of second-by-second change in the market that can be an important window into how things work on Wall Street. CNBC caught the action while it was happening and broadcast it live.

The markets are moving faster than they ever have because information is moving faster than it ever has. It reaches a much larger audience that responds with a click of the mouse.

Twelve years ago, the average volume for the NYSE was two hundred million shares a day. Today two hundred million could be the number of shares in a single stock moving on a single day. Daily volume can exceed two billion shares.

The bull market and skyrocketing investor interest have encouraged more companies to go public, with the result that there are more companies being traded on the NYSE and Nasdaq than ever before. Along with a larger number of stocks, there are many more venues to trade them. It used to be that the NYSE was the only place. Then came Nasdaq and the American Stock Exchange. Even though the NYSE continues to dominate market share, there are electronic communications networks, or ECNs, like Instinet, Island, Archipelago, and ReadyBook, that offer trading venues after the official markets close. Plus there are international exchanges in London, Frankfurt, Tokyo, Hong Kong, and Bombay that are getting linked to American exchanges. Some of the big investment banks even make their own markets in individual securities. The reason for the volume at these trading venues goes back to the information explosion.

The information explosion has changed the nature of the news that I deliver. Things that were not newsworthy ten years ago can move stocks today. Take "unlocks." When a company goes public, there's a 180-day lock-up period during which company insiders may not sell any of their stock. After those 180 days are up, the lock-up expires and an executive is free to unload some shares. That wouldn't have caused a ripple in the days before rocket-fueled IPOs. But if a hotshot fiber-optic company goes public at, say, $36, and 180 days later the stock is at $136, you would expect some of the company insiders to cash in. If enough insiders sell enough shares, that can move the stock significantly.

I always look at the lock-up expirations, but ever since the Nasdaq tanked, unlocks have become less important, because so many IPOs have fallen out of favor along with the rest of tech and telecom. It is unlikely that company insiders are going to sell shares and take advantage of the lock-up expiration if they have actually lost money on their stake.

Here's a related development: Ten years ago, not only were the lock-up expirations not newsworthy but in addition the information about the unlocks wasn't readily accessible to me. Now the information is considered so newsworthy that there's a website devoted to it: www.unlockdates.com. The government also publishes the news when an insider has filed to sell a significant amount of stock at www.fedfil.com.

The information explosion has changed the audience I report the news to. Individuals today are more sophisticated than they have ever been about the business of Wall Street. The information explosion has raised the bar for reporting on the markets. I look at lock-up expirations because the viewer demands that level of sophistication.

And because individual investors demand that level of sophistication, the Internet has become a treasure chest of information for them to play with. Investors follow stock price charts, they scrutinize company management teams, they examine balance sheets, and they listen in to webcast conference calls. More significant, as more and more information has become readily—and often freely—available online, institutions that once charged high fees for their research are now beginning   post their findings on the web.

However, the increasing "webification" of financial information and the proliferation of the number of other channels to disperse it has had another, less happy, result: the fragmentation of information. "Information now comes in tidbits," complains Arnie Berman, technology strategist for Wit Soundview Capital. "It's like trying to get educated through soundbites on the nightly news. The news reports the latest change but knowing the latest change doesn't always lead to understanding. You need context."

Another drawback is that instantaneous information can be cranked off a spreadsheet, but how do you know the quality of the data? "In our society, thanks to the impact of the media, junk in becomes junk out that's too easily disseminated to the masses without much scrutiny," cautions Paul Meeks, senior portfolio manager of Merrill Lynch's technology and Internet funds.

The shock waves of the information explosion continue to reverberate. Individual investors recently won the privilege of having access to a rich trove of information that was previously restricted to the institutional investment community. In October 2000, the Securities and Exchange Commission (SEC) mandated the Fair Disclosure Regulation, which requires companies to release important financial information to Wall

Street and Main Street at the same time. When I interviewed then SEC chairman Arthur Levitt about the full disclosure rule, this is what he said: "The reason we haven't had this before is that there's a kind of mystique that America's investors somehow need interpreters of this information, that they're not smart enough to take a mass of information that is now available to them and make their own judgments. I don't accept that. The key aspect of Regulation FD is that the individual investor is no longer going to be considered a secondary recipient of information. He and she will get the information at precisely the same time as large institutions."

The implications of Regulation FD will be tremendous. On the one hand, more information will be made available to more investors. Just after Regulation FD came into effect, Meeks listened to a conference call from Corning. "They gave far more detailed projections than they usually do," he recalls. "They said that in the future they will give more detailed industry guidance on conference calls but won't comment between conference calls."

Although that will help the retail investor, Meeks predicts that it will also lead to less informed institutional analysts and investors "because the intraquarter wink and nod won't be given." No longer will analysts try to gain important knowledge about company trends during a golf outing or lunch with the CEO. Meeks believes that will lead to more earnings surprises, either positive or negative. "And when there are earnings surprises in my world, the stock goes down 40 percent overnight." The result, many analysts believe, will be increased market volatility.

In short, the free flow of news has dramatically reshaped the investing landscape. But one thing hasn't changed: certain types of news will always move the markets.

There are four main sources of information that can move a company's stock, stocks in a particular sector, or even the entire market. I can't be completely comprehensive, but these news sources are the most obvious and common:

- news from the federal government;
- news from the company itself;
- news from market professionals, such as analysts, institutional investors and major individual investors, such as Warren Buffett and Carl Icahn; and
- news from unconventional sources, such as Internet chat rooms, journalists, columnists and your Uncle Joe.

Each of these sources delivers different sorts of information in a different way and with a different agenda. How do you evaluate the information coming from these sources? How can you tell whether it's news or noise?

I'll answer these questions in the next four chapters.

Evaluating News from the Federal Government

Every month the federal government produces vast quantities of facts, figures, and analyses to gauge what's happening in the economy. It measures consumer spending, consumer income, employment statistics, the gross domestic product (GDP), housing starts, manufacturing shipments, orders and inventories, retail and wholesale sales, and a host of other pulse points. Federal policymakers use these (and other) data to determine how to maintain the health of the economy, and their resulting decisions can move the markets. Even before the decisions are made public, however, many investors try to second-guess the implications of the data on the thinking of these policymakers. Consequently, the data itself can also move the markets.

I mentioned in Chapter 6 that every news source has an agenda or at least a bias. The government's agenda is remarkable for what one market analyst calls "absence of malice." Its goal is simply to measure every pulse point, every temperature change, and every blood pressure fluctuation that describes and determines the health of the economy.

"News from the government can generally be regarded as pretty accurate and middle-of-the-road, not slanted one way or another," comments Arthur R. Hogan III, chief market analyst for Jefferies & Company. "Sometimes the government's sources of information and the tools it uses can be a bit outdated. In factoring the

Consumer Price Index [CPI], or the inflation number, as it's called, many people would argue that the basket of goods that is measured hasn't changed a whole lot in about twenty years and probably doesn't reflect current consumer spending. So the government may be missing the mark on the CPI. And it tends to underestimate gross domestic product growth. But fortunately or unfortunately, the government uses the same yardstick on a month-after-month basis, so while it may miss the mark in terms of exactly how much inflation or growth is out there, at least it's using the same tools every time."

In short, you can generally trust news from the government. The government doesn't have any reason to put a positive spin on the average price of a quart of milk in Cleveland (part of the CPI, I kid you not) or the number of refrigerators produced in the past quarter to keep it cold (part of the Labor Department's report on nonfarm productivity) or sold (part of the Bureau of Economic Analysis's durable goods manufacturers' shipments). What's important to investors is how those data are interpreted and the decisions made as a result of those interpretations.

Which are news and which are noise?

"The Fed"

The most well known and among the most important policy decisions are those made by the board of governors of the Federal Reserve banks. Its role in controlling monetary policy and encouraging and guiding the economy through the bull market of the 1990s made "the Fed" into a colloquial term and turned its chairman, Alan Greenspan, into a star.

The Fed meets eight times a year—on the third Tuesday of January, March, May, June, August, October, November, and December—to decide whether to change the federal funds and the discount rates. The federal funds rate is the interest rate charged by banks with excess reserves at a Federal Reserve district bank to banks needing overnight loans to meet reserve requirements. The federal funds rate is the most sensitive indicator of the direction of interest rates, since it is set daily by the market. The discount rate is the interest rate that the Federal Reserve charges member banks for loans, using U.S. Treasury securities as collateral. It provides a floor on interest rates, since banks set their loan rates a notch above the discount rate.

Almost all short-term interest rates key off of the actions of the Federal Open Market Committee. The Fed raises interest rates by draining reserves from the banking system. It does this by selling Treasury securities, which absorbs reserves. Conversely, the Fed lowers interest rates by adding reserves to the banking system. It does this by buying securities.

How reliable is the Fed? "The Fed is considered by many to have more and better information about the economy than anyone else," says Robert Hormats, vice chairman of Goldman Sachs and one of Goldman's government and international economy watchers. "Apart from whether their pronouncements lead to specific policy actions at the time, the Fed is widely regarded as the best repository of economic knowledge in the country because it has so many sources of information and because its people are respected for their ability to sort out this information and draw reasonable conclusions from it. They've got a lot of information and, notwithstanding a few mistakes from time to time, they have earned the reputation for having good judgment."

Consequently, virtually everything the Fed does has the potential to move markets.

First and foremost, the Fed controls our money. "Money is the root cause of inflation and inflation is the root cause of interest-rate changes," says Lawrence Kudlow, chief economist at ING Barings. "I would say that eight times out of ten, announcements that move interest rates are the single biggest impactor on the stock market."

The amount of interest that banks charge for loaning money affects the entire economy. Higher interest rates means higher rates for the cars we lease and buy, the homes we mortgage and the credit cards we use. When interest rates go higher, we tend to spend less. Consequently, the companies that produce the goods we buy earn less, and the companies that supply the raw material for those goods are also affected.

Furthermore, what the Fed says is considered by Wall Street to foreshadow some kind of action—or inaction, as the case may be. Finally, what the Fed says is more than likely to be of some policy consequence down the road, because the Fed is likely to act on what it believes.

Investors have become so sensitive to the Fed's power to affect the markets that the quarterly meetings have spawned their own market-moving force called the Fed effect. The Fed effect is a phenomenon that has accompanied Federal Reserve meetings since the financial crisis of the summer and fall of 1998, when the Fed stopped cutting rates and began to move toward raising them again. (It also stems from the Fed's decision in 1997 to announce interest-rate decisions immediately after the meetings; before then, it often delayed the announcement, so there was no clear news on which to act.) What happens is that stocks tend to rally strongly—on average, 2.7 percent but sometimes as much as nearly 10 percent, according to the *Wall Street Journal*—in the days leading up to and on the day of the meeting, then level off or even fall afterward. It doesn't even seem to matter whether the Fed raises rates, cuts them, or leaves them alone. This trend has provided a bonanza for short-term traders who buy stocks in advance of the meetings and then sell them at a profit when the meetings end.

I tend to believe the Fed effect is noise. Trying to time what the Fed will do and trying to act on any effect, in my opinion, causes confusion, can cloud your judgment, and will distract you from the real news, that is, the actual, tangible data that move stocks.

It's much more worthwhile to try to understand the factors that the Fed thinks are important. That way, you will have a better idea of what the Fed is likely to do.

You can get a good sense of the Fed's view of the economy as well as a hint of where the Fed might go down the road by going to the Fed's website at www.federalreserve.gov. The Federal Open Market Committee publishes minutes of its meetings, as well as press releases about their decisions. There's also the Beige Book (the nickname for the quarterly *Summary of Commentary on Current Economic Conditions*), an evaluation of the economic conditions in twelve regions around the country by Fed staffers (available at www.federalreserve.gov/FOMC/beigebook/2001/default.htm). The Beige Book is pretty dense reading, but there are summaries and highlights at sites such as www.yardeni.com, a website run by Edward Yardeni, chief economic strategist of Deutsche Bank Alex Brown. Alan Greenspan also testifies to Congress several times a year.

Right now the Fed's agenda is simple: to encourage economic growth without the threat of inflation. At other times in history the Fed might be worried about something else. In 1998, when Russia devalued the ruble, the Fed worried about a worldwide recession. When Latin America's economies experienced a slowdown, the Fed worried about the impact on the United States.

More recently, worry has turned from slowing down a red-hot economy to reviving what has become a much more severe slowdown than anyone expected. When the Fed lowered interest rates for the first time during the current cycle—the first cut after six hikes—it did so between scheduled meetings, on January 3, 2001. To most people's surprise, the Fed cut both the federal funds rate and the discount rate, leading some people to speculate that the prior six rate hikes were perhaps one too many.

Some speculated that the Federal Reserve wanted to cut rates in November 2000, but could not because of the drawn-out election. The Fed is not governed by the president and never wants to appear politically charged, so it's feasible that Alan Greenspan and Company would have liked to begin a boost for the economy but could not during the thirty-four days we all waited to learn the results of the election.

One of the Fed's goals is keeping America competitive versus its international counterparts; clearly, it watches economies around the world and puts the U.S. economy into the context of the global economy. You've got to look at what's happening in the economic environment to understand the Fed's concerns.

It's hard to know what piece of data or information the Fed deems most important. Some say Alan Greenspan likes it that way, evidenced by his often-obfuscating testimonials to congressional committees.

We do know however that the Fed considers a few key factors and certain pieces of economic data in its ongoing fight against inflation. All these factors are published either in the financial press or on the Internet, and they are readily available to the average investor. (Instead of trying to remember the alphabet soup of government agencies and their website addresses, use the index at www.searchgov.com.) You should pay attention to these economic reports, because they signal a change in the landscape, and you need to be aware of the landscape in order to put individual companies' prospects in context.

Five Significant Factors the Fed Looks At

Not every report is always going to influence the thinking of the Fed—or the movement of the markets. It depends on economic conditions. But here are five consistently significant factors that individual investors should be aware of.

The Employment Report

The first Friday of every month, the U.S. Department of Labor issues a report on unemployment and wages. The report is a key snapshot of the labor market. The employment report is one of the most influential economic reports today. The reason it's so influential is partly due to the current economic landscape. During much of 2000, the employment situation happened to be tight; in other words, unemployment was at virtually unprecedented low levels, meaning jobs were plentiful. That was good news for the employee, but it was something the Fed watched closely because too tight a labor market can trigger inflation. So during that period, the employment report every month was as influential on the market as anything else. It's available at www.bls.gov.

The Employment Cost Index

The montly Employment Cost Index (ECI) measures how much employers are paying their workers. It encompasses salary, benefits, and the whole ball of wax. If it rises too much in a tight labor market, the Fed gets worried. The ECI is also available at www.bls.gov.

Consumer Price Index

The CPI, reported in the middle of the month, measures inflation pressures that are directly hitting the consumer by keeping track of what people are paying at the cash register. (You can see the items used to calculate a typical American's shopping list—milk, eggs, cereal, a computer, the cost to gas up your car, the price of a visit to the dentist—at www.bls.gov.) The government calculates what it costs to buy this stuff this month and compares it with what the cost was a month ago and a year ago. The bottom line: Has the consumer experienced inflation? Is the consumer paying more for goods? There is an argument to be made about whether the CPI in fact still encompasses what we all do every day. In today's day and age, perhaps a better gauge might include the cost of a movie ticket, a train or bus ticket, or even the cost of a stamp.

Producer Price Index

The Producer Price Index (PPI) measures the same thing at the producer level by calculating inflation pressures before they reach consumers. Did Joe Supermarket Owner pay more for his raw materials last month? And if he did, did he pass that cost on to you? Did he raise the price of milk? Are cigarettes more expensive? Has oil surged or fallen? Is the company that produces aluminum charging more for its product? If so, then you know that the company that makes aluminum cans will up its price, which will be passed on to the soft-drink bottling company. The end result: the consumer will pay more for a can of cola.

On any given month, any one of the components within any one of those reports, may flare up. In 2000, energy prices showed the biggest rise. And we all knew it. We went to fill up our gas tanks and the bill was much higher than the year before, which is why the CPI and PPI reflected increases. The PPI is available at www.bls.gov.

The Wealth Effect

A key wage-related concern for the Fed is whether consumers will use their fatter paychecks to spend more. The "wealth effect" is a reflection of consumer confidence: Do we feel richer than we are? Are you feeling wealthy enough to build a bigger house or buy a snazzier car? Are you willing to take on more debt, max out your credit card more often, invest more in the stock market because you think you are richer than you actually are, based on your wealth on paper? The wealth effect is an inflation indicator. Producers figure that if there's a strong enough demand for their goods— housing supplies, automobiles, or whatever—then they can afford to raise the prices.

The wealth effect was at the root of one of Alan Greenspan's most famous speeches, when the Fed chief claimed that there was "irrational exuberance" in the stock market. His implication was that the stock market had risen so much that investors felt richer than they actually were. We really didn't have that million dollars from stock gains that we thought we had. It was only on paper and, he warned us, could easily go up in smoke. In fact, two years later, the market did blow up, with dotcoms leading the market lower.

The wealth effect is actually a nebulous concept. However, it can be quantified through the Consumer Confidence Index (CCI). Published by the Conference Board, the CCI is based on a monthly survey of five thousand representative U.S. households. It is available at www.conference-board.org.

How Market Strategists Crunch the Government's Numbers

Different market strategists crunch the government's numbers in different ways to predict where the economy is going and how the Fed might react. Goldman Sachs's Robert Hormats looks for answers to these three questions:

1. What is the underlying growth rate of the economy? Examining retail sales, personal income, factory orders, and unemployment statistics will give you a comprehensive assessment of the direction of the economy. These, as well as information on monthly housing starts, U.S. international trade, advanced retail sales, manufacturers' shipments and inventory, and a whole host of other data, are available from the Department of Commerce (www.doc.gov), especially the Census Bureau (www.census.gov).
2. Is productivity remaining strong? That tells you how well the economy is going to do in maintaining and sustaining that growth rate without much inflation. That's reflected in unit labor costs and the productivity index reported by the Bureau of Labor Statistics (www.bls.gov).
3. What's happening with inflation? The tried-and-true inflation indicators are the CPI, PPI, and changes in personal-consumption expenditures—what economists call the PCE deflator. The Bureau of Labor Statistics (www.bls.gov) publishes the monthly CPI and PPI. The Bureau of Economic Analysis (www.bea.doc.gov) publishes the PCE deflator, which has grown in importance ever since Alan Greenspan said this inflation tracker was his preferred measure over the CPI.

Tom Galvin, chief economist for Credit Suisse First Boston, notes that different indicators raise red flags at different times. "I'm concerned about retail sales: the Fed can control consumer spending by raising interest rates and consumer spending makes up 75 percent of the gross domestic product. I look at the employment cost index, because labor tightness is significant today and the ECI is the best measure of inflation, wages, and bonuses and stock options, whereas things like hourly earnings are not. Thirdly, I look at the personal consumption deflator, which reflects what goods and services people are actually consuming on a monthly basis. It's fluid and dynamic, compared to the CPI, which is a static basket of goods.

"You can get caught up in the buzz over the CPI and PPI, but these three indicators get to the heart of the issue about labor inflation and goods and service inflation."

ING Barings's Lawrence Kudlow looks yet elsewhere for inflationary red flags. Here are his four favorite indicators that the Fed might raise rates:

1. The price of gold. "Everyone loves to hate gold, but it's a very good indicator of inflation. When gold goes up, that's a signal that higher inflation and interest rates are coming. Gold has been pretty dormant for the past decade, and that's one of the reasons we've had such a bull market. But in 1999, it went from $250 to $325 an ounce. That's pretty low, compared to 1980, when it peaked at $800 an ounce. But even a move from $250 to $325 is a signal that the Fed was inflating the money supply. And a smart investor would have known that even though stock prices were rising, in the not too distant future, higher inflation would cause the Fed to increase interest rates and stock prices would fall. What the Fed giveth, they usually taketh away. Rising gold is bad, falling gold is good. Interest rates usually follow gold in about a year."

2. Long-term bond yields. "This is sort of like financial gold. If you look at the rates for 10-year Treasury bonds, when those things start rising, it usually means higher inflation, which means that the Fed will raise short-term rates before long. Higher interest rates damage the present value of future earnings for companies; hence profits will be less, and that's bad for stocks."

3. The foreign exchange rate of the U.S. dollar. "A slumping dollar is bad; it usually means that there's something wrong with the economy. A strong dollar is good; it's telling you that everything is going to be okay."

4. The commodity futures index. "Published by the Commodity Research Bureau (at www.crbindex.com), the index measures futures on bulk goods such as grains, metals, and foods. It's a good inflation indicator. When the index goes up, it means higher rates are coming; when it goes down it means lower rates are coming."

All of these reports are published in financial newspapers and weekly business magazines. To find additional governmental economic reports on the Internet, go to www.searchgov.com. Individual investors can look up these data and do their own basic economic forecasting.

A word of reassurance: The data are surprisingly accessible. For the statistically challenged, each of the economic indicators is reported with a press release that explains the significant findings. Not at all turned off by tables of figures, Kudlow compares poring over economic statistics to reading baseball box scores and claims to get as much of a kick out of following the CPI and the GDP charts as he did tracking Willie Mays's batting average when he was a kid.

But even Kudlow admits that you could have a nervous breakdown trying to follow every economic statistic that comes out. "I do this for a living and I can't track them all," he confesses.

What makes it even more difficult is that the government issues the statistics virtually every week. Personal income and consumer spending reports come out the last Monday of the month, followed by consumer confidence reports, productivity rates and unit labor costs, and the unemployment rate. The next week brings the PPI, retail sales, and business inventories. The CPI and housing starts come out in the middle of the month. The end of the month sees the announcement of the GDP, existing home sales, durable goods orders, and the ECI. Furthermore, many of the statistics are revised two or three times in the course of a month.

How You Can Crunch the Government's Numbers

So, how should you handle the flood of economic data?

"Because they come out in this staccato fashion, the average investor doesn't look at them in their broad view and doesn't see how they relate to one another," says Robert Hormats. The average investor is looking for strategic coherence, but that isn't readily available because they come out over the course of the month. One figure may indicate that the economy is growing, another may indicate that it's weakening. It's hard to make thoughtful judgments when these figures hit you day after day.

An example of a knee-jerk reaction to one isolated piece of government data occurred when the April 2000 CPI was released. It was significantly lower than March. (The March CPI rose 0.8 percent; the April CPI rose only 0.1 percent.) "People overreacted. To them, it looked like the sky was falling," recalls Arthur R. Hogan III, chief market analyst for Jefferies & Company. "But when we looked at the May CPI, the numbers had leveled off. There wasn't inflation. Most economic data should be looked at in a time continuum. Here's April's number, so how did March look and how does May look? People didn't look at that number as part of a trend."

Hormats's solution: Sit down once a month to make sense of the numbers. Read and listen to the people who give thoughtful analysis, the serious research people at the investment banks and in the financial and economic news media. Hormats is also a big fan of *Business Week*'s regular two-page "Business Outlook" column. "In two pages, it gives a thoughtful assessment of where the economy is going. It's the first thing I read."

Some market experts make a living out of trying to predict the Fed's decisions. Should you?

Says Hormats, "The individual should be aware of Fed policy but shouldn't jump or make big trades on what the Fed says or does day to day or week to week. The Fed, don't forget, reflects the economy of the moment or at least in the relatively near term: it operates on a short- or medium-term time frame, while most investors have a longer-term, multiyear time horizon—such as saving to buy a house, to pay tuition or to fund their retirement. It's useful for an individual to understand what the Fed is saying and doing, but on most occasions it's probably counterproductive for an individual who is a long-term investor to trade on it."

Still, that doesn't mean you should ignore economic warning signs that could result in a change in interest rates. Evaluate the government numbers within the context of your own investment concerns. Ask yourself what the outlook of the economy is and how it fits into your investment outlook. If you're a retiree with a fixed-income portfolio, inflation is a big issue. You're not worried about the stock market's performance as much as the threat of inflation's eroding your savings. On the other hand, if you're a thirty-year-old with a lot of equity, you're concerned about what's going to affect stock values five years from now. You see higher interest rates and a lower market index as a good buying opportunity. As a retiree, you don't want to be exposed to that kind of risk.

The main thing is to keep in mind the old rule "Don't fight the Fed." When the Fed raises its target interest rate—the federal funds rate—that's a cautionary signal, says Kudlow. It usually takes its toll on the stock market because it slows the economy and slows profits.

Many investors ignored that rule during the heady period between 1997 and the summer of 2000, when the Dow Jones Industrial Average and the Nasdaq soared despite six interest rate hikes. There was a feeling that the New Economy was immune to Old Economic disciplines. Not so, says Kudlow. "If you took the broadest measure, which is the S&P 500, or a really broad measure, like the Wilshire 5,000, and if you drew a chart, you'll see that these measures stopped advancing in autumn of 1999, leading to the stock market slump of the second half of 2000. The Nasdaq is more volatile and there was an argument that technology would be immune to interest-rate hikes, but that proved not to be true." As economists at Morgan Stanley Dean Witter told clients in the fall of 2000, "The $32 trillion global economy has turned on a dime."

That was when virtually everyone was debating whether the United States was in an official recession, defined as two consecutive quarters of decline in a country's gross domestic product. One big negative at the time was the price of oil, which skyrocketed right at the time the Fed was raising rates. This accelerated the slowdown, making it much worse than even the Fed wanted and resulting in the change in policy in 2001, when interest rates came down.

The Federal Reserve isn't the only governmental agency whose decisions move the markets. Three regulatory agencies are critically important to some of the most dynamic sectors of the U.S. economy.

The Food and Drug Administration's (FDA's) decisions have a direct effect on the fortunes of pharmaceutical and biotechnology companies. The FDA's agenda is to evaluate the safety of drugs that are on the market, as well as those that are coming to market. By establishing the guidelines to test these drugs, it also can delay or hasten the time it takes for a company to start cashing in on its products.

Over the past decade, the FDA has speeded up the time it takes to move drugs through the safety testing pipeline. From an average of ten years, the process has been reduced to five and even three years. Even the process involved when the drug fails one of the FDA's trial phases has become much more efficient. Companies now know much more quickly what is necessary to win FDA approval of a new drug and can go back to the drawing board to fix it that much faster. That's one reason that we've been seeing so much development in the fields of biotechnology and genomics. But that's small consolation to Schering Plough. The pharmaceutical giant dropped 10 points at the opening bell on Friday, February 16, 2000, after the FDA said that manufacturing issues would delay the movement of Schering's hotly anticipated new allergy drug.

News from the FDA is not as widely reported as news from the Federal Reserve. While the major stories are covered in the news, the average investor has to dig a little deeper to keep up with the latest developments. One solution is to use the Internet to check news stories associated with various drug and biotech stocks. In addition, the FDA's website (www.fda. gov) contains press releases about the latest FDA approvals and decisions, as well as reports from its meetings.

Another federal regulatory agency operating in a key area of the U.S. economy is the Federal Communications Commission (FCC). Just a fast look at the headlines on the FCC's website (www.fcc.gov) on December 8, 2000, demonstrates why this agency's actions are significant: "FCC Monitoring Rollout of Broadband Access," "FCC Takes Steps to Allocate Additional Spectrum for New Wireless Services," "Auction of Licenses for C and F Block Broadband PCS Spectrum, 3G Wireless." Licenses to use the airwaves for wireless communications have been called the most precious natural resource of the information age. With the increased use of mobile telecommunications, the FCC's auction of part of the television broadband spectrum to cellular phone companies provides opportunities for the biggest carriers to fill in holes in their network, beef up capacity, and gain a national footprint and for second-tier players to expand, changing the competitive landscape for the entire industry.

Another area in which the FCC has an effect is in reviewing and approving mergers and acquisitions within the telecommunications and broadcast industries. The unprecedented consolidation that's been occurring, as well as the fallout from the proposed breakup of AT&T, will definitely put the FCC in a position to steer a major sector of the economy.

Overseeing all major mergers is the Federal Trade Commission (FTC), which is charged with preventing monopolies and cartels in the United States (www.ftc.gov). In recent years the FTC's trust-busters successfully prosecuted Microsoft, blocked a merger between WorldCom and Sprint, killed a proposed merger between Staples and Office Depot, and only approved the AOL and Time Warner linkup after eleven months of deliberation and the imposition of restrictions on their conduct.

The deal between AOL and Time Warner is largely believed to be the most monumental ever in terms of changing the landscape for media and telecom. Many predict that the course of this deal will dictate similar deals down the road. Consequently, you as an investor want to watch how the government responds to these big mega-mergers because they will change the competitive landscape.

You might not think the Internal Revenue Service (IRS) could move markets, but its data on tax receipts can be a rocket—or a bombshell.

During the five-year bull market, when an investor got a big tax refund, he or she typically put it back into the stock market—and with 100 million individuals investing regularly in the stock market, that created a big bounce. The IRS is an unconventional source of news, rather than a direct hit. But plenty of people use the information about tax receipts and average tax returns to predict what's going to happen with money flows into the market. That information is available at www.irs.gov.

Conversely, when people have a huge tax liability, they often are forced to sell some of their stock holdings to pay off Uncle Sam. It's no coincidence that the big market sell-off in the spring of 2000 began during tax season. People who had made significant gains from their technology investments in 1999 were faced with a huge tax liability. Of course, the tech sell-off was due to many factors and once the market began to tumble, there were plenty of elements accelerating the fall. One of the biggest was that there had been heavy amounts of buying on margin and as the values plummeted investors had to sell their stocks to cover the margins. But liquidating positions to pay the tax bill was a significant factor.

Similarly, when the market plummeted in October 2000, many people attributed it to tax liability selling on the part of mutual fund portfolio managers. The mutual fund fiscal year ends in October. Typically, if you own a mutual fund, you pay taxes on capital gains from any winning trades that were made throughout the year. It may seem like adding insult to injury, but you have to pay taxes on those gains even if the overall value of the fund declined. As the tax bill adds up toward the end of the fiscal year, mutual fund managers try to lessen the pain by selling their losers— the stocks that have not made any money—to offset their gains.

That is why we saw so much selling in the fall of 2000. Mutual fund managers were approaching the end of their fiscal year. They knew they would have a big capital gains tax for their winners but they also knew their funds were down year-to-date. So they sold their losers, which accentuated the downward slide of the market.

Investors need to watch government announcements about tax policy. Income tax rates, capital gains tax rates, and any taxes that have to do with 401(k)s, individual retirement accounts, Keoghs, and other supersaver accounts are very important to individual investors. Lawrence Kudlow explains why: "In 1997, Washington lowered the capital gains tax rate to 20 percent from 28 percent. Capital gains is the tax that liberals love to hate, but in the financial world it's probably the most important tax on stocks and wealth and the after-tax reward for taking risk. The 1990s bull market started in 1995 but really gathered force in '96, '97, and '98—those were the three big, big years—because everyone knew the capital gains tax would be cut in '96, and after the election it was cut. If you go back ten years, to the big tax reform act of 1986, even though income tax rates were reduced, the capital gains rate was raised from 20 percent to 28 percent, and I think that had a lot to do with the down market in 1987. It just didn't pay as much to take risks. Today, many expect a positive impact on the stock market from President George W. Bush's much talked about trillion-dollar-plus tax cut.

"One way to calculate this is a shorthand I use when talking to retail investor groups: At a 28 percent rate, you keep 72 cents of each extra dollar of wealth. At a 20 percent rate, you keep 80 cents. The differential is 80 over 72, or 11 percent. That's a sizable number, and investors always keep their eye on that.

"Another take to this: The capital gains tax is not indexed to offset the effects of inflation. The income tax is indexed, but not the capital gains tax. Whenever inflation goes up, that raises the capital gains tax, because you're being taxed on the inflation. I call it the illusory tax, because you didn't cause it but you have to pay it. So rising inflation is always bad for stocks, because it raises the unindexed capital gains tax and therefore reduces the rewards for risk taking."

It's also worth watching the news headlines for other government regulations that could change the competitive landscape. In 2000, Microsoft stock lost half its value almost overnight when the Justice Department suggested its antitrust breakup proposal. Microsoft stock has since come back into favor with a new political administration and the possibility of a repeal of the antitrust ruling. Back in the early 1970s, Richard Nixon proposed wage and price controls, which were devastating to the economy and the stock market. Workers couldn't get pay increases, so they had no motivation. Corporations couldn't increase their prices, so their profits were choked off. The laws of supply and demand were undermined by wage and price controls, so the entire economy was rendered inefficient.

Nixon also imposed energy price controls. That decimated incentives for oil companies to produce oil and gas, resulting in less oil and long gasoline lines. "If investors see any hint of wage, price, or energy controls, that's a very negative sign for the economy and the market," says Lawrence Kudlow. "We're seeing this now in the debate about health care and prescription drugs. If price controls are imposed on drugs, the pharmaceutical stocks will crash, as they did a few times in the 1990s when there was also a threat of price controls."

Tariffs too can affect the economy and specific industry sectors, especially in an increasingly global marketplace. A tariff is an international tax. History shows that when the government imposes high tariffs, which are taxes on imported goods and services, commerce and the economy slow down. Or if tariffs are imposed on specific industries, those companies will suffer. You can find the latest information about tariffs at the International Trade Administration's (ITA's) website at www.ita.doc.gov.

Economist Arthur Laffer argues that there are four prosperity killers: high inflation, high tax rates, significant regulatory burdens, and high tariffs. You could read those same factors as four stock market killers. So investors need to be aware of the news and see whether the government has control over these four prosperity killers—or not.

Evaluating News from a Company

Too many people confuse a good product with a good company and good management. People also assume that a good company will always turn out good products and be managed well. And many investors blindly follow managers from the company where they built stellar reputations to their next corner office, on the assumption that what worked at one company will naturally work at another.

It doesn't work that way. I think it was Warren Buffett who said that any time a manager with a great reputation meets an industry with a bad reputation, the industry is going to win. Take the oil industry. The profitability of the company depends on the imbalance between supply and demand of petroleum. That fundamental imbalance is out of the hands of management. It doesn't matter if the company brings in a great new CEO; he or she still won't be able to overcome the fundamentals of the industry.

Similarly, remember when top managers from Andersen Consulting, Citibank, and AT&T jumped to dotcoms like Webvan, Priceline, and Global Crossing? Their hires gave the fledgling Web companies real-world authority and the news goosed the stock up. But even those experienced managers couldn't keep their companies afloat when the show-me-some-profits tsunami hit Internet stocks. George Shaheen exchanged the corner office at Andersen Consulting for the same position at the online grocer

Webvan and watched the stock hit a high of $25; it recently traded at 34 cents. Citigroup chief financial officer (CFO) Heidi Miller jumped to Priceline, whose stock peaked at $104; within a year, it traded at $1. As CEO of Global Crossing, Robert Annunziata, formerly president of AT&T's $22 billion worldwide business services group, saw Global Crossing stock hit $61; he subsequently left the company, which recently traded at $19.

In short, if you want to keep a company in your portfolio, you have to know the company you keep. To do that, you must be able to evaluate the information it releases and separate the news from the noise.

Announcements from a company that move that company's stock encompass everything from a major acquisition to an important product rollout, from the management's decision to buy back stock or split the stock or issue a dividend. They can range from an important new hire to an important resignation. They can include notice of insider buying or selling large blocks of company stock or the decision to invest in a high-flying IPO.

Sometimes what makes the stock move is not the information being released but the way in which it is released. In a now infamous analyst meeting in October 2000, Oracle stock dropped 13 percent in spite of reaffirming rosy prospects for the quarter and the coming year. Instead, investors reacted to what analysts called poor body language by CFO Jeff Henley. The story going around was that Henley was less optimistic than in prior meetings and his body language reflected that. Later on that day, I interviewed Henley. His explanation for his silent message: he didn't drink enough coffee that morning. He used the interview with me as a forum, once again, to reiterate positive prospects for the coming year, but the stock continued to sell off.

These announcements may make the stock swoop or soar, but they may not necessarily hold any real significance for the future of the company. How can you tell the difference?

It helps to understand the reasoning behind the company's announcement. A company's allegiance is to its shareholders, its customers, and its employees. Shareholders are a major constituency, because as investors buy into the company's story by buying its stock, the stock will go higher, giving the company easier access to capital. The company can always tap into the public markets, buy back stock, sell shares at a better price, or use those shares to make acquisitions, so management works to enhance shareholder value.

Customers are another major constituency, obviously, because they buy the company's products. Both customers and shareholders depend on an efficient workforce, which in turn benefits from healthy revenues and a rising stock price. So a publicly traded company's agenda is, simply, to make money and get its stock price up. Consequently, it wants to deliver information that makes the company look good so that more money is raised for the company and the best talent wants to work for the company.

There are different ways of delivering that information.

How Companies Tell You What They Want You to Know

Issuing a Press Release

The most frequently used method is a press release put out on public relations or business news wires or the company's website. Today, even urgent or timely information is released on a company's website. Case in point: KLA-Tencor, a semiconductor capital equipment manufacturer, issues its earnings and future guidance by simply posting it on its website every quarter. You won't get it any other way, and it's up to the investor to look it up. That's KLA-Tencor's way of dealing with Regulation FD.

Often the company's management will call a certain reporter whom they have a relationship with and have the reporter break the news. That's typical with the *Wall Street Journal* and CNBC. A company spokesperson calls us to say, "We're making an acquisition and we'd like to announce it on air on CNBC." We're happy to do it because we want to break news.

If you keep up less frequently with your stocks, you can usually safely ignore press releases and catch up with the company news in its quarterly reports or the financial news headlines. This works better with bigger, established companies that make it into the news. But even their stocks can move significantly based on information in press releases, while volatile small-cap growth companies can see their stock values double or halve based on information in press releases.

Caveat emptor: Because they're issued by the company, press releases by their nature tend to put a positive spin on news. Furthermore, many small companies try to get in the news by flooding the news wires practically every time the CEO sneezes. Okay, I'm exaggerating, but for a while there was a fad among Internet startups to order up a fax blitz at the least provocation just to draw attention and differentiate themselves from the rest of the crowd. As Paul Meeks, portfolio manager of Merrill Lynch's Internet and technology funds, says, "Not everyone can have a great press release every day. The company probably had a public relations firm creating them or the investor relations department."

I get press releases all the time from competing wire services representing companies trying to make something out of nothing just to keep their name out there. The press releases may talk about a new product that may not even be out on the market for another two years. The company figures that just hearing its name mentioned in the news will keep consumers and investors buying its existing products and stock, or at least keep them familiar with the company. It's an intangible element in the company's growth. If you hear its name you may go to its website, and that counts as traffic generation, which, at the end of the day, actually helps the company. But it's still noise, not news.

Don't let the noise of press releases outweigh the news value of visiting the company's website for information. "One thing that investors don't do enough is go directly to the company's website," says Robert Loest, senior portfolio manager for IPS Funds. "Capstone Turbine's website has diagrams explaining how their turbines work. Ballard Towers's website has diagrams of photonic exchange membranes. These websites are not head and shoulders above everyone else. Most high-tech companies' websites have good explanations about how their technology works. The first thing people ought to do if they want to know something about a company is go to its website."

Learning about a company's technology or products or customers gives you the framework in which you can evaluate news about the company or its competition. For example, you may have discovered on the company website that Enron is involved in building high-tech windmills to turn wind power into energy. Then you read an article in the newspaper about the growth of wind farms around the world. You may think, This is an industry with room to expand and here may be a company that appears to have experience with the technology; I'll find out more and see if it's got a competitive advantage. You could even research this little nugget of news further and see which companies are involved in manufacturing the technology used in the windmills on the theory that these companies will sell the necessary machinery to all the companies in this sector.

In other words a company's website may be full of information that's not officially classified as news. After all, detailed explanations of turbines and photonic membrane exchanges isn't exactly headline stuff. But it provides a valuable tool with which to weigh those headlines and press releases, so it's anything but noise.

Calling a Meeting of the Analysts

Another way companies deliver news is to call a meeting of the financial analysts who cover the company for investment banks, mutual fund managers, pension fund families, and other investment institutions. This method has a specific advantage for the company because it is talking to the people who understand the business model best.

These also happen to be the same people who have put together their own earnings models with estimates about how much that company will make. If a company's management tells the analyst community about a particular product, the analysts will then go back to the office and write up recommendations about the stock based on what they just learned and pass it on to the investment community. It's another, secondary way of disseminating information, with the added advantage over a press release in that, like a smart bomb, the news is targeted to the people who really want to hear it and this audience can be relied on to give it an extra bounce.

Sometimes these meetings are open to the public by conference call or are broadcast live on the web. But sometimes the company wants to tell its story only to a select group of people.

That happened a while ago with Yahoo. You would think that Yahoo of all companies, being one of the main symbols of the power of free information delivered over the Internet, would broadcast its news so the world would hear it. It didn't. Instead, it announced that its analysts meeting in May 2000 would be closed to the media. Furthermore, the meeting was being held from 1:00 to 3:00 in the afternoon; because the market closes at 4:00, there would be an hour in which big investors could trade on the news while small investors would have to wait until it was delivered the next morning through the media.

This infuriated me. I made it my business to report on air what was going on and I hunted down analysts who were going to be there and asked that they please call me from their cell phones right after the meeting so I could broadcast anything that might be eventful. It turned out to be a very well attended meeting. The story was that the overall fundamentals were firing on all cylinders, usage had never been busier, and subscribers were on the upswing. Yahoo's management laid out optimistic predictions of earnings and revenue, and Wall Street came away extremely bullish on the stock. It was something that would have been great for the individual to be part of. For starters, Internet stocks remain very much a retail, or individual, area of the market. Internet investors are largely Internet users, who tend to be retail customers, not institutions. So why wasn't Yahoo inviting its own investors to its meeting? (Incidentally, within six months of the meeting, Yahoo's stock had lost 80 percent of its value.)

This sort of situation is expected to disappear now that the SEC has implemented the fair disclosure rule prohibiting companies from giving intraquarter "body language," as the Street dubs it, to a select few. Regulation FD stipulates that companies under law must divulge material information about their businesses in such a way that all the interested parties—analysts, money managers, and, most important, individual investors—receive the information at the same time.

What had happened over the years was that relationships had formed between the companies and the analysts who covered them. When you think about it, it's only natural for a company executive to become friends with one or two or three of the analysts who follow his stock. Remember, in addition to attending a company's analyst meetings, analysts are constantly calling on the company's management in an attempt to dig up new nuggets of value that will help them decide whether to recommend the stock to their clients.

Take one of the big investment banks like Morgan Stanley Dean Witter. Its institutional clients could include American Express Financial Advisors, with $3 billion under management; it could include Alliance Capital with $10 billion under management. The clients pay a big fee each month to get good investment ideas from Morgan Stanley, and Morgan Stanley relies on its analysts to find out information about these companies that could be considered proprietary. So an analyst's job is to become close to company executives so that he or she can go on what are known as fishing expeditions, looking for hints of a particular direction the company might go in or catalysts that might rock the stock. Analysts build these relationships at lunches or dinners with the company's senior management, at weekend conferences at a resort, and at on-site visits at the company itself.

The relationships pay off to the extent that information gets passed to or picked up by a select few people. Why else would Goldman Sachs come out on any given morning and downgrade a stock when the rest of the analyst community is positive on it? How did Goldman find out something about that particular stock that no one else knew? Could it be that Goldman's analyst had dinner the night before with the CEO, found out something, and surmised that it's negative for the stock?

The downside to these relationships is that so many analysts believe everything the executive tells them and their work stops there. They may simply ask management to walk them through the numbers of the company's quarterly report and pass along the CEO's translation, rather than doing their own interpretation. In addition, there's an inherent conflict of interest involved when the companies that analysts follow are also clients of the same investment bank and generate hundreds of millions of dollars in fees for those banks. I'll discuss this in more depth in Chapter 9.

I asked Arthur Levitt, then chairman of the SEC, what sparked him to implement Regulation FD. His answer: "My experiences with heads of companies who wanted to say that the price of their stock was undervalued because of visions of high stock prices. They tried to seduce analysts who would write favorable things about their company by giving the analysts information ahead of the public." Levitt says that the idea that the individual does not have the capacity to understand sensitive market information is no longer valid today. "Investors today have enough information available to them to make judgments without those judgments having to be screened first by securities analysts."

You might very well ask why the company's managers can't just come right out and make their own forecasts to the investment community. After all, they're empowered with the best information: they know how well their company is doing, they know about the industry, and they know about their competition.

One reason is that the company's management is prohibited by ancient SEC regulations from making its own prognostications. The other is that companies are afraid of lawsuits brought by shareholders who might be disappointed in their forecasts.

The result, though, according to Joseph Battipaglia, chief investment strategist at Gruntal & Co., is like trying to make a chocolate chip cookie using blueberry muffin ingredients: "The inputs are wrong for the outputs you're looking for."

Will Regulation FD change the mix?

Battipaglia has his doubts. "The fact of the matter is, up until the fair disclosure rules, analysts would have the companies confirm their estimates anyway. If you looked at the beginning of a quarter, you'd see a disparity in earnings estimates for widely held companies that was pretty substantial. But as the quarter progressed, the spread narrowed dramatically and the consensus became where everyone was. That's because analysts would go to someone in management and have the following conversation: 'How are you doing? How are the kids? Listen, I'm using 35 cents for the quarter, does that sound reasonable? Great, how about golf tomorrow?' Right then, the analyst has confirmed that what he or she is projecting in the public domain is right. If he's not, the company executive might say, 'I'm more comfortable with 34 cents.' The guidance the companies gave bridged the gap between their internal forecast and what the analysts came up with on their own. Now, in order to comply with Regulation FD, if companies want to make the same comment about what they think about the quarter, they will have to issue a press release."

Certainly, the fact that companies have already been under a severe amount of pressure to get the news out to the entire investment community at the same time is one reason that CNBC has been so successful. Companies want to use our media platform to comply with government regulations.

While ordinary investors are rarely invited to participate in a company's conference calls to analysts, as a result of Regulation FD more and more companies will broadcast those calls on the web. Then individual investors can see and hear the CFO talking and make their own interpretation of his body language. (See "Conference Calls: Tune In or Turn Off?" on page 161.)

But it's hard to believe that the relationships that have already been created and fostered will change. The jury is still out on how effective Regulation FD will be.

Keeping an Eye on Insiders

There is, however, another sort of inside information that's open to the public and, occasionally, can be significant. From time to time, company employees are allowed to sell their stock options, usually purchased at a discount, on the open market.

The SEC requires that sales of stock options must be recorded publicly. If any company director or senior executive wants to sell any amount of her stock in the company, she must file with the SEC to do so. Ordinary investors can check up on insider sales at the EDGAR (Electronic Data Gathering, Analysis and Retrieval system) section of the SEC's website (www.sec.gov), or at Freedgar.com, whose more user-friendly software makes it easier to access the SEC database, or at the site for Federal Filings Business News (www.fedfil.com), which reports the largest transactions of the day as well as those involving companies in the news. The sales are also part of the stock's daily news headlines on the major financial websites, such as CNBC, Bloomberg, and Yahoo Finance.

Sometimes when an insider sells, it's not news. Maybe the stock is up 500 percent over a year and the CEO has a window in which she can sell it. Maybe the sale is part of a regular divestiture to diversify an insider's stock holdings or maybe it's to raise money for personal reasons, such as buying a home or paying some bills.

But sometimes insider sales can signal unpleasant news. Before Dell Computer announced its 1998 fourth-quarter earnings, chairman Michael Dell unloaded a significant amount of company stock. On the one hand, his decision made a lot of sense; he owns a lot of stock and the price was near its fifty-two-week high. On the other hand, there was some question as to whether the company would be able to continue its winning streak and Dan Niles, a semiconductor and PC analyst with Lehman Brothers, had even publicly doubted it. The analyst was right. The earnings were disappointing and the stock plummeted 20 points. Had you been skeptical about the company's ability to rack up another quarter of blow-out earnings, the news of Michael Dell's sale of stock might have signaled you to reevaluate your own position and possibly follow suit.

With the information gap caused by the implementation of Regulation FD, insider sales are a potentially more significant piece of the information puzzle, says Bob Gabele, director of insider research at First Call/Thomson Financial. "If interpreted carefully, information about insider sales can help supplant what is now lacking in what used to be the normal information flow."

How do you know when insider selling is a portent and when is it merely a bunch of chicken guts? Read "How to Evaluate Insider Trading" on page 163.

No News Can Be Big News

What a company doesn't say can be as significant as what it does say. If the market is expecting to hear material news and doesn't hear it, that may mean that things are not happening the way people expect.

For example, in October 2000 I interviewed Jeff Bezos, CEO of Amazon.com. I asked him a question about the level of cash at his company coming into the holiday selling season, an especially important period that year because Amazon had yet to make money and Wall Street was beginning to question if it ever would. I knew at least two analysts who had raised the red flag about Amazon, particularly Ravi Suria of Lehman Brothers, who was worried that his cash expectations were a lot lower than what Amazon was projecting. Suria thought that Amazon would have $300 million in cash by the end of January, a sum too small to allow the company to continue operating. Amazon, in fact, did not run out of cash, but the questions about its future viability have become more urgent.

When I asked Bezos how much cash the company would have, he kept saying that at the end of the year it would have $1 billion. I asked about the end of January. He said, "Look, we deal from year to year," meaning that Amazon's fiscal year closed at the end of December. But that one-month discrepancy between the end of December and the end of January was important because while it's understandable that Amazon might reach $1 billion in revenues as a result of its Christmas season, it would have to pay all of its suppliers within thirty days. Suria, for one, didn't think there would be much left over after paying the bills—in fact, only $300 million.

My point is, Bezos would not answer my question. He would not tell me what the company's finances would be after paying back its suppliers. As I write this, the book is still out on how Amazon will do. But from a stock's perspective, you've lost 70 percent of your money if you bought a year ago. Ravi Suria's scenario is playing out. And you could have extracted a negative perspective on the stock based on the fact that Jeff Bezos didn't answer my question.

Then there was the time I tripped on a hidden nugget of news from i2 Technologies. As I mentioned earlier, I was skimming an analyst report from Credit Suisse First Boston in which the analyst wrote that the head of technology sales at i2 Technologies had resigned the week before. The salesman was highly regarded, but this analyst didn't think his departure would be bad for the stock, despite the fact that his unit accounted for 40 percent of overall sales.

Whoa! If a man whose division is responsible for nearly half of the company's sales resigns, that's significant news—yet I hadn't heard any mention about it. To make sure I hadn't missed it, I searched Bridge, Dow Jones, and AP and then looked on the press release wires to see if the company had issued any news about this man's leaving. There wasn't anything. Why had the company made no mention of it?

I called the company for explanation and while I was waiting for a response, I went on the air with the news. The stock opened down 20 points. The company called me up to complain. I said, "Clearly, investors are reacting to this news of the head of a division accounting for 40 percent of sales resigning. Could it be that once I mentioned it, people learned about it for the first time and that's why they're upset?"

"No, no, no," I was told, "this happened two weeks ago." "But you never reported it," I said. Now most people I'd spoken to about this didn't think that it would have a material impact in the long term, but it certainly had one in the short term. If the head of a unit that accounts for almost half of a company's sales resigns, that is certainly material information. One would think that i2 would have written a press release and delivered that information in a timely fashion. Instead, the company was likely going to hire a replacement and perhaps breeze over it. I just happened to trip over this nugget of news in an analyst's report and it had not been widely disseminated, intentionally or not.

Even worse than no news is the wrong news. Rumors of bad news can knock points off a company's stock faster than I can finish typing this sentence. Sometimes all a company has to do is cancel a presentation by its management at an industry conference or postpone an analyst meeting, and the resulting rumors trigger all sorts of negative expectations on the part of investors. Often, it's all just noise.

During the tech sell-off of 2000, many investors were worried that Morgan Stanley Dean Witter had underwritten a significant amount of debt in the telecom companies that had lost a large amount of their value in the previous six months. I heard rumors from a number of traders that Morgan was going to lose close to $1 billion from bad bonds. Day after day, Morgan stock was down—down 5 points, down 8 points, down 10 points. Finally, after a week of losing value from its own stock, Morgan put out a press release saying it was going to lose only 4 cents a share, for a total of $45 million. That press release stopped the rumors and staunched the bleeding.

Often, you'll see a rumor moving the stock and then see the company saying, "We don't comment on rumors." Nine times out of ten, a company says it won't comment on rumors, but I feel that it's always better for a company to comment on them and for investors to check them out, so they don't mistake the rumor for real news—or so that they don't miss the nugget of news hidden in the noise.

I was completely surprised on January 5, 2001, to see Bank of America answer morning rumors that the company was facing credit quality issues and losses in derivatives trading by issuing a press release defending its credit. I was also suspicious. As Hamlet's mother says, "The lady doth protest too much, methinks." The market was equally surprised but no less suspicious. Despite the press release, the stock still ended down more than $4 that day.

Is the Company Giving You News or Noise? How to Tell

Press releases, company websites, comments from analysts, rumors, and news reports—these are the main sources from which investors receive information about a company. But how do you determine whether that information is news or noise?

The answer: You have to know the context of the information. You have to assemble enough pieces to put the puzzle together.

To get a good picture of the company, I ask a lot of questions. I'm essentially analyzing the company, just the way the Wall Street professionals do. They call it building a model. I call it watching the stock.

There's no one way to go about doing this. I've asked top analysts and found that everyone approaches this task in his or her own way. However, the important common element in doing your analysis, according to Kevin McCarthy, co-head of technology research for Credit Suisse First Boston, is to "take as many data points and as many inputs and distill them down to some level where you can draw a conclusion, or at least come up with a reasoned analysis of where the company is today. Where it will be tomorrow could be very different. At that point, you have to trust your analysis and go with your gut."

I look at the industry the company operates in and within that evaluate its prospects for growth. Once I see how well the company competes within that industry segment, I look at the company's products. That gives me the framework that I fill in by asking questions whose answers give me the data points I need. These data points include the company's basic business model (i.e., how it makes money), its prospects for growth, its management, its customers, its suppliers, its strategic partners, its competition, and the overall economic environment for its industry sector.

You might want to keep a list of the most significant data points handy so that you know what questions to ask when assessing a company. Conversely, when a company makes an announcement, the "news" can be gauged against these data points to get a clearer picture.

The Questions I Ask

How does the company make money?

Break down the revenues of each segment of the business to see how much it contributes to the company's overall earnings. You can get this information from the company's annual report and from company profiles on Internet finance sites. Then compare those figures over the past three years. That will give you a sense of the company's growth areas and its intentions for the future.

For example, more than 90 percent of Microsoft's sales and more than 80 percent of its profits come from the PC business. The fact that the company is so dependent on one business could be alarming if that business slows. Actually, in 2000, the business did slow considerably, along with the rest of the economy. When I spoke with chairman Bill Gates about it, he was unphased. "Look, PC sales have reached a pretty amazing level, and unlike in most industries, the growth continues," said Gates. "The growth is not what it was in the early years, when things were really quite dramatic, but if you look at the opportunity, 58 percent of the homes in the U.S. have PCs, but only 10 percent do outside the U.S. If you can take a piece of software that will make people more productive, that's a smart investment no matter what the economic climate is. So I have no doubt that we are going to sell hundreds of millions of copies of Windows XP. ""

Brave words, but consider this: For several years, Microsoft earnings were growing at 30 percent or more per year. In December 2000, Microsoft preannounced weaker than expected revenue for the first time ever. In 2001, analysts were expecting no growth. That's a big difference from 30 percent. Do you believe Bill Gates or the numbers? Does Microsoft stock deserve to be trading at a premium when earnings are no longer growing at a premium rate? Investors said no, and took the stock down.

How viable is the business? Is the company putting all its eggs in one basket and relying on one sole business to grow?

Almost every sector has an organization or association that produces news about the industry. These groups provide growth expectations for both the sector as a whole and the specific components within each sector. Their reports are about as unbiased as news ever gets and, consequently, are the data on which analysts rely. (These organizations are listed, along with other sources of information for each sector, in Chapter 4.)

Unfortunately, this information is not always readily available to individual investors or is available only at a steep price. If you don't want to dig it out or pay for it, you can generally get it from the company's website or get it secondhand from the analysts' reports, from newspaper and magazine articles, or from television programs.

Where is the growth coming from?

Let's say you discovered that the semiconductor industry grew 50 percent in 1999 but only 40 percent in 2000. Growth in the semiconductor industry is obviously slowing down. The company you're interested in derives 50 percent of its revenue from semiconductors. What is it going to do?

A corollary question, one that's even more important, is, where is the next three years' growth coming from? Say a large pharmaceutical company derives much of its revenue from a drug that is due to go off patent in a year. Does it have another product in the pipeline to supplant its old one? Does it have a different way of doing business that will make it more efficient? Does it plan to open a new market?

Who are the customers?

Once you know who the customers are, you can see who the company is counting on to continue its growth. How many customers does the company have? If it relies on one large customer, then it is vulnerable if that customer cuts its orders. Witness what happened to industry giants like Lockheed Martin, McDonnell Douglas, and Grumman when the United States reduced its defense budget.

Geography also is important. Does the company reach a wide customer base, or is it restricted to a part of the country or a couple of key countries? If a company draws a significant portion of its revenues from Asia and the Asian economy tanks, then orders will be vulnerable and the company's bottom line will be affected. That's what happened to Photon Dynamics, a San Jose, California, maker of test and repair systems for the flat-panel display industry, when the notebook-computer market took a dive in late 1997. Demand for Photon's products dried up and prices were cut in half. Then the Asian economic crisis hit. By the spring of 1998, orders fell to $400,000 from $8 million. Photon managed to survive but learned its lesson. It acquired a private California maker of semiconductor inspection systems with North American and European customers, and today a third of the company's revenue comes from outside of Asia.

You can get the information about geographic breakdown from the company's annual report. It's also mentioned on investment websites like CNBC.com, Hoovers.com, Bloomberg.com and Yahoo Finance.

Sometimes information about a customer's preferences tells an important investment story. Wall Street legend has it that when Oprah Winfrey noticed a lot of people wearing Reebok athletic shoes, she decided that this would be a great investment. Similarly, I remember reading about how one investor in the Boston Market restaurant chain noticed one day that his local franchise didn't seem to be doing the booming business it once had and decided to sell—just before the stock plummeted.

Clearly, these are lucky situations, but you should not disregard the obvious. When the company's customers are consumers, you should always gauge customer satisfaction and demand. It's a little more complicated when the company's customers are other companies.

In early 2001, Schering Plough announced delays in the movement of some of its products through the FDA testing trials as a result of regulatory issues over Schering's manufacturing process. Among the delayed products was a potential blockbuster allergy drug. That drug happens to be licensed to Schering by a company called Sepracor. I was standing on the floor of the NYSE, watching the crowd at the Schering Plough post. There were so many sell orders for Schering that the stock didn't open for trading for about forty minutes. Both stocks plummeted on the news. One analyst came out with a report whose title nearly described Sepracor's dilemma: "When Schering Plough Sneezes, Sepracor Gets a Cold."

Most analysts subscribe to what's called the arms merchant theory of investing: During a war, the ones who ultimately win are the arms merchants because they supply all sides. Similarly, one of the reasons semiconductor companies were one of the best investments over a long period of time is because they supply to everyone—both pure-play PC-related business and communications companies.

There's just one problem with this theory, cautions Lehman Brothers semiconductor analyst Dan Niles: **"Their customers sometimes won't give an accurate forecast to the semiconductor companies."** Customers sometimes double-order to ensure that they get all the parts they need or to build up a lot of inventory in case the supplying company suffers a shortage. When the situation changes—either demand isn't quite as strong as was forecast or the customer has more than enough product—the supplying company can get caught off-guard.

Niles continues, **"I remember being on a Cisco conference call in the first quarter of 1996 when they announced that they would bring their inventory levels down significantly over the next six months. At the time, they had eighty-four days of inventory, compared to twenty-nine days of inventory in the same quarter a year earlier. I thought of one company in particular, Altera Corp. Their biggest customer was Cisco and their business was booming. Let's say Cisco was selling one part to their customers and ordering two to build up their inventory. At some point, they would realize that they didn't need to order at the same rates and will order only as many parts as they can sell.**

"I said, 'I think Altera has a problem and they just don't know it yet.' We downgraded Altera stock. Portfolio managers were yelling at me, saying, 'We've talked to Altera and they swear it's not an issue.' I said, 'That's because Altera hasn't gotten their phone call from Cisco yet.' They got it pretty soon after and announced that the next quarter's sales growth would be flat. That took a lot of portfolio managers by surprise but any individual investor listening to Cisco's conference call could have predicted it."

Who is the competition?

No company exists in a vacuum. When a company makes an announcement, how will that affect its status compared to its competitors? When MBNA, the specialty finance company, announced blow-out earnings one day and the stock was up sharply in the premarket, I checked up on Capital Finance, Providian, Household International, and other stocks in the specialty finance business that had not reacted yet. One thing I always do on *Squawk Box* is look for who else will be affected by this news.

You can find out the company's competitors, their strengths and weaknesses relative to each other, and how all the companies within the sector stack up right on the web. Often you will find news of all the companies in one sector under any of those individual companies' news headlines. In addition, analysts' reports, industry associations, feature articles in the financial press and on TV, as well as on most business websites, list "competition" in the companies' profiles. Caveat emptor: You're relying on other people's investigative skills and hoping that they have done the kind of research you'd like to have done. That includes the analysts' reports. The lesson: don't rely on one sole source of information.

What do the suppliers and vendors say about the company?

The companies that supply raw material and the vendors who distribute the finished products can often provide a truer picture of what's going on within an industry sector and a particular company than the company itself. Knowing what's going on with a company's key suppliers and vendors is like having a finger on the company's pulse.

Sometimes the information is right in front of you, often without your even realizing it. Recall Dan Niles's story in Chapter 4 about his visit to his local Circuit City and CompUSA computer stores, where he discovered an inventory glut just by the number of boxes of computers on the floor.

That's an example of the kind of research that anyone can do: walking around a couple of big computer retailers and asking, "Hey, how do things look?" Having a salesperson tell you that there's not enough room in the warehouse is a pretty bad sign. If you can ask, "Is this normal?" and the answer is, "No, sales are much slower than usual," then you've got some significant data points to work from.

Of course, the signals of a slowdown aren't always that obvious, but knowing what's going on with a company's main suppliers can often provide useful clues. Identifying these suppliers is just a question of keeping up with the industry news.

You don't need arcane knowledge of the industry process or an advanced degree in supply chain management to figure out that if a supplier is having a problem, it's sure to reverberate to its customer (i.e., your company). When Taiwan gets whacked by an earthquake, you know that its foundry companies will be out of commission for a while and that computer companies that rely on Taiwan Semiconductor for their motherboards will have difficulty getting an adequate supply. Consequently, those companies will have fewer PCs to sell and their quarterly sales will be affected.

In February 2000, Nike announced that its earnings would fall 24 percent from its previous forecast. The reason: problems with its i2 Technologies supply chain software. As one analyst wrote, **"The magnitude of Nike's shortfall underscores the substantial role that supply chain issues play in so many organizations' operations. Our sense is that Nike's problems were the result of difficulties associated with integrating the i2 applications with existing systems, resulting in both product shortages and overstocks."**

You are not always going to find buy and sell signals by walking around your neighborhood. However, I tend to believe that where there's smoke, there's fire. That's why with any experience I have in life, I always think about how it might relate to a particular stock.

For example, I fly US Airways and Southwest Airlines whenever I can and I like the service of both. As I write this, although the whole airline industry is showing some weakness, US Airways and Southwest stocks have done well. Conversely, I remember once flying Eastern Airlines. The flight was delayed taking off, then there were mechanical problems in the air that forced us back to the original airport, where, to top it off, customer service was indifferent to the point of rudeness. I overheard a customer service representative actually saying that she didn't care what happened to all of the grounded passengers because her shift was over. I remember wondering if that same attitude extended to the mechanics and ground crew who were responsible for our safety, and I decided then and there that I would never fly Eastern again. I wasn't surprised at all when the company went out of business a year or so later.

Who is running the company?

Lots of companies have great ideas but their management may not have the staying power to get them realized, so it's vital to examine the management team's track record. How long has it run the company? How has the stock performed? What's its modus operandi?

Dan Niles, semiconductor analyst for Lehman Brothers, loves Intel's attitude toward the competition. **"I think their chairman Andy Grove said it best: 'Only the paranoid survive.' Intel doesn't care if you're IBM or Transmeta. They think that any company, big or small, could come up and kill them. That's in comparison to one of its competitors which thinks it's the greatest thing to come along since sliced bread. All I can say is that one company has executed regularly and the other hasn't."**

(Bear in mind that Niles's comments on Intel were recorded in the late summer of 2000. He can change his opinion at any time, as can any analyst. And I stop short of giving analysts 100 percent credibility, because they are under intense pressure to say positive things about companies that are doing investment banking business with their firms, as you'll see from Tom Brown's experience, which I describe in the next chapter. The investor needs to keep analysts' comments in perspective and realize that analysts answer not just to clients but to their own companies, which derive significant fees from the companies that these analysts follow.)

Plenty of managers can successfully steer the company through calm waters, but the real test of management's skill is the decisions it makes when the wind shifts. What worked in one era won't necessarily work in the next. In the late 1980s Digital Equipment was the largest maker of minicomputers at the time, a company that had broken into a world then dominated by mainframe computers and succeeded with simply designed and inexpensive minicomputers. Its chairman, Ken Olsen, used to scoff, "Who's going to want a PC in the home?" Digital was a great company in the 1980s, but it wasn't willing to look forward. Its management was stuck in the mind-set that no one wanted a PC. The result was that Digital got killed.

If the management is willing to adapt and change with the times, the company will probably be successful. But that takes the ability to admit mistakes and learn from them. In one of the more obvious egg-in-the-face stances, Microsoft chairman Bill Gates publicly opined that the Internet was a fad that Microsoft would do best to ignore. We've since seen him do a 180-degree about-face, and Microsoft is one of the biggest proponents of the power of the Internet. That's a sign of smart thinking, not stupidity. A good leader recognizes when he or she has screwed up, retrenches, and changes the strategy.

Of course, the company can make announcements until the cows come home, but they mean nothing if investors don't have confidence in the management's ability to follow through. Has the CEO done what he said he would do? Has he delivered on his projected goals? If he promised to use the Internet to create more efficiencies, what have been the results?

There are even more fundamental questions about news from management: Is it believable? How well has the stock done under the CEO's leadership? If it hasn't done well, how much of that is due to an industry downturn or the overall economy, and how much is due to his leadership?

Scrutinizing the management and having a comfort level with it is important. You should know the people who run the company that you want to give your money to. You should have a sense of where they want to take the company and where they see fair value for the stock. For five straight quarters in 1999 and 2000, Rich McGinn, the CEO of Lucent, promised that the company would meet or exceed earnings expectations and then delivered disappointing news. For a while, Wall Street was willing to give him the benefit of the doubt, but the stock eventually lost 75 percent of its value and McGinn lost his credibility on Wall Street and, ultimately, his job.

Honest and open communications on the part of management is extremely important. If Rich McGinn had come out earlier and said, "Look, we're having a problem," it would not have shocked people as it did from quarter to quarter. Once a CEO loses credibility, it's hard to win it back. The Street sentiment is, "Why should I believe you when you don't seem to know what's going on until the eleventh hour and then you drop a bombshell and explode our expectations?" The stock becomes known as a "show-me stock," one that Wall Street won't trust until it proves worthy of investment.

At first, investors thought Lucent's slump was a buying opportunity. Given that Lucent had been one of the most widely held stocks, people wanted to see the story turn happier. In fact, it turned out to be one of those "it's cheap for a good reason" stories.

Now I know what you're saying: "It's easy for *you* to talk to management, Maria, but it's not as if I can call up the CEO of a multibillion-dollar company and chat face to face." That's true, but there are plenty of ways the ordinary investor can learn how a company's senior management thinks. You can read profiles in business magazines or newspapers, gauge his track record from the company's earnings history on the company's website, listen to interviews on television, or listen to his conference calls broadcast on the web. All you really need to do is get a handle on what the company has promised as far as earnings, revenues and growth targets, and check if he or she has delivered. You also want to have a sense of how the stock and the company have fared under his or her leadership. If you follow a company closely enough, you'll soon have a very good idea of the corporate personality and how management is likely to behave in a given situation. Tuning your radar into that frequency takes time, I admit, but the information is readily available.

Does the announcement make sense for the business?

I put a lot of faith in common sense. You trust your own judgment when you're buying a house or a car, so give yourself some credit when it comes to evaluating news about a business.

When Webvan announced it was planning to sell groceries online, some people were skeptical, given that the grocery business is a tough one. The giant companies exist on just a couple of percentage points of margin. One analyst said to me, "So how will putting this business on the Internet enable a company to make a ton of money, especially when it doesn't have the volume that the giants do?" Like many other Internet companies, its stock price initially soared, then went down to the single digits when reality struck.

Your antenna might be alerted by something as simple as a trip to the gas station. You may have noticed that you're paying more for gas than ever before. No wonder that the oil companies were the big earners in 2000.

How promising is the overall economic environment?

When you're analyzing companies, it's important to put the business into perspective relative to the overall economic environment. How is the economy growing and where do the industry and the company you're interested in fit in?

For example, the average American investor tends to have a very U.S.-centric view of the world. But if you look at the PC market, only 40 percent of all the PCs sold go to customers in the United States. A little more than 30 percent go to Asia, and Asia is the fastest-growing market in the world. There's a population of 280 million in the United States, but we forget that there are close to four billion people in India and China, and those two countries are experiencing some of the fastest Gross Domestic Product (GDP) growth they've ever seen. When the GDP per capita is going up at the rate it is, you've got a lot of people hungry for technology—whether it's cell phones or PCs or other electronic items that U.S. companies have to sell. So there are some big trends going on in those countries that will affect the stocks of companies whose products are sold there.

So let's say Hotshot Corp. announces that it's going to acquire Third Best Ltd. You as an investor want to know what significance this will have on your holding. One of the first questions analysts ask when companies merge is whether this will be accretive to earnings. Will Third Best's earnings add to Hotshot's or dilute them? If the merger is not to be accretive at some point soon, then what is the rationale for doing it? You can look over Hotshot's acquisitions over the past few years: Have they helped the company or saddled it with debt? Has the company done a good job of incorporating its acquisition, or has it choked on the extra systems and personnel? Do you agree with the management that buying Third Best makes sense? Will the acquisition give Hotshot an edge on the competition? Will it open up a new market or bring in new customers? Will it position the company well for the future?

You've heard me mention a lot of money managers, analysts, and other experts among my sources. But the most important thing you must remember is that everyone has an agenda. That is the first rule of thumb for me as a reporter, and it should be your first rule of thumb in evaluating information about a company. People don't talk about business for no apparent reason. There is always an agenda. When I interview a CEO, the analysts following a particular sector, or a money manager in charge of billions of dollars—some of which may be invested in the very company that I'm interested in—I always take everything they say to me with that rule in mind. That's why you as an individual investor *must* do your own research.

If you've done your research, you'll know whether Hotshot's announcement is hot stuff or hot air.

How to Read an Earnings Report

News that a company beat its earnings estimates can't be taken as fact; it's the quality of the earnings that really matters, not the quantity. The only way to judge a company's earnings accurately is to read its earnings report.

Evaluating an earnings report is more than simply comparing the top line to the bottom line.

How the Analysts Read Earnings Reports

"I look for a very impressive revenue growth number," says Arnie Berman, technology strategist for Wit Soundview Capital. "I like to see growth that says the opportunity is still expanding. For IBM, 10 percent revenue growth is awesome. If it's Nortel, 10 percent doesn't impress me. For JDS Uniphase, 10 percent would be a horror show. It depends on the industry.

"Then I look at the gross margins of the products or services, which are the expenses directly related to bringing those products or services to market. They're the best indicators of whether the pricing is good or deteriorating. If the gross margins are deteriorating, it could be that the cost of the components is going through the roof.

"If the margins are good, I next look to the inventory. If the gross margins go up and the amount of inventory declines, that's impressive. If the gross margins go up and the inventory goes up, then the best way to reduce average costs per unit is to make more units."

A lot of inventory is a red flag. There's a saying in the technology industry that inventory has the shelf life of lettuce; the older it gets, the worse it gets and the harder it is to sell.

"I also look at the balance sheet," says Lehman Brothers semiconductor analyst Dan Niles. "Let's say everything on the income statement looks fine, but on the balance sheet the accounts receivable have gone through the roof. If you see the accounts receivable skyrocket near the tail end of the quarter, that's a sign that the company thought demand would be better and struck a bunch of deals at the end of the quarter that allows the users to get the products sooner and pay later. That's what I call borrowing from the next quarter to make this quarter."

Conversely, if you see great sales growth but the accounts receivable goes down, then you have to question whether customers actually paid for those sales.

"Lastly, I focus on the operating margins—that's what you get when you subtract the R&D, the SG&A, and the operating expenses of a company," says Berman. "Revenue growth counts for a lot but generating cash counts for more, especially for young companies with limited maturity but seemingly great opportunities. You want to make sure that early-stage companies are getting enough momentum, that not all the revenues need to be put back into just putting more feet on the street.

"Ultimately, stocks are a lot like bonds: You want your companies to generate cash and the sooner you get it, the better. Any development at a company—which can include giant contracts, expense reductions, market acceptance of technology, a revenue growth rate that proves that market acceptance is really beginning to happen, gross margins that show they have the pricing power enabling them to put the dollars associated with their market strength into their pockets, and a balance sheet that shows that they're not making too many deals allowing customers to get the product now and pay later—basically, anything that says that the cash flow from this opportunity is going to be bigger and happen sooner than I previously thought makes me feel positive. Anything else makes me negative."

Ravi Suria, credit analyst for Lehman Brothers, looks at earnings reports in yet a different way. He focuses on the balance sheet and cash flows. "Is the company capable of generating cash flow from its operations and if it's not making money now, how does it plan to make money down the line?" When a company loses money, it can do one or two things to bolster its balance sheet: it can sell more stock to get equity money or it can raise money through debt offerings. Debt can lead a company down a slippery path. "You have to pay back the debt plus interest, but if your operations get so far out of whack that the cash flow goes down, then you have to borrow more money and the balance sheet gets screwed up."

That's what led Suria to make his headline-grabbing negative call on Amazon.com in June 2000. "When the company reported year-end numbers early in 2000, it confirmed that it was still losing money and that profitability was nowhere in sight. Then it came to the bond market to borrow $690 million by doing a debt offering that involved heavy interest payments." Suria wondered how selling books online would ever be enough to meet annual interest payments of $125 million on a total debt load of $2.1 billion. The company's first-quarter 10-Q report to the SEC didn't reassure him. **"When a company loses $355 million on $515 million in sales, something's wrong. That was my clear signal that Amazon had fallen over the cliff. If Amazon hadn't borrowed so much, it would be out of business."**

Sounds simple to decipher, right? Not so fast.

Beware the Profit Gimmicks

In an effort to deliver crowd-pleasing profits, an increasing number of companies are using various accounting games—all legal—to bolster their bottom line: making selective disclosures in earnings releases, ignoring the cost of stock-option grants, obscuring negative earnings with positive metrics such as EBIDTA (earnings before interest, taxes, depreciation, and amortization), or boosting the bottom line with gains from venture capital investments. The significance of these accounting acrobatics is that they may mask problems—problems with management's decisions and judgment, problems with product sales, problems with accounts receivable and overall problems that make the company less competitive.

These tricks aren't limited to Fly-by-Night Ltd. and other third-rate companies. Hewlett-Packard, for example, beat consensus estimates when it reported its fiscal third-quarter 2000 earnings in a press release. The stock immediately jumped 10 percent. But the next day, shareholders shot it right back down again amid concerns that the company had nudged its net with onetime gains and favorable currency and tax rates.

Beating earnings estimates is nice, but how the company did it is key; that's called the "quality of earnings."

Fortunately, the more you know about profit gimmicks, the easier you'll be able to distinguish between news and noise in an earnings report. Here's how to find the real story behind the numbers.

How to Find the Earnings in an Earnings Report

Will the real number please stand up? Companies sometimes highlight an earnings number in their earnings press releases that doesn't reflect all of their expenses. The real numbers—calculated using generally accepted accounting principles (GAAP) that have to be reported to the SEC—are usually listed at the end of the press release with little explanation or guidance. Companies defend the practice on the grounds that they're just pointing out what they feel is important in their results or they're trying to direct the investment community to a certain number they feel should be the one to value their company.

To spot these faux earnings, look for what is called an operating number or pro forma results. Traditionally, companies use pro forma numbers only for an extraordinary event, such as a merger, acquisition charges, or a corporate restructuring, to show what earnings might have been had the event not occurred. But increasingly, many companies, especially technology companies, are using pro forma earnings numbers that exclude certain items even when they aren't undergoing extraordinary events. **"Pro forma numbers have their place, but some companies are taking advantage to make their earnings look better,"** say Charles Hill, director of research at First Call, which compiles and analyzes earnings and forecasts.

One of the most common costs that companies ignore in pro forma is called goodwill. Goodwill is an accounting term for the difference between what an acquiring company pays for an acquisition and the value of the net assets of the acquired company. In the 1990s, as high-flying stocks enabled many companies to make richly priced acquisitions, some acquiring companies piled lots of goodwill onto their balance sheets.

Current accounting rules allow goodwill to be amortized over the lifetime of the acquired assets, up to a period of forty years. However, because technology becomes obsolete so quickly, tech assets are usually amortized over a period of three to five years, which can result in hefty goodwill charges. Hill points out that in Lycos's July 2000 quarter, the company reported pro forma per share earnings of 12 cents, which excluded goodwill. If goodwill had been included, the company would have had a loss of 36 cents per share.

Bad feelings engendered by goodwill don't end there. Call it a case of irrational goodwill: thanks to a combination of overpriced acquisitions, poorly executed mergers and slumping stock prices, hundreds of companies sport balance sheets that if adjusted for goodwill would show that the value of their goodwill actually exceeds the market values of the companies themselves.

Excluding goodwill as an expense has become so widespread that the Financial Accounting Standards Board (FASB) has proposed a rule that requires companies to determine if their goodwill is impaired—that is, if the fair value of the goodwill is less than what is currently reported in the companies' public financial reports. Noncash goodwill-impairment charges would essentially amount to confessions that quantify exactly how much companies overpaid for acquisitions and how much they overstated earnings for prior periods. The FASB proposal is still subject to change; if adopted, it would begin taking effect during the third quarter of 2001 at the earliest.

Goodwill is only one cost that companies commonly ignore. Companies exclude the payroll taxes they owe when employees exercise stock options, marketing expenses that are paid for with stock options, litigation charges, asset gains and losses, patent settlements, inventory adjustments, and the impact of foreign currency translation.

"Probably the majority of companies will start off with a GAAP reported number, then say, 'If you were to exclude the nonrecurring loss or gain, this is what the adjusted number would be,'" says Charles Hill. "But it may get as egregious as talking about the adjusted number throughout the text and only mentioning the GAAP number at the end.

"You've got to pay attention to the GAAP reported number and the footnotes. It's a caution flag to some degree if there's an adjusted number. When you see the pro forma number up front in the text and the company really dwells on it, especially if there's a pro forma table before the GAAP table, the chances are pretty good that the company is pushing the envelope in what they think should be excluded."

To learn what the pro formas don't reveal, go directly to the GAAP numbers at the end of the earnings press release. You'll also want to compare the release to what's said in the Form 10-Q that companies must file at the SEC within forty-five days of the quarter's end. "If there are differences, that's another caution flag," warns Hill. You can check the 10-Q at the EDGAR section of the SEC's website (www.sec.gov) or at Freedgar.com (www.freedgar.com).

Musical-chairs metrics. Another way that companies obscure actual earnings is to use a different set of metrics to value the company. EBIDTA can be a legitimate measure of financial health, but Hill cautions, "You don't want to use that because companies do have to pay taxes and interest, and those are two real expenses."

Cash flow, another measurement, usually includes the interest and the taxes but excludes depreciation and amortization. Furthermore, says Hill, "One analyst's definition of cash flow may be different from another's." In the oil industry, for example, Hill finds that 80 percent of analysts use cash flow numbers, which helps to set a standard. "But in addition to excluding depreciation and amortization, there are also dry hole charges and depletion charges, and the majority of the analysts felt that the first three charges should be excluded but not the fourth."

What constitutes revenue? Revenue growth is as important as how well the company manages its costs. You need to analyze revenue numbers carefully because revenue is based partly on price and partly on volume. The company could have raised their prices with no increase in volume, an indication that the market growth is slowing.

Different companies have different definitions of what they consider revenues. "We live in an age where there's a tremendous amount of startup activity in biotechnology and Internet companies," points out Joseph Battipaglia, chief investment strategist at Gruntal & Co. "What many companies call revenues are actually research grants, not product sales. Obviously, product sales have more value to the investor than progressive payments which can be terminated at any time."

Some companies include in their revenues products that were delivered to the customer but not accepted yet. This is frequently the case with technology products that the customer tests before deciding whether they are acceptable. "It's legitimate to book a sale before the company pays for it if they have an iron-clad obligation to pay for it, but if the obligation is conditional on the machine working, then it shouldn't be booked as a sale because it may come back," says First Call's Charles Hill.

Then there's a common trick of generating revenues by cutting core expenses like staff or R&D. The revenue line looks good and so do earnings per share, but gross margins go down and if you look at the quality of the result, it's not so hot.

The hidden cost of options. Stock options have become a regular part of employees' compensation. Current accounting rules don't require companies to list stock-option grants as an expense. In a 2000 study examining the impact of employee stock options on earnings and operating margins in S&P 500 companies, Pat McConnell, a senior managing director and head of the accounting and tax group in equity research at Bear, Stearns, found that only two of the five hundred companies in the S&P index accounted for options as a cost: Boeing and Winn-Dixie.

The impact on earnings can be substantial, McConnell reported. And, of course, the larger the option grants, the bigger the hit to a company's earnings. If options grants were counted as an expense, the study found, companies in the health care services industry would have shown a 38 percent decline in earnings in 1999; computer networking businesses, 24 percent; commercial and consumer services companies, 21 percent; and telecommunications equipment makers, 19 percent. Semiconductor manufacturers alone would have taken a hit to their 1999 earnings per share of nearly 50 percent.

The FASB requires companies to include the impact of options in a footnote in the annual report (look for a footnote concerning "diluted earnings per share"). Unfortunately, there is as yet no rule stipulating that companies list their options grants in the quarterly reports, so, not surprisingly, few do.

Boosting earnings with investment gains. It's become common for many big technology and telecom companies to make venture capital investments as part of their R&D efforts. Recently, financial services companies have also stuck a finger in the honey pot, hoping for a big bonanza when these venture-stage investments go public. Then, come earnings time, companies can sell these stocks at a profit to make sure they make their earnings. For example, Microsoft's fiscal 2000 fourth-quarter earnings of forty-four cents per share included a onetime investment gain of twenty cents a share. Intel is another tech giant that has relied on big investment gains, racking up nearly half of its June 2000 earnings per share from investment portfolio profits. Simply put, these companies buy and sell stocks like the rest of us. The difference is, their gains are added to the bottom line.

How can you find out what a company earned from its investments? Look at the "other income" figure on the profit-and-loss statement. Be sure to take note of which companies they have invested in and check the performance of those stocks. It could be meaningful when the company reports its quarterly earnings.

"Many of us take earnings reports for granted," says Battipaglia. "We focus on the bottom line and we let Wall Street be the referee. But investors should be aware of the subtle changes, and those can be found by looking at the whole income statement rather than relying on just one bottom line." It's not always easy to dig out the critical numbers, but the direction of the company is embedded in these data points, so they are well worth deciphering.

Conference Calls: Tune In or Turn Off?

Earnings reports are history reports. They describe how a company did in the past quarter. The conference call that follows the earnings report predicts how the company will do in the next quarter or coming year. It also gives management a chance to walk through the numbers and explain what areas of the business are most important to the company's future growth. How important are conference calls? "Conference calls have clearly had more impact than earnings reports over the last two years," says Arthur R. Hogan III, chief market analyst for Jefferies & Company. "Even more important than the objective data is what the company has to say about the future. Intel reports better than expected earnings but is cautious going forward and the stock sells off."

As a result of Regulation FD, an increasing number of companies are making their conference calls to analysts open to the entire investment community through telephone bridges or webcasting. "Whoopee!"

you're probably thinking. "Open access to the secret club." Well, I hate to disappoint you, but there are a couple of drawbacks.

Although the majority of conference calls for technology companies take place after the closing bell, many others are held during business hours, so it may be difficult to make the time to listen in if you've got a day job. Also, because most of these calls last a couple of hours, it's not as if you can drop in for ten minutes during your lunch hour.

Often, the analysts' questions are newsworthy because you can get an idea of their red flags and why they might downgrade the stock later. There is, however, a tremendous amount of noise from analysts' asking arcane questions, so you probably won't catch a problem unless it's blatant or you know the company really well. If you don't know the company well or you're not familiar with what the Street is looking for, you may think, "Wow, the company says earnings are up 30 percent; this sounds great!" But if everyone was waiting for 35 percent and the outlook is gloomy, there may be a downtick in the stock.

"There is a lot of minutia," agrees Battipaglia. "But that doesn't mean it's not worthwhile for investors to tune in. All the contributors to the conference call add something to the company's vision of the future. It's not uncommon to have someone who's in charge of a new product talking about his division. Now that there is a framework in which companies can articulate their forward look to everyone at the same time, if you want to be tied closely to your investments, this is the way to do it."

What should you look for in a conference call? "I like to use conference calls as a data point to confirm what I already believe to be true from my fundamental research," says Henry McVey, equity research analyst for the asset management and brokerage industry at Morgan Stanley Dean Witter. "In rapidly emerging industries, conference calls can be much more informative, whereas in more mature industries, they are more like signposts along an established road.

"Focus on the tone of the management and how they project future earnings potential. Most industries have a couple of key metrics that everyone from Wall Street to Main Street watches. The conference calls are an excellent forum for how the firm is performing against those benchmarks."

Listen to comments about the business that might have an impact on other companies. Maybe the company has been experiencing shortages of key components, and as a result the component makers are seeing a huge jump in their business.

Note too that conference calls get interesting when there's a major strategic shift in the company's business or the competitive environment. If you're trying to edit your research time, then this is a good way to determine which calls to listen to and which to ignore.

"Here's what I'm skeptical about," says Arnie Berman, technology strategist for Wit Soundview Capital. "Too much management enthusiasm. They're running the company, they ought to be enthusiastic. I'm also skeptical about all information about new contracts. The company's generating revenues, they ought to be getting contracts. If you open your doors for business every day, there ought to be contracts. That's not something that ought to be hyped."

It is also a good idea to check the stock's performance before, during, and after the conference call, particularly if it is held in the extended hours. That tells you whether investors believe the executives' sales pitch or not.

"Will everyone turn into a financial analyst with a deep-seated understanding of the industries they're invested in?" asks Battipaglia. "I'd say not. But a person who's clear-thinking and logical with a modicum of training can glean a lot from these conference calls."

How to Evaluate Insider Trading

What does it mean when employees of a company buy or sell large blocks of company stock? Do they know something the ordinary investor has yet to learn? Or are they unloading shares as part of a routine reallocation of their portfolio?

When is insider trading a portent and when is it merely a bunch of chicken guts? Bob Gabele, director of insider research at First Call/Thomson Financial, explains how to tell when insider trading is news and when it is noise:

"Investors tend to oversimplify the game. In the early 1980s, there were two common conclusions drawn about insider trading: that insiders buy for one motive but can sell for many reasons (therefore buying was more significant than selling) and that ordinary investors should follow the trades of the chairman, CEO, and president, because these are the trades that are the most profitable to mimic. That's changed dramatically. Neither of these are the case any longer.

"There's an old adage about Wall Street: whenever investors figure out the key, someone changes the lock. That is so true with insider trading. What happened was that insiders became cognizant of the fact that everyone was watching them and in the early 1990s, you started to see changes in behavior. You saw companies announcing insider buys with press releases. You saw companies loan money to insiders to buy more shares. You saw companies establishing executive ownership guidelines, which required senior executives to take a certain multiple of their salary in stock.

"We started questioning the motivation behind insider buys. Were these being driven by an investment motive? Or were they occurring to paint a good picture to investors?

"In this current environment, class action suits have become rampant and volatility in the stock market much higher. It's not uncommon to see a stock fall 30 percent to 50 percent in a day—and if any insider sales occurred prior to that drop, you're likely to see a class action suit. Consequently, we see a lot of class action repellent buying.

"Investors need to be aware that there's a possibility that someone who was a huge seller over the past year is sticking his toe back in the water just to make things look good. Back in the 1980s, there was quite a bit of insider selling in a Los Angeles–based company called House of Fabrics. The chairman called me and gave me a spin about the selling, but the more spin there is, the more I want to keep my eye on things. The stock went from $50 to $40 to $20 to the teens, and then it was $3. Then the next thing you knew, the chairman bought ten thousand shares at $3. The investment community jumped on it. But when you looked at it, it was a $30,000 investment; meanwhile the amount of money he pulled out by selling when the stock was in the $30s and $20s was in excess of $200,000. That $30,000 was a class action repellent and cheap at the price. Meanwhile, the company went into Chapter 11.

"Another example of corporate spin: When Anthony J. F. O'Reilly was the chairman of Heinz Corporation, he held over 4 million stock options, which he exercised and promptly sold 3.2 million of the shares. But the press release publicized another transaction instead: 'Chairman O'Reilly Increases His Stake by 100,000 Shares.'

"Be aware of that kind of smokescreen when a company puts out a press release saying that someone is increasing his position. It shows how the company tries to make things look like buys when they're actually a sell. Options are part of insider holdings, too and cashing out options can represent a big reduction in an insider's holdings.

"In short, not all buying is because things are good or because insiders are investing real dollars. Corporations are getting trickier in buying, and insiders too. Be suspicious of situations where corporations are heralding insider buys with press releases. Be suspicious of any excessive corporate spin. And always try to find out whether loans were involved in the transaction.

"Insider sales used to be considered total noise. But thanks to a 1991 SEC rule change requiring insiders to file evidence of all options holdings, they have actually gotten easier to interpret. After 1991 we were finally able to identify all the options that insiders held. Before 1991 if an insider sold one hundred thousand shares, we knew they had options but we didn't know how many. Now we can understand how much of their real holdings they're getting rid of. [You can check this out at the EDGAR section of the SEC's website (www.sec.gov), at Freedgar. com (www.freedgar.com), or at the site for Federal Filings Business News (www.fedfil.com).]

"The public tends to look at insider selling as a story unto itself: Oh, my god, Michael Dell is selling so I must sell too. We view insider trading as an aspect of the insider's behavior. Once we view the transactions as 'behavior' as opposed to 'trades,' we're looking at a picture that is an ongoing story that reflects this aspect of this individual's behavior. I don't read a lot into one transaction; if someone sells seventy-five thousand shares, it could be because he or she is adding five thousand square feet to their house or diversifying their portfolio or, if he's getting older, thinking of estate planning. You need to establish what is normal for the individual. Then, given what is known about his or her trading behavior, you can ask if the current activity represents a change.

"Here are some points to keep in mind about insider selling:

1. "Expect to see a certain level of insider selling after the lock-up period has expired.

2. "Do get concerned when you see insiders selling at prices off the highs. Many insiders have programs where they sell a certain amount of shares every quarter. To a certain extent, this explains the selling off the highs. But it's unlikely that all insiders in a company will have these programs. And in periods of extreme volatility, it's unlikely that you would see insiders retaining a certain programmed selling strategy if the stock has been dramatically reduced in value. If the selling continues when the stock is depressed, I become concerned. Just because insiders have a program to sell stock doesn't mean they have to do it. If the stock is getting decimated, you'd think they'd pull back from their plan if the stock was going to turn around.

3. "Watch out when you see insider selling around significant rumors. There was a lot of selling by insiders at Continental Airlines in the summer of 1999, when rumor had it that Northwest Airlines was going to buy it. The stock fell down to $40 by September, and in fact there was so much insider selling that I had to believe that even if there were a deal, it wouldn't show much premium over $50. Sure enough, no deal materialized. If everyone on the Street is saying there's a deal, or if there's a piece of news that will make the shares move higher, but insiders are selling at the same time, then I must believe that the insider expectations don't match those of the people who are bidding the stock up. This is especially true if the expectations are event driven, such as by a takeover. Then I strongly suspect that the event won't be as dramatic or won't happen. Insider selling patterns help me decide how much credence to put in the rumors I'm hearing.

4. "Conversely, lack of insider selling can also mean something. When Intel had its Pentium chip problem in 1993, there was some insider selling and the media came to me saying that it must be related to the Pentium problem. When we checked Intel insider activity over the prior ten years, it turned out that the shares were at an all-time high in 1992 and insider selling was at the lowest level in a decade. So, yes, there was selling but on the whole, insiders must have felt good about what they saw. So we put out a report saying, 'Of course, they're selling but they're actually selling less. This must be a good sign.' It was a good example of when insider behavior was actually changing. The reduction in selling was a reflection of insiders' ability and desire to expose themselves to stock market risk. And it paid off.

5. **"**However, while we always expect to see a certain amount of profit taking when the stock is moving higher, you can get lulled to sleep by steady insider selling. If the overall holdings start to decrease—if there's been selling every month for eighteen months—then a picture is evolving of a significant change in sentiment.

"These aren't easy things to pick out of the data. You have to do your homework.**"**

Evaluating News from Market Professionals

"Follow the smart money." I'm sure you've heard this a hundred times. The "smart money" refers to the market professionals whose perspicacity is so revered that their buy and sell decisions move individual stocks, sectors, and sometimes even the entire market.

There are the individual investors praised for their prescient picks: Saudi Arabian Prince Alwaleed bin Talal, who bailed out Citibank in the early 1990s and reaped a 2,250 percent return on his investment; Carl Icahn, whose reputation caused shares of GM to rise 7 percent on the rumor that he intended to expand his stake; and, of course, Warren Buffett, a.k.a. "the Oracle from Omaha."

There are the "lead steers," the star analysts whose calls cause Wall Street's thundering herd to change direction, such as when Goldman Sachs analyst Abby Joseph Cohen's recommendation to reduce holdings of tech stocks helped spark the Nasdaq's spring 2000 sell-off.

There are the highly regarded mutual fund families, whose picks can push stocks to new heights. This phenomenon was so pronounced with Janus Funds's moves in the late 1990s, that when it took a big position in a stock, the share price could triple or even quadruple in as many weeks, a surge known as the Janus effect.

There are venture capital firms and publicly owned companies, like Intel and Microsoft, which act as venture capital firms. There are technology seers like George Gilder who stand on a particularly prominent pulpit. In a demonstration of "the Gilder effect," stocks routinely soar 15 percent and 20 percent after being discussed favorably in his $295-a-year monthly newsletter, *The Gilder Technology Report.* On April 24, 2000, Gilder recommended Avanex. Within minutes of the report's publication, Avanex's stock rose from $55 to $80. By the end of the week, it had passed $140. Shares in New Focus rose 58 percent over two days following Gilder's recommendation in December 2000.

It's as if other investors kowtow to these market gods and goddesses, intoning, "We are not worthy" like the two guys in the movie *Wayne's World.* Imitation may be the sincerest form of flattery, but it's not the smartest way to invest.

To be sure, there's always the suspicion that the supersuccessful investors know something that the rest of us don't. Maybe they do. Maybe they're the "go-to guys," the ones who are first in the company's call-back list. Maybe they've got a close relationship with a member of the company's board of directors, who mentioned that a big customer is going to stop ordering from this company. This type of situation is expected to lessen, if not fade out entirely, with the SEC's fair disclosure ruling stipulating that a company can't allow one person to know something before the rest of the market does). Maybe they can see farther through a millstone than most and are able to extract newsworthy information out of data the rest of us deem unimportant.

To a certain extent, it makes sense to follow the smart money. They're studying the 10-Ks and 10-Qs, the thinking goes. They're dissecting the balance sheets. They're doing the work for us and they know what they're doing. Onward!

But it's not smart thinking to follow the smart money blindly; otherwise you won't know whether you're making decisions based on news or noise. You never want to take someone's investment advice at face value—certainly not without knowing his or her agenda.

I'm no mind reader, so I can't pretend to know what the agendas of people like Warren Buffett and Prince Alwaleed bin Talal are, other than the fact that they are known as top value investors who snap up brand-name companies at depressed prices and hang in for the long term. I do know that what's right for princes with portfolios in the billions of dollars may not be an appropriate strategy to follow for average retail investors.

While it's part of human nature to search for a superhero with all the answers, ordinary investors should remember that nobody bats 1,000 in this business. Look at some of the Oracle of Omaha's longtime winners just over the past year. He's had a couple of duds.

The gurus and the single investors, the venture capital firms and the companies with venture capital divisions, and even the mutual fund firms that invest millions of dollars make the high-profile decisions on an intermittent basis. The group of professionals whose calls are routinely reported in the financial news and move the markets as a result are Wall Street's analysts. They have a definite agenda, and being aware of that agenda can help you discriminate between calls that are news and calls that are noise.

When I talk about analysts here, I'm primarily discussing financial analysts, the people who examine and evaluate companies and industry sectors and who then write reports that include the analyst's rating of the stock as well as estimates of future earnings and other prognostications. (I'm not going to talk about the people who analyze overall economic trends, because we're talking about evaluating specific companies and industries, rather than the overall economy.)

Most financial analysts are employed by what's called the sell side—big brokerage firms and investment banks that sell their research. That research is bought by the buy side—institutional investors, pension accounts, mutual funds, hedge funds, and retail investors.

Many of the big fund families boast that they don't listen to the Street; they have large staffs of their own analysts. Those analysts do almost exactly what an investment firm's analysts do, except that the fund firm's analyst advises only the fund's portfolio managers on what to buy. Consequently, analysts at big, highly capitalized fund firms like Janus and Fidelity can affect the market as much as—if not more than—their counterparts at Lehman Brothers or Merrill Lynch. The difference is that the buy-side analysts don't publicly release their ratings the way sell-side ones do; in fact, they do not want outsiders to know their position.

But the biggest difference between buy-side and sell-side analysts, from my point of view, is that the sell-side analysts work for firms that often do business with the companies the analysts cover. Consequently, a sell-side analyst has two allegiances: one to her investment clients and one to the firm, which has an allegiance to its corporate clients.

The problem is that sometimes those two interests conflict.

How Close Is Too Close?

One of the most common criticisms of the analyst community is that analysts talk only about the stocks that their investment firm has a relationship with. Consider the fact that although so many of the telecom and Internet stocks lost so much value in 2000 and 2001, so few analysts downgraded their ratings on those stocks. Why would analysts issue a downgrade or make negative comments on a company that their firm took public and generated tens of millions of dollars in fees for doing so?

Still, that intimacy can have certain benefits, as Credit Suisse First Boston's co-director of technology research Kevin McCarthy explains: "Those analysts usually have very good contact with management, and investors have to listen to what they say because they have a close relationship with the company." On the other hand, McCarthy warns, "If an analyst is part of a deal or if his firm participated in a company's public offering, then they're universally bullish on that particular story."

A quick word about the rating system. Each firm has its own language for rating stocks. Few of them use "buy," "sell," and "hold" only. Typically, analysts rate stocks the following way: strong buy, moderate buy, outperform, accumulate, speculative buy, speculative hold, hold or neutral (which equals a sell in Wall Street parlance), moderate sell, and strong sell.

Different terms mean different things to different analysts, a situation that has led to what Joseph Battipaglia, chief investment strategist at Gruntal & Co., calls "an extreme level of disconnect" between what analysts say and what they think you should do. "I'm afraid we've created a language for analysts that obfuscates what they really mean to say about a company. When you hear a rating go from a strong buy to a buy, what the analyst is really saying is that it was a buy and now it's a sell."

The reason? The range of ratings offers analysts a way to hedge their bets without offending the investment firm's clients. According to Battipaglia, "If there's a corporate finance investment relationship, the analyst will speak one way to keep that relationship on firm ground while trying to send a subliminal message to the investor. That's why there's so much skepticism by the individual investor about the institutional marketplace. The public gets this obfuscated description while institutions get direct information. "

The vast majority—McCarthy estimates 98 percent—of all recommendations are either buys or holds. You almost never see a sell. That's because if an analyst puts a sell on a company, the company may react by knocking her off the regular conference calls so that she won't be able to get first dibs on even the most basic news of the company. The analyst can be shut out—or worse.

Tom Brown covered financial stocks for Paine Webber back in the early 1990s. For nine out of ten years, he was top ranked by *Institutional Investor*, a magazine whose rankings are highly prized by the analyst community. One of the companies he analyzed was First Union Corp., one of the country's ten largest banks. "I met the CEO, Edward Crutchfield, back in 1984," Brown recalls. "I liked the company and had a buy recommendation on it. But then they went on a buying spree beginning in the second half of 1985 and they never stopped." Brown felt that Crutchfield's acquisitions were diluting First Union's earnings and criticized the company accordingly.

It turned out that First Union did business with Paine Webber. Now remember that an investment firm's bread and butter is investment banking, that is, taking companies public and raising money through secondary offerings and bond offerings. All this banking business commands enormous fees for the investment bank.

An analyst walks a tightrope of coming up with good investment ideas for his clients as well as answering to the bank's corporate clients. Crutchfield threatened to stop using Paine Webber for First Union's bond offerings unless Brown changed his calls. Paine Webber backed Brown, and First Union pulled its business.

But the story didn't stop there. A few years later Brown got a job at Donaldson Lufkin Jenrette, where he continued to cover the financial sector. Again, his picks were good. Again, he won the top *Institutional Investor* ranking. Meanwhile, First Union continued its string of acquisitions and again, after First Union purchased Core States Financial in 1997, Brown criticized the company. This time, he rated the stock as neutral, which is the equivalent of a sell.

Once more, Crutchfield threatened to stop doing business with Brown's firm and even went so far as to publicly refer to him at an analyst meeting as "that little red-haired boy." The upshot: Donaldson Lufkin Jenrette fired Brown in March 1998. (Two years later First Union stock hit an all-time low as investors realized that the company had indeed made too many acquisitions that were dilutive—exactly what Tom Brown had warned of. Brown ultimately started a hedge fund using his own money, so he could be his own analyst and make investment recommendations without worrying about offending an important client.)

Right there is an example of how agendas can conflict. The investment bank's agenda is to make money by generating high fees from regular clients. It can't afford to lose those clients because of a negative rating from one of its analysts. When Jonathan Joseph, semiconductor analyst at Salomon Smith Barney, made a controversial call downgrading the semiconductor sector in July 2000, one of the reasons his call was so controversial was that Salomon Smith Barney was the third largest underwriter of semiconductors on a dollar basis. "Virtually every company I downgraded had some kind of corporate finance relationship with the firm," he recalls. "We did lose some corporate finance business because of it."

Consequently, he explains, "The reason the analysts downgrade stocks so little is not because they're idiots or because they're spineless. Analysts are businesspeople like everyone else, so they'll do anything to maintain their business."

Why Analysts Avoid Controversial Calls

The corollary is that some of the big investment firms will only rate companies who either are already clients or whom they would like to make into clients. That's why you rarely see small companies being rated by the analyst community. The reason is that those companies can't afford to hire the major investment banks, and if they can't afford to hire them, the major investment banks can't afford the time to cover their stocks. Consequently, many small stocks have no coverage on Wall Street and many large companies are treated with kid gloves.

A classic example of that "if you don't have anything nice to say, don't say anything" attitude occurred in the summer of 2000. Ravi Suria is the credit analyst for the telecom and tech sector at Lehman Brothers. As the credit analyst, he focuses only companies' credit and cash outlook, as opposed to his equity analyst counterpart, Holly Becker, who looks at a company's fundamental earnings and expectations. In June 2000, Suria came out with a negative report on Amazon.com, saying that the company could run out of cash sometime in the first half of January 2001 and be unable to operate. The report sent Amazon stock swooning.

While in retrospect it was probably the best call on the Internet on the Street, Lehman Brothers did not want to be vocal about it. In fact, they started pushing Holly Becker forward. Becker was also turning cautious on the stock, but it was not her call that raised everyone's awareness of Amazon. However, because Suria's call was so much more harsh, the management at Lehman Brothers did not push it aggressively in the media. Suria was asked not to do television interviews and not to be so vocal about it.

That autumn I did a special report on Amazon. I wanted to get a bull-bear debate on the stock. On the bull side, I invited Henry Blodget of Merrill Lynch, who is the analyst who became a star by putting a $400 price tag on Amazon when it was at $250 (it hit the $400 level two weeks later). On the bear side, I wanted Ravi Suria. Lehman Brothers wouldn't let him come on my program and instead gave me Holly Becker, who was cautious but not nearly as negative as Suria.

Similarly, in the summer of 2000, when Jonathan Joseph at Salomon Smith Barney predicted the end of the semiconductor cycle, sending semiconductor stocks sharply lower, he didn't do any press. I called him several times to come on my show, but he said that he couldn't because it was such a controversial call. It was such a controversial call that Joseph actually received death threats. Every other analyst in the semiconductor sector disagreed with him and said that there were at least twelve months left in the semiconductor upswing. Three months later the semiconductor stocks were down 20 percent from where they were when he made his call. Since then, the entire tech sector has undergone a major correction and it became clear that Jonathan Joseph was right. In the middle of the correction, I tried once more to get him on the show. This time he came.

The outcries coming from controversial calls aren't limited to companies in the affected sectors. When Suria made his call on Amazon, he recalls, prominent Internet analysts ranging from Merrill Lynch's Henry Blodget to Morgan Stanley Dean Witter's Mary Meeker, a.k.a. "Queen of the Internet," to Suria's own colleague, Becker, went public saying, "He doesn't know what he's talking about."

George Strachan, senior retail analyst for Goldman Sachs, had a similar experience when he downgraded the retail sector in May 2000 due to such macroeconomic factors as decelerating consumer spending growth and rising oil prices in conjunction with rising costs within the sector. **"You want to know the fundamentals of retail stocks, but if you can detect changes in the sector and real changes in the big picture, you can make valuable calls."** Strachan made his call on May 2, 2000, and the stocks promptly reacted. The next day Gary Balter, his counterpart at what was then Donaldson Lufkin Jenrette (now Credit Suisse First Boston), held a conference call at which he listed the ten best reasons not to listen to the Goldman Sachs call.

Now these stories make the whole business of Wall Street seem tainted, and I don't want to say that. I think there are some professional analysts affiliated with investment banking firms who make great stock picks. Just because an analyst works for an investment firm doesn't mean she hasn't done her homework, hasn't researched the company and the industry aggressively, hasn't talked to the customers and the suppliers and the vendors and the management, and concluded that this is a terrific company that's well run and has great prospects in an expanding industry. Think of all the research that was done on the Ciscos, the Intels, the Sun Microsystems, the Oracles, and the EMCs that turned out to be pretty accurate throughout much of the 1990s.

However, a recent survey by *Institutional Investor* magazine in which investors were asked to rank the overall quality of sell-side research gave Wall Street research a mediocre 5.9 grade on a scale of 1 to 10. Forty-four percent of the portfolio managers, buy-side research directors, and buy-side equity analysts felt that the quality of research had deteriorated over the previous year, with just 6 percent saying it had improved and 50 percent seeing no change. The complaints are familiar: far too many buy recommendations; sell recommendations that come too late, if ever—even in a down market; and, above all, the pressure to generate investment banking fees for the parent firm.

Not all ratings come from investment firms. There are analysts who recommend stocks based on their own proprietary research. And there are research firms, such as Standard & Poors, Sanford Bernstein, Suntrust Equitable Securities, First Albany Corp., Wit Soundview Capital, First Analysis Corp., Sands Brothers & Co., and others that don't do any investment banking at all, so they're free from potential conflicts of interest.

Interestingly, a study by Kent L. Womack, a finance professor at Dartmouth's Amos Tuck School of Business, and Roni Michaely, a Cornell University finance professor, found that the stock recommendations of brokerages without investment banking ties tend to be more accurate. Their stocks rose an average of 3.5 percent within a year, versus a decline of 11.6 percent over the same period in stocks recommended by brokerages involved in investment banking with the companies they cover.

In short, you always want to remember that clients may be part of the story when an investment firm pushes that stock. As Kevin McCarthy says, "Skepticism is very healthy in this business." You can't rely exclusively on an analyst who's bullish on a stock. You need to know the story behind the rating. You need to know the amount of work an analyst put into coming up with the rating. The role of the individual investor is to treat every data point as just one more piece of the puzzle. You have to be ready to hoist your red flags. Frankly, you're better off being a skeptic than not.

The Realities of Research

You'd like to think that every analyst is going whole hog, checking every single data point in a company's supply chain, personally questioning customers in the field or by phone, and relentlessly interviewing many layers of the company's management. Unfortunately, that's not always the case.

On the Street, sell-side analysts often are too busy doing deals for the investment firm to have time for painstaking research, but that's not necessarily their fault. Many of them are assigned an onerous number of deals that have to be done within the stringent requirements of the banking calendar. Consequently, their research is limited to "fishing expeditions."

A fishing expedition is when an analyst calls up a company to fish for news. There's nothing inherently wrong with going fishing. As McCarthy points out, "Depending on the relationship you have with the company, oftentimes you can get pretty good body language on whether the trends are playing out the way you think. For the analyst who does his work, that body language call should be the last call. It should be the check against the things you've already researched and resourced. You've come up with the conclusion and are looking for just one more data point."

The problem is if that last call is the first and only call.

Here's a good example: In October 1999, Donaldson Lufkin Jenrette and Merrill Lynch surveyed about two thousand information technology managers about their company's spending plans for Y2K. The research indicated, among other findings, that IBM's customers were getting ready to shut down purchasing to prepare for Y2K. IBM didn't agree. Other analysts who listened to IBM also rebutted the findings. Who was the average investor to believe?

"It's a classic complaint about the sell side," McCarthy explains. "The sell side calls up the company and asks, 'Are you worried about Y2K?' And the investor relations director replies, 'No, we're not worried.'

"That's why the sell side is notoriously wrong. That's why after a company announces a shortfall and opens down 20 points, you'll see twelve downgrades from 'buy' to 'hold.' The Street wasn't doing its job. That's not saying that if you don't do your homework, you won't be right every time. But the vast majority of those downgrades are from analysts who relied almost exclusively on the company for news on how things are going. They're told that things are fine—and the next day the company preannounces and catches them by surprise."

The upshot of the survey, as McCarthy recalls, was that "it gave us the right call on the industry's quarter." IBM got hammered and the analysts who exclusively relied on IBM for information had egg on their faces. McCarthy concludes, "If the SEC's fair disclosure rules stick, analysts who rely only on companies for information will be stuck."

In concept, at least, Regulation FD will put a premium on the hard-working analysts who do the nitty-gritty research on a company's or an industry's prospects rather than those analysts who rely on friends in high places. But how do you know which analysts to trust and which to ignore? You need to track their record the way you would track a favorite movie reviewer. Learn their investment style. Familiarize yourself with their spin. Understand their underlying bias.

Certain analysts have attained rock-star status. They are what's known as the lead steers, or the axes, in their sector. They're called an axe because a negative call from them will chop the stock. The axes often have the best relationship among the entire analyst community with the companies they cover; they are the ones who get the story right most frequently.

Axes don't have to be individuals. Certain investment banks also act as axes. Major investment banks, such as Goldman Sachs, J.P. Morgan Chase,

Morgan Stanley Dean Witter, Merrill Lynch, Credit Suisse First Boston, and Salomon Smith Barney, have much more clout in terms of moving the market than an A.G. Edwards, Joseph Stephens, or another regional investment bank. A call from Goldman or Merrill Lynch will move the stock even if the bank's analyst is not the main axe in the stock. The reason is that the clients of these investment banks are institutions themselves, so when one of the banks make a call on a stock and their clients buy into that call, their clients' money will move the stock.

Furthermore, certain investment firms are strong in certain sectors. CSFB, for example, has a very large department of bankers in its technology and telecom group. With banks comes a large group of analysts, so when CSFB makes a controversial call on a telecom stock, the stock typically moves.

By the way, when I talk about making a call, I don't mean changing estimates. Analysts will raise or lower estimates based on company guidance, but a change in estimates doesn't necessarily move a stock. I don't mean making a change after company management already gave guidance. I don't even mean a downgrade from strong buy to buy, because that is weak; it shows that the analyst is on the fence about it and doesn't want to upset company management but wants to give a signal to investors that something is going on. After all, how do you downgrade to buy? No, I mean an aggressive call, like downgrading a stock from buy to hold or upgrading it from hold to buy.

Not every sector has a clear axe, but most do. Sometimes a sector will have a couple of axes. Sometimes an individual company has its own axe, someone who knows the company intimately, the way Rick Sherlund of Goldman Sachs knows Microsoft, Merrill Lynch's Steve Milunovich knows IBM or Jessica Reif Cohen of Merrill Lynch knows Disney.

Once someone has a reputation as an axe, he may remain an axe for a long time. But just as circumstances on Wall Street can change quickly, so too can axes. A few years ago, Tom Kurlak of Merrill Lynch was the acknowledged axe in semiconductors; today one rarely hears from him, and Jonathan Joseph of Salomon Smith Barney has replaced him after that controversial downgrade. When Internet stocks were soaring, Merrill Lynch's Henry Blodget and Morgan Stanley Dean Witter's Mary Meeker were the hotshots. With the dissolution of their sector, they promptly went into the hot seat.

Analyze Your Analysts

Analysts are rarely identified as axes per se, but you can come up with your own list of names gleaned from the financial news. Every year, *Institutional Investor* and the *Wall Street Journal* come out with annual lists of top analysts; often the listed analyst is considered an axe for his or her sector. Make your list as large as you like; then cull the initial group to a list whose names light up your research radar screen and make your news-gathering more efficient. In putting together your basic list, check out these sources:

Institutional Investor's "All-America Research Team" (www.iimagazine.com)

This list is published every year at the beginning of October. To select the 363 members of the 2000 All-America Research Team, *Institutional Investor* sent questionnaires covering eighty-two industry groups and investment specialties to the directors of research and chief investment officers of major money management institutions, as well as analysts and portfolio managers at top institutions and key institutional clients from lists submitted by Wall Street research directors. Analysts were rated in six of their primary activities: accessibility and responsiveness to client requests, estimating corporate earnings, industry knowledge, initiating useful and timely calls to investors, picking stocks, and writing reports. Rankings were determined by using the numerical score each analyst received.

Many analysts pride themselves on getting a high ranking in *Institutional Investor*'s annual listing. Kevin McCarthy isn't so wowed by this, even though he's been on the list a couple of times. "It's a popularity poll. A ballot goes out to institutional investors who list the top four analysts from their perspective. *Institutional Investor* tries to focus on who's providing the best service to the institutional investor. But that could be defined as an analyst who organizes great field trips for investors to see the company's management, or someone who does great weekly round-up reports. Some analysts are given a lot of positive credit because they write really well, or because they pull apart every piece of the company and dissect and analyze major trends. It's not about stock picking. We joke that *Institutional Investor* focuses on who's the best concierge, not the best analyst."

Be that as it may, getting tapped for top pick on this magazine's lists is highly coveted and not just for the honor alone. CSFB's Tom Galvin made

Institutional Investor's 2000 list as the second best strategist of the year. Most people would be pretty thrilled, but Tom told me that missing the number one spot cost him money. He said that his contract stipulates that he gets a bonus if he wins the top ranking. (Incidentally, Ed Kerschner of UBS Warburg got the top spot, after talking down techs and the market just days before the beginning of the March 2000 sell-off.) Many other firms have similar incentives.

The *Wall Street Journal*'s "Best on the Street" (www.wsj.com)

Published every year at the end of July, this list is one of the most watched rankings in the analyst community. This list measures the performance of more than 3,000 analysts to come up with 275 winners in stock picking and 275 analysts who scored bull's-eyes on earnings forecasts over the past year.

By taking a rigorously quantitative approach, the survey prides itself on the fact that it givers no credit for reputations, just results. Having good telephone manners and calling clients back quickly doesn't boost analysts' chances to make "Best on the Street." They either make winning picks or don't. Consequently, an unknown analyst from a small regional firm has as much chance of winning as a well-known Wall Street veteran.

Comparing the two lists is useful for a number of reasons. First of all, while top analysts like CSFB's Kevin McCarthy and Merrill Lynch's Steven Milunovich in computer hardware, Lehman Brothers's Dan Niles in computer peripherals, Goldman Sachs's Maykin Ho in biotechnology, Merrill Lynch's Ken Hoexter in telecommunications carriers, and Merrill Lynch's Jessica Reif Cohen in entertainment make the finals in both lists, what makes the lists truly valuable is that you're not seeing the same names all the time (and that's a good thing too, because while the research done by the major investment firms is restricted to clients who pay big bucks for it, research reports from lesser players is often available on the Internet for free).

www.bulldogresearch.com and www.validea.com

These two Internet sites track analysts' investment suggestions and rate the analysts accordingly. The sites are helpful tools in winnowing down a preliminary list of names. You can find out which analysts cover which industries, then track the record of both a specific analyst and a firm against the S&P 500. You can see that a particular analyst upgraded Ciena at $50 and maybe it's now $150. So if he issues a recommendation for Ciena's competitor, Nortel, at least there's evidence of good performance.

How Can You Analyze the Analysts?

With the amount of information available to the average investor, you can do your own research and then use the analyst's report as one of your final data points, just as a good analyst makes a chat with the company's CFO one of his or her telephone calls. In other words, do your homework then use your common sense to analyze the analyst's recommendation.

If you see some PC analyst on television in July or August telling you that demand doesn't look good, semiconductor analyst Dan Niles of Lehman Brothers says your response should be, "He's an idiot." He explains, **"Demand never looks good in July and August because all of Europe's on vacation, you're on vacation, your kids are at summer camp, and you're not shopping for computers or much of anything else. In late August you're getting ready to send your kids off to school or college, so you're buying clothes and computers as well. That's when you should see demand getting better. It's like wondering why it's cold in January. Well, no kidding, it's the middle of winter. It should be cold.**

"The problem is that the average investor sees an analyst being interviewed on television and thinks that since he's on TV, he should be smart. Instead, it's like football players. You've got some good ones and you've got some bad ones. For every Joe Montana, there's a Bubby Brister."

Niles says that if you see an analyst constantly changing her mind on large companies, flip-flopping from positive one week to negative another, your response should be, "She's an idiot too." **"You don't change your mind based on one day of bad results. Just because it's raining in June doesn't mean it will rain the entire summer."** People forget that companies like Microsoft and Intel and General Electric are huge. Getting them to change course is like trying to turn a battleship. If you've got a lot of momentum going in one direction, it will take a lot to stop you. When things are going well, they'll stay good for a while. Conversely, the company can go through cycles when the stock is flat for a year.

If you see analysts doing an about-face on their ratings after a company reports earnings, especially if those earnings are disappointing, your response should be, "They're not doing their homework." As the bottom was dropping out of PC stocks in the autumn of 2000, Gretchen Morgenson of the *New York Times* wrote an article, scathingly titled, "Memo to

Analysts: Thanks for Nothing," in response to the latest crack-up, in which Gateway shares dropped 32 percent in one day. "Evidence that personal computer sales were sliding has been pouring in recently from independent research concerns like PC Data, NPD Intelect and Dataquest. . . . What we don't understand is why you think equity analysis consists of dialing up company management and smiling when they tell you how great things are."

Similarly, it's a no-brainer for an analyst to make "momentum" calls, that is, negative calls on stocks that have already been beaten down. Sure, the outlook may no longer look rosy, but such downgrades are often a day late and a dollar short.

When I choose analysts to talk to on my show, I look at their past picks and present calls to evaluate their record. I want to know what companies they follow and the ratings on those stocks. I want to know how close their predictions are to reality. Do they get the industry or are they missing something?

Every morning, I quote a lot of analysts' upgrades and downgrades. I try very hard to find the most notable reports, the ones that *will* move a stock. Make no mistake: I have a lot of information that flows across my desk every day and I have to do a lot of editing before I go on the air. How do I choose whom to highlight?

First, I look for the axes in the stock. I want to know what the best analysts in the sector are saying. I like to put their calls in context, so I go on the web and pick out the top institutional and mutual fund holders of the stock. Right off the bat, that tells me who owns the stock and who could be influential in moving it, and it gives me a basis of comparison for the analyst's call.

A second thing that helps me make up my mind is the report itself. I think there's something newsworthy if a formerly steadfast analyst changes his mind. Let's say he's been a long-term bull and all of a sudden his opinion is to sell. That's a fundamental change in conviction and could be very important.

For example, Whirlpool is not a company I normally follow. But I led off the show with it on August 28, 2000, because Prudential analyst Nicholas Heymann downgraded the stock from a hold to a sell. That's almost never done. Hold is not a great rating, but sell? The investment firm might as well dump the company from its client list. Whirlpool denounced his report, but three days later reduced its profit estimates for the next quarter by more than a third. Now I ask you, Is Heymann a mind reader? Or does he have a relationship with Whirlpool that's intimate enough that he could extract the fact that something is going wrong? That's why we have to watch the axes. They are the ones who get the story right most frequently.

Remember, though, that even a market guru isn't infallible, and the other analysts' track records are even worse. Over the three-year period from 1998 through 2000, only 35 percent of money managers beat the S&P 500 index.

I think it's a good thing that we have so many analysts' opinions readily available, but it's easy to lose sight of what the opinions are based on and which opinions are important for which reasons. I think it's good that investors can extract what they think is important and make their own decisions as to what is newsworthy. But you're making a big mistake if you think a particular analyst is God, even if he is an axe. You also want to make sure you know what he is specifically looking at. Is any of his research noise that is clouding your investment scenario? Are you looking at all of the important nuggets of information? You might want to create a list of your news criteria. Do they mesh with his? Yes, you want to hear from the most influential analysts in the field, but you have to have enough conviction to say, "This is what *I* think."

Evaluating News from Unconventional Sources

"Plastics." The word, whispered by a party guest to befuddled graduate Dustin Hoffman in the 1967 movie, *The Graduate,* has become part of every investor's vocabulary, code and shorthand for a stock tip from an unconventional source. Today "plastics" has been replaced by "fiber optics" and a face-to-face suggestion with anonymous advice from Internet message boards. But unconventional sources of news continue to intrigue the investor and, more than ever, move the markets.

When I talk about unconventional sources of news, I mean information that doesn't come from market professionals: Internet message boards, reporters doubling as investors, your Uncle Joe, and your own observations.

Just because information doesn't come from conventional sources doesn't mean it's not valid. Stories abound of people who noticed the growing popularity of a certain product—Tampax tampons, L'eggs panty hose, Reebok sneakers, Starbucks coffee, to name some of the top consumer brands of the past four decades—and profited from it. Peter Lynch, legendary manager of Fidelity's Magellan Fund in the 1980s, became one of the first mutual fund managers to achieve rock-star status by practicing the theory "buy what you know." It's stories like these that make unconventional sources so seductive.

But it's precisely because the sources are unconventional that they are questionable. When information comes from the government, a corporation, or the financial community, you have a pretty good idea of the source's agenda and bias. That's not always the case with other unconventional sources of news. That the sources are unconventional means that you have to bring sharpened critical faculties and more than the usual skepticism to the analysis. That's why it's especially important to examine these market tips carefully so that you can distinguish between news and noise.

Evaluating News from the Net

It's hard to believe that just a few years ago, Internet message boards and chat rooms were on the fringes of the investment world, populated mostly by tech-stock groupies. Today they have become mainstream and impossible to ignore.

For investors trolling for information about small- and mid-cap companies that get little coverage from the analyst community, the message boards offer a chance to dig a little deeper, to track down a lead, to compare notes, and to add one more data point to the overall picture. And because of heavy use of the boards by computer and software geeks, who often provide the lowdown on their own companies and their competitors, they can be valuable sources of information on high-tech stocks.

Or that's what I'm told. I have to be honest: I never go on message boards and I don't hang out in chat rooms. The reason is the underlying problem with the message boards and chat rooms: You just don't know whom you're talking to. You're never sure of the credibility of the information.

When I asked outgoing SEC chair Arthur Levitt for a few must-dos for investors, he said, "They should avoid chat rooms like the plague. Material in chat rooms is like graffiti on the walls of a bathroom. It's garbage."

If I had forty-eight hours in a day, I might scan through the message boards to keep abreast of what people are saying. I call that weekend time. That's not your precious time. Your precious time is the time you cherish and allocate to the fundamentals. This stuff is gravy—and pretty thin gravy at that when the credibility of the news is absolutely in question and is impossible to monitor.

There are dozens of message boards out there. Even CNBC.com now hosts message boards. Sites like Yahoo Finance (www.yahoo.com, then click on "Finance/Quotes") and The Motley Fool (www.fool.com) tend to cast the widest net, with messages on both Old Economy and even low P/E ratio "value" stocks, as well as hotshot high-tech issues. Other sites, such as Silicon Investor (www.siliconinvestor.com), began as an exchange for information on tech stocks, while Individual Investor (www.individualinvestor.com) and Raging Bull (www.ragingbull.com) built their reputation early on for their postings on break-out small-cap companies. Both have since branched out considerably, although the volume of traffic continues to be the highest for Internet and high-tech companies.

There are message boards that enable you to search other message boards for postings on companies you're tracking. There are message boards that allow you to bet on a company's earnings expectations. There are message boards that allow the community to vote on likely winners and others that feature "analyst reports" written by ordinary people and for sale at $5 each.

That's where things can get dicey.

The old computer axiom "garbage in, garbage out" is particularly true on the message boards and chat rooms. A recent thread on The Motley Fool was devoted to whether the proper postal code for the state of Missouri was MI or MO.

If the *gigo* doesn't get you, the anonymity might. We've all snickered at the caption of *The New Yorker* cartoon: "On the Internet, no one knows you're a dog." The truth is, it's easy to be snookered. You never know if the person who identifies himself as an employee of the company or an industry consultant really is one. You can scan the message for internal evidence or even try zapping an e-mail at the person to see what comes back. But the truth is, you never really know who is on the other side of the computer.

That's a problem. You don't know this person's agenda. Sure, Joe Schmo may be saying that IBM is going to miss earnings. But why is this person saying this? He may not be lying, but he may also be shorting IBM because he wants the stock to go down.

This uncertainty is especially prevalent at sites like Whispernumber.com (www.whispernumber.com), which reports the analysts' consensus on company earnings estimates as well as whisper numbers from the investment community. What's a whisper number? As a company approaches the time when it reports quarterly earnings, the analyst community engages in a game in which the analysts try to predict the exact dollar figure that's going to be announced. As more and more analysts place their bets, companies like First Call collect them and come up with what's known as a consensus number. At websites like Whispernumber.com, however, anyone who logs on to the site can contribute a number.

In the quiet period of two weeks leading up to the actual earnings announcement, the company isn't allowed to let out so much as a peep about the accuracy of the consensus. But everyone else in the financial community is free to speculate, and the resulting rumors are what's known as whisper numbers. The consensus on Oracle's earnings may be $1.57, but the whisper number may be $1.58 or $1.59—or higher or lower.

Often, a whisper number is the more optimistic number than the consensus. But in a sign of the times, take the case the case of Yahoo, back in January 2001. The consensus on Wall Street looked for Yahoo to generate $315 million of revenue in the fourth quarter. But the whisper number was lower, at $296 million. Analyst Holly Becker of Lehman Brothers told clients to lighten up on Yahoo stock a week before the company reported. She said that revenue would probably hit the whisper. The company reported earnings and just missed the whisper number at $294 million.

Whisper numbers can churn and billow like smoke in the wind. The problem is when they obscure the consensus number to the point where the investment community now expects the company's earnings to match or beat the whisper number. That can lead to the paradoxical situation when the company's earnings beat the consensus but not the whisper, and the stock gets punished as a result. That's noise if I've ever heard it.

Now what if you wanted to short the stock? Wouldn't it be great if there were a way to skew the whisper numbers higher so that earnings would have to be disappointing and the stock would go down? Whispernumber. com claims that it has safeguards to prevent that from happening. But how do I know whether the person putting in her estimate has any knowledge whatsoever about the company? It's helpful to see what the highest and lowest expectations are, because whisper numbers are a good gauge of market sentiment, but then again, how do I trust this?

Obviously, one anonymous whisper number or comment in a chat room is not going to make IBM plummet, but the fact is Internet messages really do move stocks in the short term, in a day-trading situation, for better or for worse.

Most of the time we hear about the "worse" examples. For instance, in May 2000, the SEC alleged that the shares of a micro-cap stock, Rentech, doubled as a result of enthusiastic message board postings on Yahoo and Raging Bull.

How did that happen? It's a contemporary version of an old Wall Street trading strategy of "reading the tape" and buying stock on the basis of order flows.

Say you start prowling at www.iExchange.com, which features both message boards and a unique feature—"analyst reports" that are written by ordinary people and are for sale at $5 each—and you find a tip that you like. Double-check the recommendations at www.clearstation.com, which also showcases stock picks from amateur analysts. Then see whether this initial wave of enthusiasm has gathered steam on the Big Three—Silicon Investor, Raging Bull, and Yahoo Finance. If the board-prompted buying is strong, you can catch the wave and ride the run-up for short-term profits.

This is a classic example of momentum buying, and it's one of the reasons that market swings have increased in both force and frequency. But it's a chancy stratagem that can easily go the other way. (By the way, I am completely against this and would avoid it.)

That's what happened on August 25, 2000, to Emulex, a California company that makes fiber-optic communications equipment. A fake news release stating that the company's CEO had resigned amid questions about the company's accounting practices appeared that morning on Internet Wire, a web-based news-release service. The release was automatically posted on some websites, including the well-regarded and widely read CBS Marketwatch, and within minutes the "news" hit the Internet message boards. "Emlx to RESTATE EARNINGS DOWN," warned one posting on Yahoo Finance, while another said, "EMLX SEC investigation SELLLLL." As the stock began to fall, the "news" of the press release was picked up by the business press, giving it legitimacy and driving the stock down further. (The main culprits were Bloomberg, CBS Marketwatch, and Dow Jones Newswires; CNBC anchor Joe Kernan noted Emulex's plunge on air but emphasized that he was uncertain about the source and that the information didn't look right. I wasn't in the office that day. Kernan was the only reporter to get it right.)

You might think that news organizations would check their sources, but they were caught in a trap of their own making. Because they are able to deliver the news almost as soon as it happens, their audience now expects and demands that news be delivered instantaneously. As a result, many news organizations use information from press release agencies without checking directly with the companies mentioned in the releases. In any case, the East Coast–based news organizations claimed their reporters couldn't call the California-based Emulex because its offices weren't yet open.

Within one hour of the opening bell, the price of Emulex stock had dropped 60 percent from the day before and Nasdaq halted trading. Half an hour later, Emulex declared the news release to be a hoax. When trading resumed, the stock rebounded and by the end of the day, it was down only 6.5 percent. But in the process, it roiled the markets and dragged down the stocks of other fiber-optic companies.

Later it was discovered that the hoax was perpetrated by a former employee of the news-release service who had made a bad bet on the stock and decided to short it to recoup his losses. Investors who held on through the roller-coaster ride suffered little more than a bad case of high anxiety, but those who sold on the way down were out of luck. The former employee was later indicted.

There's something to be said for the plethora of message boards. Message boards are another reflection of the information explosion. Even though the chat rooms and discussion groups can be noise generators, more noise means the likelihood of more data points, and the more data points there are, the better chance you have of getting to the true story. You make more educated guesses with more inputs. But is the news worth all the noise?

Paul Meeks dedicated a lot of time to trolling the message boards at one point. "They're a haven for short-sellers and they're sometimes a haven for disgruntled employees, so you can find some real blasphemous stuff," concludes the senior portfolio manager of Merrill Lynch's technology and Internet funds. "I don't mind if there's an employee talking about the technology or the lack of a product's success in a certain channel. If the trend is overwhelmingly positive or negative after many, many postings, there might be something to it. I think the message boards can add value in certain situations, but I would not rely solely on them for information. They're just one arrow in your quiver."

Meeks agrees with me that separating the few nuggets of news on the message boards from all the noise takes a huge commitment of time. For my part, I'm not sure it's worth it.

Arnie Berman, technology strategist for Wit Soundview Capital, compares the chances of finding real news in a chat room with the likelihood of meeting your soulmate in a bar. "There's no screen. I always found it easier to meet girls at a party than at a bar. If I was at this party, then I was already prescreened. Anyone can walk into a bar. When I read information in the financial press or hear something on one of the financial networks, those comments aren't always right, but at least the people who are speaking are prescreened."

How much credence does he give to what he picks up online? "Zero. The message boards are interesting to read because you want to know what's being rumored. But believing a message in a chat room is like hearing something in a bar and automatically believing it."

Berman thinks that the influence of chat rooms and anonymous messages on stocks is less profound than a year ago. "People now understand that anyone can stand up in a movie theater and yell 'Fire!' and anyone can write on the Internet and send it anywhere," he says. That may be true, but plenty of people still implicitly trust what they read on the message boards and get taken to the cleaners as a result.

Part of the problem is a certain mind-set that comes from spending a lot of time in chat rooms or on message boards. "I call it the lemming effect," says Robert Loest, senior portfolio manager for IPS Funds. "They all go in the same direction at the same instant. I think the more time you spend on these things, the more powerful the lemming effect becomes."

That's how unwary investors fall prey to so-called pump-and-dump operations. One such scheme that made headlines recently was run by a fifteen-year-old boy who used the Internet to buy obscure penny stocks, hype them in a barrage of false e-mail messages to various web bulletin boards, and then sell them as soon as the price rose, ultimately reaping gains of almost $800,000 over six months. Jonathan Lebed would buy a large share—17 percent to 46 percent—of a day's volume of a thinly traded stock and then, using numerous fictitious names to create the impression that other investors were interested, post hundreds of false messages touting the stock from the computer in his bedroom. One typical message noted that Man Sang Holdings was "the most undervalued stock in history," and its price—then $2 a share—would hit $20 "very soon." As his buying and messages created a flurry of activity and drew other investors, Lebed would sell out. The SEC ultimately charged Lebed with stock manipulation—making false statements with the intent of moving the market, then defrauding others by trading the shares. Examples like these have made us all smarter about message boards and about the implications that the Internet can have for investors. The SEC has also come down hard on improprieties. As they say, eventually everything comes out in the wash.

This example is one of the reasons that I have a problem listening to someone whom I don't know talking about investments. True, I get calls from traders and brokers whom I haven't met. I'm not going to say that I don't take their calls. I do. I want to listen to everything. But I don't want to put something in my head that might sway me without knowing that person's agenda, and I certainly would not go on the air with something a broker has called me about without checking it out.

Similarly, I'm not going to say that some of the people on chat rooms aren't smart or well informed or making wise decisions. But I don't know them and I don't know their agenda or their bias. I don't follow a tip from someone I don't know without verifying it and you shouldn't either.

Neither would Arthur Levitt. "I wouldn't invest with someone who called me over the phone. I would want to look that person in the eye and make a determination of what his or her motives are."

Levitt also warns us to beware of get-rich-quick schemes, fast-talking brokers urging you to "do it now or you'll miss this opportunity," country club or barroom information, hot IPOs, and analysts who have never met a stock they didn't like.

If you think their advice might be worthwhile, use it as one data point—and only one. Don't buy or sell stocks solely on the basis of messages. Compare the messages with news articles and company filings and reports from real analysts, not the self-styled amateurs. Just remember: you have no idea how amateur the person writing the message is, and you probably never will.

One way in which the message boards are useful is that they offer a full 360-degree view of a prospect, not just the conventional point of view but also a contrarian view. I mentioned earlier that I'll often choose an analyst to talk with on my show if he or she is making a controversial call. If an analyst comes out with a sell, that's going against the grain; it's announcing to the world that he truly believes the company has a problem and is willing to back that against his allegiance to the investment bank.

I think message boards can perform a similar service. It's all too easy for the average investor to fall in love with a stock or fall in love with his opinion of a stock. When that happens, you just tend to ignore views that you don't agree with, like a kid sticking his fingers in his ears so he won't hear something he doesn't like. If you pay attention only to the messages you agree with, you might as well stick your fingers in your ears. The contrarian views on message boards can force you to think things through a second time and maybe see them a little more clearly.

So yank your fingers out of your ears and pay attention to the contrarian views, even if you don't want to. You might pick up some useful news.

Evaluating News from the Headlines

There's a ton of noise in the news headlines, especially in what I call opinion news. That's what you see a lot of on many financial websites that bill themselves as delivering news but in fact are delivering opinions. Why take any one person's opinion for fact when you can make an equally firm opinion for yourself?

There are so many opinion reports that I get in the morning: *Bulls, Bears and Bloch, Schaeffer's Investment Letter, The Gay Financial News Network,* and *Art Cashin's Morning Letter* (written by the lead broker for Paine Webber, who has been on the floor for forty years and has his own take on the market). These are all written by professionals who have been on Wall Street for decades.

The difference between some of these smaller newsletters and, say, Tom Galvin's weekly report from CSFB is that Galvin's report goes to paying clients with billions of dollars under management. The smaller newsletters don't have that kind of buying power behind them, so the opinion could be well taken but it won't impact the stock market.

Having said that, are they worth reading? Sure, as one piece of the puzzle. Not every report is worth reading, though. Content has become commoditized, and there's so much content out there. Some of it is news; some of it is noise. You have to learn whose opinions you value and whose analysis you trust. It's much like finding a good movie reviewer, except that you're investing a lot more than the cost of a movie ticket.

You need to ask yourself some questions: Who is this person answering to? What is the source of his opinions? What is this person's agenda and why should I listen to him? Is he trading on his own stock picks? Is he pushing his firm's stock or investing for anyone else other than himself? Is he a hedge fund manager who might be promoting the holdings in his own portfolio? Is he trying to interest investors in companies that are politically correct or environmentally sensitive or known for doing the right thing? If you can't figure out what his agenda is, you're wasting your time reading his newsletter.

How do you differentiate what's opinion from what's actual news? You scrutinize the source. Who is the person writing it? What is he basing his statements on? Are they fact or are they opinion? Can you verify this fact anywhere else?

Now you're probably saying, "Maria, you work in the financial news business. Do you have an agenda?" Sure, I do. My agenda is that I get paid to help the individual get on the same playing field as the institutional investor. My agenda is to give you, the individual investor, access to people whom I have access to because of my job. I want to add value. I want you to say, "She just told me something I didn't know" or "Thanks to her interview, I just met the CEO of a company I've been thinking of investing in."

My agenda is to give you both sides of every story so that you can make a decision. I would like to think of myself as a symbol of free information, because a lot of information comes my way. But I would like to think of myself as a gatekeeper, because I make the distinction between news and noise. It's an issue that I deal with every day, in some cases, every hour. I sift through information and I try to pick out valuable nuggets. I try to assess whose information can make money for my viewers and whose information is a waste of time. Remember who pays me. General Electric (GE) is the parent company of NBC and CNBC. I have an allegiance to GE, which is why you constantly hear me and others on CNBC saying, "the parent of this network" when referring to GE. We have a legal obligation to constantly reiterate that. Does this mean that I or any of my colleagues will cover GE or NBC differently than the way we would cover other companies? Of course not. But we want you to know right from the beginning that there is a relationship here.

My agenda is also to break news and be the first to have the right story. When I call my sources on the trading desks, they know that I need the results of their morning call or their midday call first, before they disseminate it to their top clients. I make it clear that if they call me later than 9:00 a.m., I won't do their call; it's too late. It's just not as valuable. The individual investor deserves to have the information as soon as it comes out.

What you see when I go on the air is a digest of the most important news of the day. I've already edited out what I think is noise. But you may want to edit me further, because you want to organize and prioritize the things you look at when it comes to your money. You have a responsibility to use some of the news that I deliver as just one data point in your investment plan and decide what you deem as noise.

And just for the record, I do not trade stocks. Early in my career, I realized that I speak about so many companies and interview so many CEOs that it would be a gray area to own shares in a company and interview its executives without full disclosure. And, frankly, I didn't want to come out and say, "I own this or that." I concluded that the best way to handle any confusion about my agenda was not to trade at all. I do own mutual funds and I have equity positions in GE in my 401(k), because that's the company that owns CNBC. But I don't trade GE stock and I don't trade my 401(k). Trading stocks and doing my job do not go hand-in-hand. CNBC has strict rules about employees investing in stocks. We have to hold stocks that we own for at least ninety days, we have to notify top personnel about large purchases or sales, we are not allowed to trade options, and we are not allowed to short anything or do anything considered exotic. Although it is legal for me to own stocks, I think the potential for conflict of interest is an overriding concern.

Evaluating News from Family or Friends or Your Own Finds

Every investor has heard the theory espoused by Peter Lynch, the former Fidelity Investments portfolio manager under whose leadership the Magellan Fund clocked unparalleled returns: Buy what you know.

Lynch's favorite example of the power of common knowledge is L'eggs panty hose, one of the most successful consumer products of the 1970s. He didn't find the stock through analysts' research or computer models. Instead, he was tipped off to its potential by his wife, Carolyn, who found it by going to the grocery store. At the time, panty hose was sold in department stores, which meant making a special trip when you wanted to buy a pair. By putting their product in grocery stores, Hanes, the company that sold L'eggs, saved consumers a lot of time. To the convenience was added superior quality and stand-out packaging in signature colorful plastic eggs. The result: L'eggs became a sell-out success—and Hanes stock soared 600 percent. (The company was then taken over by Consolidated Foods, now Sara Lee.)

Can you spot your own version of L'eggs? Probably. You might notice that your electricity bills are routinely higher than they used to be and it's not just because it was a hot summer. You look around the house and realize how much you've got plugged in that sucks up the juice: PCs, microwave ovens, VCRs, CD players, you name it. Electricity is in high demand in your house—and in every other house like yours across the country. You look around the office and realize that every desk has a computer humming all day long, and those computers are wired to big storage units that gulp electricity. So it's not surprising that the energy and utility stocks have done particularly well in the past year. Even alternative energy companies were in high demand; Fuel Cell, an alternative to natural gas, went up 466 percent in 2000.

Or your neighbor might mention that practically all of her teenaged son's friends are toting a cell phone and they're using their cell phones to access the Internet. Hmmm, you think. These young people are tech savvy and trend oriented. If they're using wireless devices for more and more activities, then it might be worth investigating the wireless and cell phone companies for investment opportunities.

These are perfect examples of unconventional sources. An unconventional source provides tidbits rather than investment tips. It's up to you to decide whether these tidbits are worth pursuing.

Some people don't consider themselves (or their friends or families) legitimate sources. They tend to discount these tidbits of unconventional information until they are validated by a market professional. The problem is that they can then become a victim of what Lynch calls "Street lag."

Street lag is a symptom of the don't-stick-your-neck-out, me-too attitude that still prevails on Wall Street. As Lynch explains in *One Up on Wall Street*, the professional investment community tends to be a homogeneous bunch of people who all read the same newspapers and magazines and listen to the same economists. The few exceptions are, he writes, "entirely outnumbered by the run-of-the-mill fund managers, dull fund managers, comatose fund managers, sycophantic fund managers, timid fund managers, plus other assorted camp followers, fuddy-duddies, and copycats hemmed in by the rules."

Don't look to these people to pluck a promising stock out of obscurity. It just won't happen, as Lynch explains: "Under the current system, a stock isn't truly attractive until a number of large institutions have recognized its suitability and an equal number of respected Wall Street analysts have put it on the recommended list." It can literally take years before that happens, years during which the company was too small to have investment banking needs and therefore was too small to be followed by the investment firms' analysts, years during which the company may have prospered—along with the individual investors who picked up on it before Wall Street did. That's Street lag.

Peter Lynch is famous for leap-frogging Street lag. You can too—but you can just as easily trip and fall in a heap.

Let's say it's tax season and you see that tax returns are up significantly from a year ago. Americans have more money in their pockets, you conclude, and that could be a positive for the stock market and for the retail sector. But how do you know that the American public is going to spend that money in buying stocks or new clothing? You don't.

I noticed in the summer of 2000 that Intel and Texas Instruments were selling their shares of Micron Technology, a company in which both corporations had hefty stakes. Yet over a three-month period, according to SEC filings, they were cutting their positions. Could this be because something had gone awry at Micron? Or could it be that Micron stock was already up 300 percent over the previous year and Intel and Texas Instruments just wanted to cash in some chips? The Micron sales could have been a red flag, but they didn't have to be.

Some people have the exact opposite reaction to Street lag. They place greater emphasis on their unconventional sources precisely because they are unconventional. They may indeed have discovered a hidden gold mine, but they will still need the proper tools to determine whether what they've got is fool's gold or the real thing.

Don't go dashing off into some unfamiliar sector precisely because it sounds exotic and seductive. Ask yourself what products you use a lot of. Where do you spend most of your time and your energy and your money? My sister is a nurse, yet when she looks to buy stocks, she talks about technology and telecom companies. I said to her one day, "Theresa, you're a nurse, why don't you stick to what you know, since you don't have the time to start from scratch with a company you know nothing about? Why stick your neck out when some things are easier to do because that's what you live and breathe?" She decided to use her nursing background as a jumping-off point to research medical-related companies.

I think unconventional sources can be helpful, but I don't think you can rely solely on them. They are the first blip on your radar screen, and you wouldn't commit your resources on a little blip. While I give those blips a high regard in terms of getting me to notice something I might otherwise have ignored, I don't regard them as a trigger to buy or sell a certain stock.

When your antenna starts buzzing from an unconventional source, treat it as you would any other source of information. Check it out with the same degree of diligence you would apply to other sources. Ask yourself all the fundamental questions about the company and the industry.

Unconventional information is just as legitimate as any other form of information—and just as likely to be either news or noise. It's up to you to decide which.

My Top Thirteen Noisemakers

Noise in the market doesn't happen by itself. Just as a thundercloud doesn't suddenly appear in a clear sky, noise doesn't just rumble out of nowhere and unleash a downpour of confusion and bother. There are very definite events and situations that trigger a noisy market.

What happens to stocks in a noisy market? They behave uncharacteristically. They swoop and soar and swoon again for what seems like no good reason. The fundamentals of the company haven't changed. There may not be a news trigger or, if there is, a rational investor will not be overly concerned about its effect on the company's basic business. In most cases, despite its wild gyrations, the stock ends up almost exactly where it started.

But when the drums begin beating, when the daily volume bursts out of its normal parameters, and when momentum overwhelms the market, it's hard to remain rational. Whether you call it a knee-jerk reaction or Robert Loest's lemming effect, sentiment has a huge impact on the stock market. It was market sentiment, after all, more than fundamentals, that drove technology share prices up so rapidly in 1998 and 1999. That's the danger to investors in a noisy market: it's difficult to stay clear-headed when the Nasdaq and Dow sirens are calling, even though you know they could be luring you onto the rocks.

You could simply plug up your ears. But then you might miss the significant snippets of news that are generated amid the noise. That's one of the paradoxes of most noisemakers: while they generate mostly noise, they can also be a source of useful news.

Rumors are a classic form of noise that may or may not be masking important news. I hear tons of rumors every day. I get calls from hedge fund managers and day-traders who make their living off noisy markets. Often a rumor gets started and day traders will whisper the rumor to other traders until the stock moves; by the end of the day, the rumor is found not to be true and the stock goes back to its original level, but the day-trader got out hours ago, profit securely in hand. I personally do not report a rumor unless it has already had a material impact on the stock. That's my rule.

Consequently, even though I had a source tell me a month before it happened that Donaldson Lufkin Jenrette was going to be taken over by Credit Suisse First Boston, I kept my mouth shut. This source told me, "I'm sure this firm is for sale and I'm sure the deal is done." I asked why. He said, "Joe Roby, the CEO of DLJ, came in before Labor Day weekend with a suit on." I said, *"What?"* He insisted, "I'm telling you, Maria, the firm is sold. You do not walk around on a Friday before Labor Day with a suit on."

Now there had been a lot of consolidation among the investment firms all summer and the brokerages were on fire, but trading in DLJ had not heated up much. I called various sources and tried to get more solid information than the CEO's choice of wardrobe on a slow day, but I could only get speculation: yes, the industry would continue to consolidate and DLJ probably would be affected. Obviously, I couldn't go with that rumor. But it turned out that my source was correct; a month later, DLJ was taken over by Credit Suisse.

Another time, however, I got a call to check out an item on www. briefing.com. Briefing.com was quoting *Electronic Buyers' News,* which had obtained a confidential map saying that Intel would drop Rambus from the majority of its computing platforms by the middle of 2001. I called *Electronic Buyers' News* to get a copy of the story. I called Rambus and Intel. Why go with the story? It was important because Rambus relies heavily on Intel business and this would be material information for both Rambus and Intel shareholders. At one point during the day, Rambus stock was down $17; it ended up down $9 for the day. After my report, the investment bank SG Cowen came out with a report saying that the article in *Electronic Buyers' News* confirmed the neutral rating on Rambus and reiterating Intel's plans to cancel the yet-to-be introduced Rambus 850 chipset in the third quarter of 2001.

Certain news events can also confuse investors by cloaking significant nuggets of news within a thick layer of noise. Take, for example, 1997's Asian economic meltdown and the 1998 collapse of the Long-Term Capital Management hedge fund. **"People believed the sky was going to fall,"** recalls Tom Galvin, chief strategist of Credit Suisse First Boston. **"You could have gotten caught up in the noise and emotion of the moment and sold stocks, which a lot of people did. In retrospect, that was a bad idea. Instead, you could look at the problems in Asia and say, 'These are good for the U.S. We're a net-importing country. These countries are going to have to produce goods and cut prices because they need the cash flow to pay down debt, and that means the U.S. is going to have low inflation and a consumer deflationary boom,' which was the case. With Long-Term Capital, I knew the Fed was going to have to cut rates to provide adequate liquidity, because the markets had become overemotionalized and, as a result, fragile. In both those cases, the information created noise but at the same time it also created opportunities for investors who could filter it and recognize the implications."**

"A reaction to a data point isn't necessarily driven by a proper analysis of a data point," concludes Joseph Battipaglia, chief investment strategist at Gruntal & Co.

Thanks to the massive proliferation of information, there are more data points available to individual investors than ever before. Some noisemakers are nothing but noise. They roil the markets but have little or no effect on the long-term individual investor. You can ignore them entirely. Other noisemakers are a bit more dicey: they too stir up the markets unnecessarily, but in doing so they reveal useful news that could affect your portfolio.

So don't plug up your ears as soon as you hear the noisemaker's siren. Learn to recognize each one's call, and then you'll know whether to stop for a look or sail on by.

To help you navigate your course, here are thirteen of the most common noisemakers in the market today.

1. Confession Period

Two to three weeks before the quarterly onslaught of earnings announcements comes the confession period when many companies give the investment community a sense of what to expect. The companies then retreat into the so-called quiet period, before unleashing the official announcement.

Confessions can be both news and noise. Their newsworthiness is clear: you get a sense of how well the company did over the past quarter and whether it will meet the Street's expectations. Confessions are a way to help the analyst community fine-tune its earnings models. Knowing how well one company is doing gives individual investors a sense of its direct competitors. If Compaq preannounces that it's seeing weakness in Europe, maybe Dell and IBM are experiencing the same thing.

If the company is a bellwether for its sector, then its confession can give you a sense of the entire industry. Bellwether stocks include IBM for computers and semiconductors, Merck and Pfizer for pharmaceuticals, Amgen in biotechnology, Citigroup and J.P. Morgan Chase for financials, Wal-Mart in retail, EMC in information storage, Yahoo in the Internet, Morgan Stanley Dean Witter in brokerages, Cisco in networking, ExxonMobil in oil, Schlumberger in drilling, and GM and Ford in automotive. General Electric is a bellwether for the entire market because it is so diversified and has one of the largest market caps in the world. Basically, the largest and most liquid stocks are the market's bellwethers.

Confession periods can be noise because the company may not be announcing anything new. It's preannouncing to give the analyst community a more accurate sense of where the business stands in that quarter. The confession may be along the lines of "We still believe that the guidance we gave you one month ago holds" (big deal) or "We're still comfortable with the current estimates on the Street." Or the company may say, "There was a hurricane and we've got high insurance liabilities." Or the confession may be a sector-specific issue that everyone already knew about, such as an earthquake in Taiwan that hit all the fab plants, which means that all the companies that bought their motherboards from Taiwan can no longer get any.

Some companies never preannounce. Sun Microsystems, for example, does a scheduled midquarter update every quarter rather than making a confession. In its call in early February 2001, Sun did, in fact, tell investors that business would slow down for the year. Earnings estimates dropped further—and so did the stock.

What I don't like about the confession period is that it encourages the day-trader mentality. Some people overreact and view confessions as a trading opportunity, which can lead to volatility in the market. When Computer Associates preannounced disappointing second-quarter earnings in 2000 as a result of a slowdown in mainframe sales, it set off a chain reaction with first IBM, then Hewlett-Packard, falling out of bed. There was no good reason for that; Computer Associates is not a bellwether stock and its problems had more to do with the company than with the overall environment. That's why you have to look at the confession period and the confessions themselves with caution.

2. Economic Data

CPI, CCI, PPI, GDP. There's an alphabet soup of economic data released by the government every month (*Business Week* lists the week's upcoming releases in its "Figures of the Week" column at the end of the magazine; many of them are published regularly on page A2 of the *Wall Street Journal*).

"There are fads with information, based on what the consensus thinks are the most important bits of data," says Gruntal & Co.'s Joseph Battipaglia. "In the 1980s, we would spend an inordinate amount of time waiting for the Fed data on the money supply. The feeling was that excess growth in the money supply would lead to inflation because you'd have too many dollars chasing too few goods. That didn't happen because of confidence by the consumer and global markets that the U.S. economy was on the right track. Then in the 1990s, we spent time talking about employment data and the relation between unemployment and inflation. Right now, it's the Consumer Price Index (CPI), the Producer Price Index (PPI), and employment data. Housing data is less important and money supply doesn't even come into the conversation."

Which data should you watch?

I think it depends on two factors: how the index is skewed and how it affects the prime interest rates set by the Federal Reserve's Board of Governors. Most of the indexes look to the past to predict the future. For example, every month the Conference Board releases the Composite Index of 10 Leading Economic Indicators. It's designed to predict the economy's path in the coming six months based on data gathered over the previous month. The index, whose components are adjusted for inflation, has accurately forecast the ups and downs in the business cycle since its creation in 1959.

Other indexes merely report on past events but the data may be too old or key factors may change too quickly to extrapolate future trends.

Information on factory inventories and construction spending, for example, have a two-month lag period.

Furthermore, many of the statistics coming out of the government are revised a number of times. The original numbers in the Gross Domestic Product (GDP), for example, are revised twice each month. **"If you look at the GDP, you see a wide disparity of the numbers, yet the market reacts to each one as if it's the final answer,"** says Battipaglia.

Probably the most important indexes are the ones that give you a sense of what might happen to interest rates. Some people say that all economic data give you a sense of interest rates. I think it depends on what the Fed is looking at, and what the Fed looks at will change with every shift of the economy. Some of the major factors affecting economic growth and inflation in 2001 are an inventory buildup, high energy prices, and weak consumer confidence, so the Fed is watching the GDP. The slowdown in the economy has also been the cause of a variety of industries missing their earnings targets, so the growth of the GDP is what many people focus on every month—and that's why the market reacts so strongly to each revision. Merely one year earlier, the main economic crimp was a tight labor force, so the Fed at that time was focusing on the Employment Cost Index.

You can't plunk one set of government reports in a bucket labeled "news," and another set in a bucket labeled "noise," and forget about them. With economic data, it all depends on where we are in the overall cycle.

3. Headline Grabbers

News items act as triggers. The Federal Reserve ponders an interest-rate hike and the overall market swoons. Something hits the headlines and investors are faked out into thinking that it's important, when in reality it's only drama. A good example a few years ago was the Monica Lewinsky scandal. Some investors got the idea that the economy was going to fall apart in its wake and panicked. The fact was that the economy had less to do with Bill Clinton's infidelities than with decisions made by then Treasury secretary Robert Rubin and Fed chairman Alan Greenspan.

More recently, Halliburton stock slumped when its CEO, Richard Cheney, was named to be George W. Bush's vice presidential running mate. The investment community surmised that the departure of the

CEO would be a negative for Halliburton stock. It was a total headline grabber and it meant nothing. What people hadn't realized was that Cheney's second-in-command, who stepped in to replace him, was the guy who was really running Halliburton.

Another headline that stirs stocks is the publicity given to every analyst rating change. Because we hope that analysts know something that we don't know, there's often a huge response from a high-profile analyst working at a high-profile firm. It's not that some analysts don't have good opinions. But ultimately, the only information that really matters is the information that tells whether your company is going to generate more cash sooner or less cash later. There may be proprietary insight behind the rating change that says, "Gee, the cash is being raised sooner rather than later," but often the ratings don't include recent estimate changes or estimate changes that were dialed into the stock price long ago. There are many times when stocks are smarter than people and rating changes can be a lagging indicator.

You often hear how one company's announcement will drag down the Dow or goose the Nasdaq. IBM announces solid earnings and the tech sector soars. Conversely, Nortel in the third quarter of 2000 reported revenue that was just short of some people's expectations, as a result of inventory buildup and a onetime nonrecurring charge. The entire fiber-optics sector blew up. It was scary because it happened right in the middle of a sell-off that had claimed every other sector of high-tech stocks, and Nortel's shortfall was the last straw. Corning, JDS Uniphase, and all the technology contract manufacturers sagged as well.

It's easy to fall into the trap of cause-and-effect thinking. But, claims Charles Biderman, that's rarely the case. **"It always comes down to money flows. Market liquidity could be strong and the market is flat, then some news story breaks and people start to buy. Because there's all this cash lying around, the market goes up, so people say that the news item or earnings announcement is responsible. Similarly, if money is already flowing out and the market isn't doing much, bad news can make the market crater."** The news item merely accelerates the money flows in a sensitive market; in a market that's not susceptible, it would just be a blip.

Biderman would say, Watch the flows, not the news. I say, Watch both. If you already have money coming out of the tech sector and IBM pre-announces with bad news, you can bet that the flow will accelerate. If there's no significant trend in the money flows, however, then headlines may roil the market but the effect will be noise, not news.

4. Initial Public Offerings

Every investor has heard about the IPO that got away: theglobe.com, priced at $9 and opening at $90; Foundry Networks quintupling in price on its first day of trading; VA Linux scoring a nearly 700 percent gain right out of the gate. It's enough to make almost any investor throw caution to the winds and plunge into the market to make sure that the *next* one *doesn't* get away.

The result? Too often, an individual investor puts in the buy order for, say, Palm's IPO price of $38, but the stock may open, as Palm did, at $145—and that's the bill the investor is stuck with. That's all well and good if the stock continues to rise—as Palm briefly did, before heading south, breaking its IPO price and trading down to a low of $19.88 all within its first month.

The fact is, for most individual investors, the chance to get in at the bottom of a hot IPO is gone long before they have ever heard of the fledgling company. "IPOs are strictly about limited supply for in many cases sometimes virtually unlimited demand," explains David Menlow, president of IPOFinancial.com. "It is a rigged game, and the individual investor is, for the most part, eliminated from the process."

Here's how it works: The lead underwriting firm doles out only so much stock to other brokerage firms involved in the deal and it's never enough stock to meet the demand of those firms' customers. Consequently, the brokerages first call the customers who have given them the biggest orders and therefore the biggest commissions. After all, that's what the big-money customers pay for: research, investment ideas, execution of trades, and allocation of new stock. Those customers are usually institutional investors, hedge funds, mutual funds, and, maybe, their biggest individual clients. They are almost never ordinary investors.

Wall Street has a saying about IPOs, Menlow explains. "When you want 'em, you can't get 'em, and when you can get 'em, you don't want 'em. The IPOs that are in high demand, you can't get. The ones that are not, you can, but there's no institutional sponsorship, so the stock is destined to trade lower.

"IPOs have definitely added to the noise in the market. The scales are weighted very heavily in terms of hyperbole. The level of misinformation and the heightened state of emotionalism that prevent an IPO investor from making an intellectual decision is rampant." Yet because of all the hype and sense of urgency surrounding IPOs, individual investors just can't leave them alone.

Still, while IPOs add noise to the market, interpreting the noise can often produce some valuable nuggets of news. A hot IPO can give you a sense of the health of the market. The number of IPOs and the quality of an IPO are other good indicators.

A quality deal includes three fundamental factors. The company must have what Menlow calls "the eyebrow factor," the quality that makes potential investors read the business description and say, "Wow, this is cool." It must be not just a company with growth potential but be in a sector with strong growth. "The investor might say that wireless applications or fiber optics are a good market, but if the level of saturation within the sector has been strong, the sector may not be worth the investment," says Menlow. Finally, the IPO must have a strong underwriter—one of Wall Street's big names.

When you have a deal like that and it does well—not necessarily up $100 but up $10—my takeaway is that the market is healthy. Quality deals will get bought.

5. January Effect and Other Seasonal Stock Rockers

Stocks, especially small ones, have historically tended to rise markedly during the period starting on the last day of December and ending on the fourth trading day of January. The January effect is due to year-end selling to create tax losses; recognize capital gains; raise holiday cash; and, especially on the part of mutual fund managers, engage in window dressing (see page 215). Because such selling depresses the stocks but has nothing to do with their fundamental value, bargain hunters quickly jump in, causing the January rally.

Since the dynamic of mass public involvement in the market began in the mid-1990s, the January effect has spread backward into December, as investors try to get a head start on the rally, and into February, as they extend the rally. Different sectors will trade differently toward the end of the year. E-commerce and retail stocks may move up in anticipation of the holidays. The tech sector often moves to the upside from mid-October through mid-March, as a result of information technology managers bucking up their budgets.

September often sparks its own version of a January effect. Investors are coming back from vacations and want to invest, so a lot of money goes into the market in September. The financial community too is back at work, so there is often a spate of new offerings toward the end of the month. And virtually all the major investment banks and brokerage houses host industry conferences at which companies flaunt their strong points to an audience of investors and analysts. Portfolio managers have new money coming in, no money going out, and are looking for ideas, so they go to these conferences and buy into the companies they like.

Many of those gains are reversed in October. It's not just that October is traditionally the spooky month of the year, the time when the market crashes. These days, it's because mutual funds are a bigger factor in the market. Their fiscal year ends in October and November, so the reasons that prompt a sell-off in December—portfolio managers' dumping losers to minimize the taxes on the gains they give their shareholders—now occur three months sooner.

Dan Niles, Lehman Brothers semiconductor analyst, concludes, "You pick up a good 60 percent to 70 percent of the movement in the stock market between October and January. If stocks are depressed but there aren't fundamental problems with either the company or the economy, then you might do well to invest in the summer. And if you sell most of the stuff you bought in January and February, you'll probably do pretty well."

So, is this seasonality news or noise? Depending on what happens with the market, it can be either. I'm including it in this list because it will help you understand what the stock market is doing, but you can't count on it enough to put in a trade order.

6. Round Numbers

Round numbers are enticing and have a certain allure; investors tend to egg each other on when a new 100 mark is in sight, and they get really anxious when the indexes slip below the previous mark. The fact is, these are just numbers. They give you a rough idea of what the averages have done, but what moved the average is a whole other story.

In 1999 and 2000, investors were ecstatic each time the market ticked off a new round number: 11,000, 11,100, 11,200. Actually, "the market" meant the Dow Jones Industrial Average, a price-weighted average of thirty actively traded, blue-chip stocks, so investors were thrilled from the results of just thirty stocks, most of them industrials. The dirty secret was that when the Dow 30 was at 11,000, most of the industrial stocks were trading down.

When something happens to one of the companies that make up the Dow, things get exciting. To give you an example, on June 13, 2000, I heard from an analyst at Sanford Bernstein that he didn't think Hewlett-Packard could live up to its rosy expectations. Now Hewlett-Packard had been flying high and was up 18 percent for the year. Its projections for future growth and revenue looked promising, and the stock price was heading higher. But this analyst didn't agree and the firm downgraded the stock in its morning call. I went on the air that morning with the news and the Bernstein report had an impact. The stock dropped 8 points at the opening bell. Hewlett-Packard is a Dow component, so if it's down that much, you know it would affect industrials, and it did. That news began to drag down the Dow. People surmised that if Hewlett-Packard wasn't doing well, then maybe earnings growth would fall off the board across the technology sector, so they started selling other technology stocks. Hewlett-Packard and IBM are both major components in the Dow weighting, so the next thing you knew, the Dow as off 50 points.

A quick explanation of how the Dow is calculated: The impact of the performance of each of the thirty stocks in the Dow on the index is calculated according to their price (IBM is a more expensive stock than United Technologies, so it has a heavier weighting) and a number called the "Dow divisor." Changes in Hewlett-Packard and IBM stock are multiplied by six, so if Hewlett-Packard or IBM is down 2 points, the Dow will be off by 12 points.

The Nasdaq Composite Index comprises all of the four-thousand-plus stocks traded on the Nasdaq stock market. Compare that to the Nasdaq 100, which is a sampling of the one hundred largest Nasdaq companies. The S&P 500 is broader, because it is a composite index of 500 stocks, but the main components of its 100 Stock Index are, like the Dow, mostly industrials, transportation, utility, and financial stocks.

If you're an index investor and the Nasdaq is above 3,000 and the Dow is kissing 11,000 and the S&P 500 is hitting an all-time high, then you're a happy camper. But if the majority of your portfolio is in biotechnology and biotech stocks are lagging, then a round number doesn't mean a thing to you.

What's more newsworthy than the round numbers of the indexes is the round number of a particular stock. When a particular stock goes to $100 or $150, typically it will split, an action that often sends it higher. But it's questionable whether stock splits over the long term are news or noise.

7. Short-Term Deadlines

Money managers have to worry about short-term gains and losses because their quarterly and yearly performance is constantly compared to that of the S&P 500; if they're not showing better returns than the major averages, then their clients may look elsewhere. So money managers are under continuous pressure to buy stocks that are going to move *now.*

The individual investor doesn't have to worry about short-term deadlines. You don't have to be married to what a stock is going to do over the next week or month or quarter or year, and you shouldn't be (unless, of course, you are a short-term or day-trader, but you already know how I feel about that). You've got the luxury of time, and there will be plenty of times when you will need that luxury. There was a two-year period from 1992 to 1994 when Microsoft went absolutely nowhere—and then it split four times over the next six years.

Remind yourself of this when you feel inclined to make a knee-jerk reaction. The one thing you don't want to do is make a rash decision on a stock because of one piece of information or because you've been infected by the mood of the market and are thinking, "Oh, my God, I'm going to miss a crucial opportunity to trade." I think the risk associated with being afraid to miss one day's situation has much more downside than the reward potential. It's a lot riskier to trade on something you've just heard than taking the time to think it through. The only thing you'll accomplish is increasing the amount of noise.

In January 2001, I asked Jonathan Joseph, a semiconductor analyst at Salomon Smith Barney, if he thought semiconductor stocks had bottomed out. Remember, he was the first to downgrade the sector in July 2000. He told me not to be in such a rush to find bottoms just because the stocks have sold off. Then he pointed out that when you try to find a bottom or try to buy on what so many people call compelling valuations because the stocks have plummeted, just remember the story of National Semiconductor. The stock went from $85 to $30 in 2000 in the tech sell-off. Many investors figured that was the bottom and bought, and the stock recovered to $37. Then the company preannounced disappointing earnings and the stock went down to $20. It's interesting to hear an analyst saying that he doesn't know where the bottom is. It reminds you that not even the market professionals know for sure. In Joseph's case, he looks at company- and sector-specific factors, such as whether inventory has been used up and capital spending has decreased, rather than the stock's price.

8. Spin Cycles and Road Shows

Wall Street has an amazing capacity to regurgitate the same piece of information several different times. Here's how Dan Niles does it: **"We'll start with an earnings release with a company that's doing well. The company releases earnings after the market closes. The next morning, you've got thirty-five analysts all talking about how good the quarter was, so there's no way you can differentiate yourself unless the quarter was great and you downgrade the stock. So you wait a couple of weeks or a month, and then the company's not in the news as much anymore. That's when you come out and talk about certain trends you've seen. Then you wait a couple more weeks; if things continue to do well, you can come out and raise your estimates for the next quarter. Now the quarter's almost finished, so you say, 'If the last few weeks stay on track, we think this company's going to do well and you should buy the stock.' It's essentially the same message you've been putting out all along, but with more data to back it up. And that works on the negative side as well."**

Companies try to drum up interest in their stock by holding a road show. That's when the management makes the rounds of analysts and institutional investors in different cities around the country and, in the case of global corporations, around the world. When Alcatel did a road show at the beginning of September 2000, it presented its view of the future to analysts in London, New York, and Boston. In each case, the message was the same: the company was looking for 35 percent growth in their optics division, 32 percent growth in overall revenue in 2000 and 35 percent growth in revenue in 2001.

Now, do you think the company's spiel was different in any of those meetings? Of course not. What an extended road show does is cause a lot of noise for a company. After each presentation, analysts will put out reports. The market will likely view the information as something new and there will be more volume than usual in the stock for as long as the road show continues, which helps put the stock in the news and brings it more attention from investors who might have ignored it earlier.

I like road shows. I think they're important and helpful because you get to hear from management and it's not often that you have that chance. However, because the management team is delivering the same message over and over, the road show can quickly devolve from news to noise. If the company hosts a road show on Monday and analysts in one city report on it on Tuesday, and then the next week another analyst in another city comes out with more information that he says is news, it's really not. By that time, it's noise.

Road shows are not open to individual investors, but if you like what you hear through the grapevine, I suggest scrutinizing a chart of the stock. See if it has moved and ask yourself how much of the good news presented in the road show is already built into the stock.

Road shows and spin cycles aren't a clear-cut case of news or noise. They are more of an amplification process that focuses the market's interest on both the stock and, I should add, the analyst. With so many people getting caught up in the excitement and banging the jungle drums for this stock, it's easy to dismiss the spin cycle as noise fueling a momentum rally. But when you sift through the analysts' remarks, you may discover the tidbits of true news that you can rely on.

9. Stock Splits and Other Company Announcements

Stock splits may seem like nothing more than meaningless paper shuffling. In a two-for-one split, for instance, shareholders end up with twice as many shares. But each share's claim on the company's dividends and earnings is halved, so shareholders are no better off.

Nonetheless, splits almost always boost the company's stock when they're announced. Partly that's a result of the publicity surrounding the split and the greater sponsorship by brokers who generally prefer to push a stock that's more affordable. But a split may also be a sign of management's confidence in the company. A study by David Ikenberry and Sundaresh Ramnath, both professors at Rice University's Jones Graduate School of Management, showed that in the year following the announcement of the split, the split stocks outperformed comparable companies by an average of 9 percentage points.

So, despite the "so what" argument that a two-for-one split only cuts the stock in half and doubles the amount of shares, I happen to think it's news when a stock splits. But to take a split announcement as a buy signal is just noise.

Other corporate announcements that may move the markets but don't really mean anything include rumors of mergers and acquisitions; promotions that change the person's title but not the fundamental job description, such as the president getting an anticipated promotion to CEO; and corporate buybacks. "Although corporate buybacks can have an effect, they're usually more bark than bite," says Arthur R. Hogan III, chief market analyst for Jefferies & Company. "Companies can announce as much or as many as they like, but they don't have to execute them. It's an old trick—the company announces with great fanfare that the board has approved a $2 bajillion buyback. Well, the board may have approved it but the treasurer never implemented it."

When you hear a buyback announced, scrutinize the stock to see where it is relative to its fifty-two-week high and low. Try to understand the management's thinking: Will they really execute that $10 billion buyback with the stock at a fifty-two-week high? Buybacks become news only when the company actually starts executing.

10. "The Stock's Telling You Something" and Other Wall Street Jargon

Just about every day, you'll see stocks persistently gapping up or down on a swirl of expectations but with the absence of real news. The explanation for this is encapsulated in the adage, "The stock's telling you something." What the stock is telling you is that it's sensitive to rumors.

A couple of years ago, there was a high correlation between the way the stock behaved and actual news that ultimately came out. The stock was telling you that there might be a leak in confidential information: an acquisition, negative earnings, or an analyst's doing grassroots research with customers and concluding that the company hadn't closed on its business goals for the quarter.

Today someone in a chat room may be telling you something. A hedge fund may be trying to create uncertainty to short out its position. Perhaps the corporation isn't very communicative and investors are sniffing out their own leads. Or it could just be that there's a big seller. Maybe a corporation owns this stock heavily and is selling it. Sometimes there's just selling pressure that needs to finish in order for it to go back up. In short, a lot of times the stock's message may be right, but it may not be telling you anything significant. It's pure noise.

In fact, beware of all Wall Street jargon. Phrases like "It's a stock picker's market," "The market's nervous today," and "We use proprietary trading techniques" are nothing but a lot of hot air once you think about it. Here's why:

Phrase 1: When stock prices fall—and that's generally when the call for careful stock picking goes out—stock investors as a group won't beat the market because they *are* the market. Studies have shown time and time again that active investors almost never beat the market, no matter what its direction.

Phrase 2: Who's officially gauging investor sentiment to justify claiming market anxiety? It's like saying that the market is down because of profit taking. Says who? Maybe investors are selling their losers instead.

Phrase 3: This is one of my favorites. It basically means that they have an oh-so-secret strategy that you, the individual investor, are too dumb to understand, and it involves charging you fat fees and making you lose money in ways you never could have imagined.

11. Triple Witching

Once every quarter—on the third Friday of March, June, September, and December—stock options, stock index options, and stock index futures all expire on the same day. Massive trades in index futures, options, and underlying stocks by hedge strategists and arbitrageurs can throw the markets into turmoil as traders scramble to offset buy and sell orders. Smaller-scale witching hours occur in the other eight months, usually on the third Friday, when index futures or options expire.

These are about as clear an indication of noise as you'll ever see, since the witching-related activity has absolutely nothing to do with market sentiment. In fact, you'll frequently see a complete reversal in the market momentum on the following Monday. It's totally technical, totally noise.

12. Whisper Numbers

As a company approaches the time when it reports quarterly earnings, the analyst community engages in a game in which the analysts try to predict the exact dollar figure that's going to be announced. As more and more analysts place their bets, companies like First Call and I/B/E/S International collect them and come up with what's known as a consensus number. Companies are not allowed to speak during that two-week quiet period, but everyone else in the financial community *is* free to speculate. The resulting rumors are known as whisper numbers. You can check the latest whisper numbers at www.firstcall.com, ww.ibes.com, and www.whispernumber.com.

Whisper numbers are important, says CSFB's Kevin McCarthy, because they set expectations. In fact, whisper numbers got started because certain companies set a pattern of underestimating earnings guidance so that they could develop a reputation for "beating the numbers."

But whispers can also raise expectations to unrealistic heights. Charles Hill, director of research at First Call, gives an example: "In [the first quarter of 2000], GE preannounced that it would do better than expected and guided analysts up from 75 to 77. That matched the consensus figure, which was 77. But just before GE reported, people cited a whisper website that had a whisper number of 85 cents for GE. Now anyone who knows the company knows that GE wouldn't surprise by 8 cents even in a normal quarter, and especially not after they had put out a preannouncement two weeks earlier guiding people to 77. They actually came in at 78."

Inflated whisper numbers can lead to the paradoxical situation when the company's earnings beat the consensus but not the whisper, and the stock gets punished as a result. "If the whisper is 55 [cents] and the original consensus number was 50 and the company comes in at 55, that's good," says

McCarthy. "But if it comes in at 52, the stock will be down. The company beat the consensus but it didn't beat the whisper."

Whisper numbers can come from a variety of sources. McCarthy explains: "Sometimes whispers are put out by hedge funds that are looking to change expectations to fit their advantage. They'll set a high whisper to short the stock if the company can't make it. Or they'll set a low whisper if they're long on the stock to enable the company to beat it."

Sometimes a company is responsible for lowering its whisper number. Companies like Cisco and Intel routinely try to be conservative when giving guidance so that when they do come out with their earnings, they beat the whisper number handsomely.

Sometimes an analyst is purposely putting a positive spin on the quarter in order to make it look good. If he puts out a whisper number of 45 cents and the company reports 50 cents, then the analyst can say, "Hey, this is a great performance. They beat us by a nickel." Of course, since analysts are rated by how well they target their estimates, it seems paradoxical that they should advertise the fact that they were off the mark. "Even if you're expected to come in at $1.10 and come in at $1.09 instead, if you're Cisco, then that's a problem," says Hill. "A penny means a lot in today's market."

Ultimately, the fundamental problem with whisper numbers that they are basically rumors with a fancy name. People won't tell you what they're basing their estimate on. The combination of the amorphous nature of the whisper and the anonymity of whisper websites can be inflammatory. "Anyone can come onto the site and submit a number," says Hill. "That's open season for manipulation. In fact, I've talked to some reporters who have gone onto these websites and manipulated the number to significantly change what the whisper number was. So buyer beware."

13. Window Dressing

You'll often see violent market rallies at the end of a quarter. Stocks suddenly pop to new highs in the absence of any real news. Has some vital piece of information just been released? Is the stock just going on its own momentum? Or could it be that it's the end of the quarter and mutual fund portfolio managers are engaging in the practice known as window dressing?

Portfolio managers are under pressure to turn in a good performance, quarter after quarter. They can polish it by engaging in window dressing. Many mutual funds hold large positions in certain companies. To bump up the performance as the calendar deadline approaches, the portfolio managers sometimes buy a lot of shares of those companies that they already own. Let's say a portfolio manager owns ten million shares of Nortel. Over the last few days of the quarter, he might buy half a million shares more. Sure, he's paying a lot of money for those five hundred thousand shares, but the laws of supply and demand will increase the overall price of the stock, so the return on his original ten million shares will come in higher.

Window dressing sounds sneaky, but it implies a positive outlook for the stock. A portfolio manager can't single-handedly boost a bad stock out of the doldrums.

The flip side of window dressing occurs at the end of a mutual fund's fiscal year, which ends October 31 for some and November 30 for others. Let's say you've invested in a mutual fund that is down for the year, and you've lost money overall. If the portfolio manager did a lot of trading and some of the stocks were big winners, you will still have to pay capital gains taxes. Now the portfolio manager is well aware that when you are told that you lost money but also have to pay taxes, you will not be a happy customer. Portfolio managers are looking for ways to offset the tax gains, so they will blow out the stocks that have crashed and burned in order to record the loss. Consequently, they sell so that they can offset those capital gains with losses.

Putting It All Together

There is more than enough information out there to keep you tuned in. The problem is sorting through it and learning what to tune out. One of your most useful tools in organizing and handling the information explosion is a personalized investment calendar on which you note important market-moving events. Those events could range from news that is specific to one company, such as an upcoming stock split, to broad-ranging economic news, such as the eight annual meetings of the Federal Reserve's Board of Governors.

Every Wall Street firm puts out an economic calendar, most of which are free on the firm's website. But I'm not talking about a general calendar; I'm talking about one that's personalized for your investment philosophy and portfolio.

An investment calendar is a way of making sure that you're up-to-date about the news of your investments. Knowing beforehand which market-moving events are coming up helps you predict how the market might react and avoid knee-jerk reactions that could harm your portfolio.

But an investment calendar serves another purpose. People often tell you to pick your battles. Well, I'm telling you to pick your information. Noting down events on my investment calendar helps me organize all the clutter and makes me feel that I've got everything in order. Once you've got things organized, you can tune out the noise and focus only on the news that is important to the particular investment idea that you're working on.

When I construct my investment calendar, I divide up the information in three ways:

- specific events that might be a catalyst to the stock or the sector are marked on the days on which they occur, as are also the dates of reports of broader economic indicators;
- general market trends which occur in a known time period, such as the Fed effect, are shaded in over the weeks when they tend to occur; and
- other notes and reminders, such as comments about changes in the management team or thoughts about the valuation of the stock, which I scribble in the margins.

My investment calendar is not all that different from my regular calendar, on which I might note my husband's birthday on the actual date but scribble in the margins my thoughts about how we should celebrate it and what presents he might like.

I try to make this calendar as simple as I can, because I don't want it to be too crowded or unwieldy. You want to be able to update the calendar at least every week or every other week, so you don't want it to be too much to handle. For example, on January 1 you may not know that Home Depot is having a meeting on February 1. You may not know that until January 20. And going into those meetings, you want to have a sense of the important topics to be discussed. You may not own the stock but it may impact your investments in another company. Home Depot is a Dow component; if something unexpected is said at an analyst meeting, that will impact the stock, the retailing sector, and the Dow in a nanosecond. So you want to know about things that may not be directly linked to your portfolio but are directly linked to the market.

At a minimum, your calendar should include information about the stocks you own. If you'd like to take it up a level—and I strongly recommend that you do—you should also note information about other leading stocks in the sector.

You don't have to be all-inclusive. Jack Welch, the chairman of GE, likes to tell his division heads that if their company isn't number one or number two in its field, they should get out of the industry. I think the same applies to your information gathering within a sector. Follow your own investment and one or two of its top competitors; that's enough to give you a good picture of what's happening in that sector.

What to Jot Down on Your Investment Calendar

Stock- and Sector-Specific Events

Earnings Announcements

Earnings announcements are one of the strongest catalysts on a stock's performance, affecting not only the specific stock but also the sector and, sometimes, the entire market. Mark when the quarterly earnings are announced, not just of your stock but the bellwether stocks in the key Dow and Nasdaq sectors. If IBM has a bad quarter, that could sway the market; it will certainly affect the PC, semiconductor, and storage sectors. Similarly, during the week that brokerage firms report earnings, you can bet there will be movement in the financial sector. That's because, of course, many of the same reasons that Morgan Stanley Dean Witter exceeded estimates—or missed them—will likely drive Goldman Sachs.

One of the major shocks in the tech sell-off of 2000 was disappointing earnings in July from cell phone manufacturers Nokia, Motorola, and Ericsson. The shock wave next hit the telecom equipment makers; then the semiconductor industry; and, almost inevitably, the EMS (electronics manufacturing services) companies, which manufacture many of the products for the equipment companies on an outsourcing basis. It's no secret that the financial services industry felt the implications of rising losses from telecom services companies defaulting on their loans. Could you have foreseen the sell-off? Maybe, maybe not. But I firmly believe that noting the dates of the earnings releases from the other related sectors would have given you a heads-up reminder to be extra alert and might have enabled you to take precautions to protect your portfolio.

Obviously, not every earnings announcement has such dire implications—quite the opposite occurred during the boom years between 1995 and 1999. But events like this past year's dramatically demonstrate how earnings—good or bad—are the most fundamental factor in evaluating financial news. That's why earnings announcements should be the first and foremost element on your investment calendar.

How do you learn the date of the announcements? Sources include First Call (www.firstcall.com); the business news shows; press releases from the company, which are usually posted on the company's website; and the company's investor relations department.

If you'd like to take your research to the next level, try to get an idea of what the market is looking for and what might affect its opinion. While you're talking with investor relations, inquire about any catalysts that might rock the stock: analyst meetings, product announcements or acquisitions, and even preannouncements about earnings. Don't be shy about bothering them; that's what they're there for.

Also, check out the consensus on www.firstcall.com and www.ibes.com, as well as First Call's preannouncement scorecard and list of catalysts at www.earningswire.com. I don't want to sound self-serving, but on CNBC's *Market Week,* I put together a calendar of earnings announcements, conferences, road shows, and analyst meetings occurring in the week coming, so you can have a sense of what events might move the market.

If you want to be more aggressive, you could get a whole calendar of when each of the market sectors reports from First Call. Some groups have a bigger impact on the market than others. Financial stocks, for example, have been a leadership group for some time. As a source of capital to the economy and the underwriters of new companies, they have been at the nucleus of the market. The investment bank and brokerage numbers give you a sense of what's happening in the rest of the market and mirror the sentiment of the investment community.

All you had to do was look at financial stocks in the latter half of 2000 and early 2001, and you knew what was happening on Wall Street. The banks had been facing issues of bad credit. Bank of America and First Union had secured loans for the failed Sunbeam Corp., among others. In addition, Goldman Sachs, Merrill Lynch, Morgan Stanley Dean Witter, and J.P. Morgan Chase all issued bonds for telecom companies. Many of these bonds are now under water. Many of the brokerages took Internet companies public. Many of those stocks are down sharply. Many banks have investment units that own telecom and Internet stocks; those returns are down, dragging down the companies' bottom lines.

Company Conference Calls

With Regulation FD in effect, individual investors can now listen to (or use the Internet to tune into) the conference calls that companies often hold in conjunction with their earnings announcements. As I've mentioned earlier, conference calls can be very time-consuming as analysts painstakingly pick through a mountain of minutiae. They are, however, one of the best sources of information explaining the reason for the past quarter's performance, as well as giving a glimpse of the company's expectations for the near future. I won't say that they're a must-do, but they definitely should be listed on your calendar so that you have the option of making that decision yourself.

Analyst Meetings and Industry Conferences

These are red-letter days on an investment calendar for two reasons: all sorts of interesting information from both the company and the analyst community will be generated, and the stock typically moves as a result.

Sometimes an analyst meeting merely confirms what you already know about the company; sometimes you'll learn something new. I remember an Enron analyst meeting in 2000, when the company introduced its new online unit, which trades everything from oil futures to broadband. Executives—and analysts—were so optimistic about Enron Online that the stock shot up $12 that same day.

Sometimes even the announcement of an analyst meeting can be enough to tickle your antennae. For example, any of the investment banks publishes periodic lists of upcoming market events that will trigger trading. (You have to be a client to get this information directly, but I try to get my hands on it whenever I can so that I can broadcast it—and you'd better believe that I do.)

Early on in 2000, a particular firm mentioned that Minnesota Mining and Manufacturing was going to have an analyst meeting. It struck me as odd, because this firm was big into New Economy stocks. Why was it interested in an Old Economy standby like 3M? The information spurred me to do a little research. First, I found that over the previous months, more and more analysts had become bullish on 3M. Then I read that 3M planned to focus on the telecommunications section of their business at the analyst meeting. Finally, at the actual meeting, 3M announced that it would derive 50 percent of its revenue over the next five years from telecommunications technology. Wow! Now *that's* news, especially when you see what has already happened with similar companies like Corning that have made comparable decisions. Not surprisingly, the analyst meeting put a spark under 3M's stock and it traded up significantly. Two months later, the company announced that it had hired W. James McNerney Jr., from GE, as its new CEO. That news added a spark to the New Economy story that was already going on and further boosted the stock.

Sometimes what *doesn't* happen at an analyst meeting or industry conference can be significant. Three days before J.P. Morgan announced that it would be acquired by Chase Manhattan, Merrill Lynch was hosting a banking and financial services conference at which the CEOs of all the major banks and brokerage houses were supposed to speak. At the eleventh hour, the CEO of J.P. Morgan canceled and sent a lower-ranked person to speak in his place. Now when a CEO has a major speaking engagement on his calendar and he cancels, it could be important. I heard about this from a source at another firm, checked it with Merrill Lynch, and then reported it on my 2:00 show. By then, the market speculated that something was going on and sent the stock up. Three days later, the CEO announced that J.P. Morgan was going to be taken over by Chase.

Should you speculate that a company is being taken over every time a CEO cancels an appearance? Of course not. But when you're looking at a particular investment, you need to be aware of all of the pieces of the puzzle. If this were the only piece of information that I had, I would not trade J.P. Morgan stock. It's obviously not enough. But it could have been a crucial piece that filled in the picture I had been building, and I wouldn't have known about it if my investment calendar hadn't alerted me to pay attention to the Merrill Lynch conference.

How do you know when analyst meetings and industry conferences are going to occur? Check out www.bestcalls.com and www.smartmoney.com, which also does its own look-ahead. CNBC.com also posts a list of upcoming conference calls. Or you can watch the business news and make notes (yup, that includes *Market Week;* I always mention important meetings and conferences for the coming week).

Trade Shows

Industry trade shows are great generators of news, since that's where companies routinely introduce their latest, whizziest products. These shows typically do not move stocks. There's more of a focus on products and less of a focus on the impact that those products will have on earnings. However, the trade shows offer a great opportunity to compare different products, get a sense of a company's strategic direction, and learn about industry trends.

PC and electronics companies strut their stuff at Comdex in November and the Consumer Electronics Show in January. You don't have to attend in person, but you should definitely keep up with them to find out the latest developments and innovations. While the geekfests always garner a lot of print, every sector has its own series of shows that are worth following.

Go to the auto shows to get a gut feel of the success of the new models, urges Lehman Brothers' senior analyst Nick Lobaccaro. **" It's an opportunity to beat the institutional investors, who tend to wait until after the earnings are being generated. People who study the auto industry for a job get desensitized to new vehicles, so putting on a consumer hat instead of an analyst hat gives you a better perspective. "**

Not only will you get a sense of which companies are doing something exciting, but you'll also learn which companies are falling behind. If a company that is historically known for being right on top of the wave shows up with what's only a tweaked version of the same-old same-old, then you should raise a red flag. Has it cut its R&D budget? Has it lost crucial customers? What's going on?

At the 2001 auto show, many people talked about some impressive new trucks coming from Toyota and BMW. For a long time the U.S. automakers relied on their light trucks for their bread and butter because those were higher-margin products. But the other automakers have since figured it out, and now BMW, Toyota, and others all manufacture light trucks. After going to the auto show, I decided to do a little research on auto stocks. After seeing the new products, I wasn't surprised to learn that U.S. automakers, which commanded 75 percent of the global market in 1999, had dropped down to 68 percent global market share in 2000.

The New Issue Calendar: Initial Public Offerings and Secondaries

The market for IPOs is a good indicator of market sentiment. If the environment is favorable for more companies to go public, (i.e., if companies feel they can get a good response from investment community if they go public), there will be a lot of big deals and quality deals. Quality deals share two elements: a big-name underwriter, like Goldman Sachs, Merrill

Lynch, Morgan Stanley, or one of the other major investment firms, and an offering of a large amount of stock, such as AT&T Wireless's 360-million-share deal.

Even quality deals need a willing market in order to succeed. When you see an IPO announcement of a lot of stock coming into the market, you'll want to know whether the market has enough money to absorb it. So, your first questions should be: How is the IPO market looking? Are you seeing a lot of deals? Are they underwritten by big-name investment firms? You can find this information in the *Wall Street Journal,* which lists the upcoming week's IPOs every Monday; www.ipopros.com; and www. IPOFinancial.com.

Then inquire about market liquidity, which is simply a matter of looking up the weekly money flows. After all, if a new bunch of stock is coming out but we've been seeing money leaving the market and going into cash or bond funds, then it's likely that the IPO—and the market—will go down in that environment. It's simple supply and demand.

Secondaries tell you something else. A secondary offering refers to the public sale of previously owned securities held by large investors, usually corporations, institutions or other affiliated persons. (One difference between a secondary offering and an IPO, or new issue, is that in an IPO, the seller is the issuing corporation, and the money goes back to the company. In a secondary offering, the money goes back to the individuals who are selling their stock.)

When a company first goes public, much of its offering is owned by insiders and large investors. A secondary offering is an opportunity for some of those investors to sell some shares and cash in.

Krispy Kreme Doughnuts stock more than tripled in the year since it went public in April 2000. In January it filed a planned stock offering to sell two million shares, including 1.85 million owned by existing shareholders and only 150,000 shares to be issued and sold by the corporation. Similarly, Human Genome Sciences recently did a secondary offering of eight million shares, giving insiders a chance to cash in, at least partially.

Both companies hire an investment bank to handle the secondary offering. What that means is that the insiders—the large investors who own at least 10 percent of the stock and the company's management—sell their stock to the investment bank. What will the investment bank do with it?

They'll turn around and sell it to their clients and on the open market. The people who get the cream of the proceeds are the insiders.

All of that is par for the course. But something interesting happened with Human Genome Sciences—and what happened is why secondary offerings are significant and should be noted on your investment calendar.

Human Genome stock was selling at $81, but rather than sell 8 million shares at $81, the company announced that it would sell shares at $75. Now, say that you see that Human Genome Sciences just announced that it's going to sell eight million shares at $6 below the current trading price. Obviously, you'd want to know why the company is valuing itself at a discount to the market price. Here's what happened: Human Genome Sciences had so much demand for the stock that the bankers decided to raise the offering. They sold twelve million shares at $75; the stock went up to $88 and continued to go up. That was a reflection that good things were going on at Human Genome and a very good signal for the near term. The fact that twelve million additional shares were received so well was a big positive.

When you see an announcement of a secondary offering, ask these questions: Is there a lot of new supply coming to the market and is there money to absorb it? Why is this company raising money and why now? Does it seem likely that the stock will continue to go up if they have a secondary offering? For bond offerings, it is important to know how much interest the company will have to pay once the offering is done. Are they borrowing just to pay back interest payments from the last round of offerings? For example, at a certain point, Amazon could no longer raise money in the public markets because investors refused to bite. Finally, and most important, ask what the company is doing with the money it's raising. Will it go to the company or will it reward insider investors?

Like IPOs, secondary offerings will give you a feel for the supply and demand of the current market. The sources of information are the same: the *Wall Street Journal,* IPOFinancial.com, and the general financial press. I also mention significant secondary offerings on *Market Week.*

A corollary to secondary offerings are unlocks. Insiders who bought shares in a company prior to its public offering must hold on to their shares for ninety days after the IPO. After that initial lock-up period, their shares "unlock."

Unlocks are material to the stock that you own. Often when a lot of inside stock comes onto market, it will pressure the stock. The fact that the secondary offering did not pressure Human Genome Sciences was a reflection of that company's strength. But many high-flying stocks have been known to sag significantly immediately after the stock unlocks.

Whenever you buy stock in a company that recently went public, you should know when a large holder of the stock has an opportunity to sell it and note the unlock date in the calendar. You can find lists of unlock dates at www.unlockdates.com and www.IPOlockup.com. You can also see which insiders have filed to sell large blocks of stock in the financial press; the *Wall Street Journal,* for example, notes this in a box titled "Insider Holdings" in its C section. You will also want to make a judgment call to see if the insider will, in fact, use that window to sell. If she bought the stock at $10 a share, for example, and now it is trading at, say 75 cents, maybe she will not sell at all. If however, it cost her $10 and is now trading at $200, there is a likely shot she'll want to cash in some chips.

General Market Trends

No industrial sector exists in a vacuum. After examining the specifics of a company and its competitors within its sector, you have to put that picture within the context of larger trends that move the market: both the domestic economy and the global economy, interest-rate changes, and other macro issues.

For example, back in 1999, Jerome Heppelmann, portfolio manager of three PBHG value funds, made a note to evaluate energy companies. "There was great long-term growth because of the electricity demands of the U.S. market. The near-term dynamic I thought was compelling was that the U.S. as a whole had 20 percent less natural gas in storage than it had the year before and over a five-year average. That was compelling, rather than just interesting, data because three out of the past four winters had been some of the warmest winters on record. So we were coming off an unusually warm spell while at the same time demand was going up and storage levels were hitting new lows." Heppelmann significantly overweighted his portfolio with natural gas companies, and his bet paid off. All three of his funds notched more than 20 percent returns in 2000, despite the overall down market.

This information is not difficult to come by. Every Tuesday, the American Petroleum Institute issues statistics about the U.S. oil inventory, which I typically report on *Market Wrap,* on CNBC at 5:00 (if you miss it, it's reported in Wednesday's *Wall Street Journal*). The statistics detail oil stocks in everything from motor gasoline to fuel oil to the daily domestic output and the daily import of crude oil for the previous week, with comparisons to the week before and the same week a year ago. When there's plenty of inventory, prices go down. Conversely, when the inventory goes down, prices goes up.

What are some of the broad economic pacesetters that you should mark on your calendar?

Meetings of the Federal Reserve Board of Governors

We've already discussed the immediate impact that the Fed effect has on the market in the weeks just prior to the regular meetings of the Fed. But you also want to note the dates of the eight regularly scheduled meetings as a way to remind yourself to periodically assess the state of the economy. Ask yourself whether there have been any significant changes in the broader economic landscape and how those changes might affect your portfolio. Use this opportunity to look over the broader trend of the market since the last meeting of the Federal Open Market Committee and try to extrapolate which sectors stand out and why.

Of course, you can't predict when Alan Greenspan might utter one of his market-moving pronouncements. On any given day Greenspan speaks at any number of conferences and dictates that day's market activity. Certainly, that's what happened on January 3, 2001, when the Federal Reserve called an irregular meeting and cut interest rates by a half point, goosing the Dow more than 400 points and pushing the Nasdaq to its biggest one-day gain. But if you'd been following the general economic trends, you would have been expecting a rate cut at some point soon.

Economic News

Every month, like clockwork, the government releases a barrage of economic data. Should you trade on every PPI or CPI report that comes out? Of course not. Should you be aware of the changing inflationary landscape? Absolutely. You need to be aware of big-picture trends, and the government's data provide an electrocardiogram of the health of the economy.

Ask yourself these questions: Has inflation become a problem? Did we see prices go higher for three months in a row? Is unemployment steady, rising or falling? Is the cost of raw materials rising? In short, is the economic landscape changing? You can get this information only by tracking several months' worth of data.

Seasonal Market Movers

Analysts have noted seasonal effects that move the markets. Some are news, some are noise, but all are worth noting on your investment calendar.

- The January effect. "December and January are two of the biggest months for income tax collections (as reported on company wage statements, which means that income is up), so mutual fund inflows are big in those months as well," says Charles Biderman of TrimTabs.com.
- Paying the IRS. Investors who did especially well in the prior year sometimes need to sell stocks to pay the taxes on their capital gains. That was one of the factors in the April 2000 sell-off of technology shares.
- Summer tech doldrums. Often big corporations take a summer break from their usual pace. In other words, people are on vacation, so you don't see a lot of big ordering going on for information technology. As a result, tech stocks have typically traded down in the summer. The past few years' heightened activity were exceptions that prove the rule. First we had the Y2K scare, which impelled many information technology managers to upgrade their systems to head off any millenium bugs; then in the summer of 2000, we had monster merger announcements like Deutsche Telekom's $55 billion acquisition of VoiceStream Wireless and JDS Uniphase's $40 billion acquisition of SDL Inc. going on. So the last couple of summers were atypical, but for the most part the summer brings about a slowdown.
- Earnings season. Earning season happens four times a year, at the end of every quarter. As soon as the quarter ends, companies have ninety days to report their earnings. Usually the first month after the end of the quarter is jam-packed with earnings announcements, so expect some movement in the market.

- Conference season. Every quarter, after the peak three weeks when most companies report their earnings, earnings announcements slow down, and conferences pick up. The reason is that big brokerages do not want to have conferences before companies announce earnings, because the companies are in their quiet period and can't say anything at their conferences. They don't want to have conferences during earnings season, because there's just too much else going on. That leaves the month in the middle of the quarter. Be aware of what conferences are going on and which companies are making presentations at those conferences; you can pick up the agendas on the firms' websites.

  Today, companies often report bad news, such as a preannouncement of disappointing earnings, a few days before they are scheduled to speak at conference in order to comply with Regulation FD. In a groundbreaking move in late February 2001, Applied Micro Circuits used CNBC as a forum to drop bad news. CEO David Rickey deliberately announced during a *Market Week* interview that he was lowering revenue guidance for the next quarter. Even though the show wasn't scheduled to air for a couple of days, he expected us to broadcast the news that day—which we did. It was the first time a company had used CNBC as an open forum to comply with Regulation FD; I'm sure it won't be the last.

- Autumn slump. "There are periods of the year when the IPO calendar is hot, which can foster selling stocks to raise cash to buy these IPOs," says Tom Galvin of CSFB. "Typically, mid-September to mid-November is very heavy, then the end of January to the end of May. Things cool off in the other periods because of vacations and because you can fit a road show around the Christmas/New Year's holiday."

- October hex. "Before the market was heavily invested in mutual funds, stocks that had been down for the year got weaker in December as investors sold their losers so they could have a tax deduction against their winners," Charles Biderman explains. "That doesn't work so much anymore because the fiscal year for mutual funds, which are now a bigger factor in the market, ends in October and November. So shares that have been going down going into October go lower." Certainly, mutual fund tax selling was one of the factors in the sharp slump the market took in October 2000. We saw a lot of activity in the losers, such as Internet and telecom stocks, which further exacerbated the ongoing sell-off. We know this happens every October, so it's a good idea to assess your mutual fund portfolio every September, so you know what your mutual fund was holding at the end of the quarter and can have some idea of what the portfolio manager might do come October 31.

- Winter tech rally. The opposite of the summer tech doldrums happens in the period from mid-October through mid-March. That is the period when corporate buyers do most of their information technology purchasing. They either have to use up money left in the previous year's budget, or they get their budgets for the new year and promptly do most of their ordering. Research has shown that nearly 100 percent of the gains for the year in technology happen during those five months. Certainly expect to see the tech sector move.
- Back-ended quarters. Many companies derive much of their business in the third month, or the back end, of the quarter. Software companies in particular derive 50 to 80 percent of their revenue in the back end and have scant visibility about their earnings expectations until that final month. For example, in the first quarter of 2001, while much of the technology sector had already preannounced weak conditions, Microsoft, PeopleSoft, Manugistics, and Oracle did not preannounce, because they would not know whether business had slowed until March.

In the Margins

In addition to the events and broad market trends, one of the most important elements of your investment calendar are your notes in the margin. These are the personalized memoranda that provide insight into your portfolio. Every investor has his or her own set of margin notes—maybe it's a scribbled comment from a favorite analyst, maybe a reminder of a new product introduction, maybe a list of the top five websites to check regularly.

Here's a good example of what would go in the margins: After I went to the 2001 auto show that I described earlier, I then did a little more research on auto stocks. Wendy Beale Needham, the auto analyst at CSFB, upgraded Ford Motor and all the auto supplier stocks in the beginning of January 2001. She told me that because these stocks were early cycle stocks; they were going to move as interest rates came down. No one else on Wall Street agreed with her; in fact, many of her counterparts at other firms pointed to the fact that U.S. automakers had been losing market share steadily, had been manufacturing stale products, and would probably see more of a negative impact from the weakening economy than a positive impact from lower interest rates.

These stocks typically trade at a discount to the market, something that infuriates auto executives. Ford and GM, in particular, trade at between eight and ten times next year's earnings estimates. One would think of that as a value opportunity, given the fact that the S&P's multiple exceeds twenty-five times next year's earnings. Ford is sitting on more than $19 billion of cash, it pays a high dividend, and it's in the middle of a $5 billion stock buyback plan. In addition, the company has been ramping up its high-margin products, with brands such as Volvo, Land Rover, and Jaguar. So why is the stock so cheap? Do these stocks trade at such low multiples for a good reason?

Yes, I want all the catalysts that might move a stock on my calendar. But I also want to know the background to the entire investment story. That sort of information goes on the margins.

No matter whether you want to scribble down background notes, everyone should have a set of margin notes of the red flags that signal potential problems with the stock or the sector. A red flag isn't necessarily a signal to sell, but it should cause you to start delving a little deeper.

Micro Red Flags

When I talk to analysts, I always ask these two questions: What are the main issues we should look at for a possible turn in the business? What would change your bullish perception of this stock?

It might be deterioration in the operating margins, a sudden deceleration in top-line growth, a downward earnings estimate revision by analysts, short interest going way up on the stock, or even the company becoming very quiet when typically it has been out there pounding its corporate chest and giving lots of guidance to the investment community. It might be a change in the management team, such as the departure of the head of an important division of the company. It might be when the company starts talking about how the business environment is becoming more difficult than it was, say, six months ago, or if a competitor has difficulty with a similar product. If the industry is not buying that product right now from the competition, you have to think about what your own company is doing.

Ravi Suria, who worked for Lehman Brothers before leaving to manage money at a hedge fund, says his red flags are often bond offerings, because of the interest payments associated with them. But there's another red flag associated with bonds, says PBHG portfolio manager Jerome Heppelmann. Sometimes in higher-leveraged stocks, the company's bonds may turn into high-yield bonds. Say the bonds the company issued originally had a 6 percent yield on them. If the bond investors start believing that the odds of the company going bankrupt are increasing, they will sell the bonds, which pushes the price down and the yield up. As the yield rises, to 8 percent or 10 percent or even higher, that's a red flag that there's more of a risk premium that needs to be priced in. "Whether the bond gets marked down to junk status by one of the rating agencies is almost superfluous information," says Heppelmann. "Bond watchers will have already spotted the red flag before the rating changed. The bond investors are often the first to dig into the financials and realize that there's a financial problem with meeting payments."

A corollary to bond prices as an indication of financial imbalance: "If the company switches auditors, that's a huge red flag," says Heppelmann.

Insider selling may or may not be a red flag, as we already discussed in Chapter 8. Some people say it's necessary because stock options are a portion of an executive's compensation package, and it's only prudent to reallocate one's assets. "I typically have better luck when buying with the company rather than buying against the company's stock," says Heppelmann. When he saw that Halliburton announced plans to buy back 5 percent of the company's stock at the end of 2000, he jumped in. That way, he pointed out, "When other people try to buy, there won't be a lot of excess stock out there."

Sometimes, the red flag is embedded in a company announcement of disappointing news. In the first quarter of 2001, Gateway preannounced that earnings would fall below estimates, as had happened at many other PC companies. Now in the fall of 2000, the CEO of Gateway came on *Market Week* and told me that things were going extremely well and that his company was not feeling the slowdown as so many of his competitors were. I specifically asked him, "How can you continue to excel when so many companies in your space—Apple, Dell, Hewlett-Packard, and Compaq, just to name four—said that the slowdown would hurt their business?"

Why didn't the CEO know such important news earlier? My news nugget was that maybe there was a bigger issue going on within the company, something bigger than a quarter's miss. In fact, soon after, Gateway announced that CEO Jeff Whiteson was being replaced by Gateway founder Ted Waitt.

Red flags may not necessarily appear to be negative at first. For Robert Loest, senior portfolio manager at IPS Funds, what alerts his antenna are anomalies in the very factors that once made the stock fit his investment framework of companies that create value. "When Yahoo first came along, it was clearly creating a huge amount of value, whether it made money or not, because it made it so much easier for people to get information from the web," he recalls. "It expanded rapidly to all Internet users at a time when the Internet sector itself was expanding rapidly. It was a no-brainer. But once Yahoo reached the limits of all the people who were using the Internet, that component of its growth fell off a cliff. At the same time, the rate of growth of the Internet user base began to slow too, so that component of value dropped also."

Loest's red flag? Yahoo started adding incremental services, such as paying bills online and checking one's stock portfolio, as a way to try to create more value. "The simple fact is, their days of raging value creation were a function of their place within the sector and that sector itself."

When a company starts expanding outside of its core area of expertise, that can be an indicator that its growth rate is slowing. It means it may have expanded as far as it was likely to in terms of market share within its space, so its management is looking for new markets. It may introduce a lot of new products, like Amazon offering everything from Palm Pilots to flowers or Starbucks trying to sell home furnishings. Management may attempt big mergers to try to wring more growth from a sector that's already mature, as was the underlying reason behind AOL's marriage with Time Warner. Dell and Gateway have moved into peripherals, because everyone who can afford to buy a PC already owns one, so these companies can make more money selling CD-ROM burners and the like. Cisco has switched to optical networks. Intel is trying to get into communications chips.

Actions like these make Loest take a closer look at the company. They signal that the company has taken advantage of all the easy growth creation within its sector. Succeeding in a different sector isn't impossible but, says Loest, "it's going to be a lot harder. They will no longer be the eight-hundred-pound gorilla. They may be a big company but now they're the new kid on the block."

Every industry sector also has a red flag that alerts you to an especially market-sensitive issue. For the pharmaceutical industry, it's FDA regulations; for media companies, it's the advertising environment. We discussed these sector red flags in Chapter 4. Once you identify the red flags, put them on your investment calendar and make sure to check them regularly.

Macro Red Flags

There can also be red flags on the macro level. "I think we can get good signals from the markets themselves," says Edward Yardeni, chief investment strategist for Deutsche Bank Alex. Brown. "If we're talking about the stock market, it's important to keep your eye on the bond market. These markets do not operate independently of one another. The trend of bond yields and changes in those trends are critically important for understanding market sentiment. It's an important variable that influences P/E ratios and the value of earnings, as well as giving you insight into inflationary sentiment and whether the economy is too strong or maybe weakening."

When bond yields go up, that's usually not a good environment for stocks, Yardeni points out. "It's conceivable that bond yields would go up and stocks would go up, but the leaders in that situation would likely be inflation-hedged stocks like oil companies. But at a minimum, rising bonds should raise a flag about rotating away from consumer staples and interest-rate-sensitive stocks towards energy and basic materials."

Falling interest rates should usually be positive for the stock market. However, as many economists fretted in the wake of the surprise rate cut in January 2001, falling interest rates can imply a weakening economy, which is bad for earnings. In that case, Yardeni says, buying interest-rate-sensitive stocks, such as banks, brokerages, and insurance companies, would make sense.

Yardeni's advice is only one data point. When the Fed cut rates in 2001, one would have expected a rally for brokerage stocks. Instead, the group traded down for much of the first half, as industry fundamentals dominated the environment. Trading volume had slowed because of tough market conditions, and the IPO market—a brokerage firm's bread and butter—had all but dried up. So this time around, falling interest rates could not save the day for brokerages.

What Would an Investment Calendar Look Like? Two Samples

Let's say you're interested in investing in the retail sector. You want to clear the paths in your head of all the other noise and other information that is immaterial to the one investment you're thinking about. You want to look only at the events or possible catalysts that affect retail stocks.

We go back to the fundamentals: when the company reports earnings, when it reports comparable store sales, when its sector holds analyst meetings. Put in the red flags for the sector.

So what's important? If I'm looking to invest in retail, the holiday selling season represents in many cases 70 percent to 80 percent of sales. The fundamentals of the retail sector are centered around the holiday season, so I'd want to get a sense of what the season might be like: How is the economy doing? How is the consumer spending her money? Is the holiday selling season expected to be strong? What type of sales figures are we expecting from this company? Are people looking for high-margin products or low-margin products to be the hot sellers? Valuation is the other major component to look at in any group. You want to make a note to do a valuation check: What is the fifty-two-week range on the stock? What does the overall chart look like? Is it being pummeled unfairly or should it be down? People often say, "This stock is so attractive; it's down 50 percent from its high." But, you know, sometimes stocks are down for good reason. Sometimes the message of the market is that this stock *should* be down. As Jerome Heppelmann says, **"Just because a company has a low P/E does not mean it has a good value; it just means it's cheap."**

When you're breaking down the valuations, don't be taken in by the fact that the stock is down. Otherwise you may get sucked into the value trap, which occurs when a company that looks cheap goes down, you buy it, it goes down more, it looks cheaper, and you buy more. That's called catching a falling knife. Look for good values, not cheap stocks.

It happens that the valuations of the retail companies right now are low. In 2000, retail stocks got crushed and are now selling at a discount to the S&P 500. Whether that is a buy signal is arguable. Yes, the stocks are selling cheaply, but are they selling cheaply for a good reason? That's what you need to decide.

Auto stocks also fall into this category. Auto stocks have always traded at a discount to the market, possibly because they are directly linked to the economy. Along with the slowdown in the economy, we have seen negative sentiment regarding the autos. Yet as I mentioned earlier, Ford has more than $19 billion in cash on hand, is buying back stock, pays a dividend, and trades at eight times next year's earnings. Why is the stock so cheap?

I've heard both sides of the story. Some analysts and portfolio managers like the retail and auto groups; others believe it's too early to buy because the economy will continue to weaken. This is the sort of comment that goes on the margins of your investment calendar—not any specific date, just a memo to stay aware of the valuation issues.

Once you have your main themes—holiday sales and valuations—you can break down those themes further. Breaking down the fundamentals includes looking at the sales and earnings growth leading up to the holidays as well as during the rest of the year. I'd want to find out when the companies within the sector report same-store sales, because this is one of the ways that the retail group gauges itself.

You also want to narrowly focus in on the company you're looking at. Do your basic homework. Start by breaking down the numbers: What is the record of annual and holiday revenue growth? How has the company performed during past holiday seasons? What's the projected earnings growth for the quarter? For the year? What is the projected five-year growth rate? Break down the management: How long has the CEO been in charge? How has the stock done under his or her leadership? How have the business prospects changed? Are there rumors of an impending change in management? How much debt does the company have?

You also want to note broader economic trends that could affect the sector. For example, people say that it typically takes one year for the economy to be affected by a move in interest rates. In the last interest-rate-rising cycle, the most recent rate hike came in June 2000, suggesting we may not feel the impact until the following June. Already we've seen a slowdown in the economy based on the hikes that were set a year previously. We haven't seen the full impact yet, and that impact will definitely affect the retail and auto sectors, despite the fact that we are now in an interest-rate-falling environment.

If you were looking to invest in the formerly hot area of electronics manufacturing services, or EMS, there would be a completely different set of issues. Just as Intel made the chips that helped drive the PC revolution, these companies—Solectron, Flextronics, Jabil Circuits—make the components that drive the Internet. Although their end-use customers are ultimately consumers, their immediate customers are companies like Sun Microsystems and IBM, as well as the telecom equipment companies like Cisco and Nortel. The fortunes of the EMS sector are intimately tied to the fortunes of their customers, so the market events that affect Cisco and Sun, such a slowdown in info-tech spending, must be factored into the other fundamental elements on an EMS investment calendar.

Because the stocks in this sector have been on a roll, the fundamentals are going to look different from retail or other value stocks. When you look at the fifty-two-week charts, which stock within the group has not kept on the path?

There has been a lot of momentum in this group. Is there anything on the horizon that could break this momentum? A technical analyst might predict future indications for the stock. Analysts who follow the company or the sector might point out potential problems that could trip up the stock.

Definitely note stock buybacks and stock splits. You want to note the last time that company split its stock and at what price so that you can keep abreast of where the stock is trading and whether it is nearing a point when it might split. Similarly, look up the company's history of buying back stock. How likely is the management to announce a buyback? How many buybacks has the company had? How did they affect the company's performance?

The answers to all these questions that I put out to you are readily available to individual investors. You must be aware of these issues, even if your money is being handled by a mutual fund manager. Granted, finding out the answers to all these questions for every one of your stocks might be too much for one person, but if you're heavily invested in a couple of stocks, you need to know their history.

For example, the one stock I'm heavily invested in is GE, because it's my parent company. I have options in GE, I have GE in my 401(k), and GE owns CNBC, so I'm always watching the stock and gauging the health of the company's business. That's a stock that I know well, and I want to know it well. It's information I have a stake in.

The news you glean can help reinforce your sentiments about the stock or can change your mind. You need to constantly look for support for your investment story. If you can't find support, that's a red flag too.

CSFB's chief strategist, Tom Galvin, likes to say that when you are on a driving trip, you gauge your distance by looking at the mile markers. Similarly, when you put your money in the market, you need to set up certain benchmarks to gauge whether the companies whose stock you own are meeting your expectations, whether the reasons that you bought that stock still hold true, and whether there are alternatives or additional opportunities.

The point of an investment calendar is that it helps you familiarize yourself with the stocks you own to the point at which you can set reasonable benchmarks, make realistic expectations, and recognize certain patterns. That way, you'll be able to distinguish between news and noise. You'll understand when you're tempted to make knee-jerk reactions—and you'll be able to avoid them.

Use the News

You should now have a good sense of how Wall Street works. You know the main forces that move the markets. You know how to get a handle on a particular company or industry sector by "interviewing" the sources. You know what bias each source is likely to take and how to compensate for it. You know which news to ignore as noise and which noise might contain some nuggets of useful news. And you know how to extract those nuggets.

All that you need to know now is how to use the news: how to put the fruits of your research—and the actual task of gathering it—in context.

With more and more information available, the most valuable commodity today is not the data per se but how you interpret them. Robert Hormats, vice chairman of Goldman Sachs, likes to say that all the facts and figures spewed out every day by the government and Wall Street firms should come with an Investor General's warning, "judgment not included."

"A culture of gamesmanship has developed in the markets, so that individuals are obliged to make decisions and judgments not just in terms of separating good information from bad but of gauging objectivity from bias," says former SEC chairman Arthur Levitt. "This makes it difficult to tell the difference between salesmanship and advice."

Good judgment enables you to decide how to customize the news-gathering process so that it works for your schedule and your interests—in other words, how to put it within the context of the rest of your life. Once you've done the research, good judgment helps you distinguish between news and noise. It allows you to match what you've found to your personal investment style, so you know what to use and what to ignore. Last but not least, good judgment will leach some of the emotion out of market volatility, so you'll avoid knee-jerk reactions.

How Much Is Enough?

There used to be a bar in New York City whose motto was "Too much ain't never enough." If I were putting together an individual investment calendar for myself, that would probably be my motto too. Given my druthers and the kind of thirst for information that I have, I would probably keep researching items until I ran out of sources.

Realistically, though, it would be difficult to indulge my investigative itch to the fullest because I have a job that takes up a lot of my time. Even though my job involves a lot of research, I can't possibly screen everything that's out there. That's why each show at CNBC has its own team that researches upcoming guests and subjects. On *Market Week,* we scan the web looking for important events that might affect the market and read all the major brokerage firms' analysis reports for important catalysts.

Now I know that you are one person, not an entire research team. Furthermore, you've probably got a regular day job, just as I do, which doesn't leave you time to scan a lot of websites. Looking over wads of information *is* the *Market Week* team's day job; asking you to do something similar would be absurd—and you might not even have the inclination, let alone the time, to do that anyway.

When you are setting up your investment calendar, you have to ask yourself at what point the research process becomes too overwhelming. How much research *is* enough? At what point do the means detract from the end? How do you drink from the fire hose and satisfy your thirst for information without getting flattened in the process?

"There really is no substitute for experience," says Wit Soundview Capital managing director Jonathan Cohen. **"It would be almost impossible for someone who hasn't looked at stocks before to be confronted with the enormity and complexity of the public equity markets, and come up with a cogent investment rationale.**

But it's not impossible for someone to devote time to gaining a knowledge of the ways the market works and the ways stocks trade and the types of information that do and don't affect the value of publicly traded equities. You only get more expert over time. "

That said, there's no need to jump in the deep end right at the start. It's perfectly acceptable to get your feet wet by focusing on only one or two sectors at first; you can gradually ease into more depth as you feel more comfortable.

Even if you can't get all the details into your investment calendar, a little is better than nothing. It may not fill in all the pieces in the jigsaw puzzle, but it will at least give you the overall picture. That way, you'll know whether you're dealing with a square jigsaw puzzle or a circular one and whether the picture is of the Grand Canyon or a Jackson Pollock painting.

Now I know what your next question is going to be. How much is "a little"? (If you've read this far, you already know how much is "a lot.") What is the bare minimum amount of work you need to do in order to stay on top of things? How do you recognize the fundamental catalysts for your portfolio? What will enable you to tailor your news gathering to your investment style? How do you hone your antenna to separate news from noise?

Start by reviewing and reiterating your investment philosophy. Why do you want to own certain stocks? Will buying a certain security or a specific sector keep you awake at night, worrying that you're going to lose your money? How old are you and when will you need the money that you're trying to make?

Think like a portfolio manager first, an analyst second, and a reporter third. Set up the framework of your investment philosophy; then—*and only then*—start screening for specific stocks in sectors that fit your philosophy. "I have investors who ask me stupefyingly detailed questions about the company," says Robert Loest, who, granted, *is* a portfolio manager. "I tell them, 'That's the analyst's job.' There's too much information out there to do a dissertation on every single stock. That's why you have thousands of analysts, because it takes that kind of horsepower. All I care about is what the company does and whether it fits my model in terms of my criteria. "

Remind yourself of the key drivers that make up your screening mechanism. Maybe they're similar to the factors Loest considers when he decides which sectors and which stocks within those sectors are right for his IPS Funds (which we discussed in Chapter 2): Will this sector expand rapidly and create a huge amount of value? Which stock within that sector stands the greatest chance of grabbing the biggest hunk of market share and creating the largest amount of value? Often it's the industry leader, but sometimes it's the smallest player that happens to own the right to a hot product.

Maybe your investment philosophy is similar to Jerome Heppelmann's at PBHG's Small-Cap, Mid-Cap, and Focused Value Funds. Value investing means buying companies that have good fundamentals and are growing earnings but are selling cheaply relative to the rest of the market. When you look for a value story, you're looking for low P/E ratios and Cinderella companies that possibly have been unfairly punished or simply haven't yet been discovered by the rest of the market.

Traditional value investors tended to set certain parameters to define a "value" stock, the most important being a P/E ratio below 26, the average P/E of the S&P 500. Investing in those stocks made sense during the high-interest-rate, slow-growth environment of the 1970s and 1980s. In the bull market of the 1990s, value stocks were trounced by "growth" stocks, or those with the fastest sales growth, and technology proved to be the fastest-growing area of the economy. That's why Cisco was considered an attractive growth stock even when it was trading at 126 times earnings and investors were snapping up Yahoo at a 600 P/E ratio. Today after over a year of heavy selling, many longtime "growth" stocks are considered "value" because they fell to low valuations.

Heppelmann's definition of value doesn't use the S&P P/E ratio parameter for traditional valuation metrics. He measures what the company is worth based on long-term growth characteristics, its position in its industry, the competitiveness of its products, and how well those products are protected by barriers to entry by other competitors. "I look at the same things that growth people do, but I pay a valuation that I think is less than the company deserves," he explains. "It's not traditional value. It's more commonsense value. If a company is worth twenty-five times earnings and is only trading at eighteen, then I want to buy it." In other words, defining your investment philosophy by traditional labels may help you focus but, like putting blinders on a horse, it definitely limits your overall perspective.

Or maybe your investment philosophy is similar to Dennis McKechnie's at the PIMCO Innovation and Global Innovation Funds. McKechnie's Global Innovation Fund was the best-performing technology fund in 2000. In a year that saw the Nasdaq lose 40 percent, this fund gained 40 percent.

Here's how he did it: "We view our work as being 85 percent fundamental and 15 percent valuation. We try to determine the four or five drivers that really matter for a company's business. Many people focus only on the company itself and only on its product line or management. We think that only captures about 30 percent of what drives a company's success. We try to look at the other 70 percent as well: the competition, the customers, the state of the economy, the direction of the economy, interest rates, and other potential investments in the stock market. We often hear that a company's management is great or lousy; the reality is that management dictates only 30 percent of a company's fortune. It's much more important to see what environment they operate in.

"With every company that we analyze, we try to simplify what we're looking for and boil down every investment idea to the four or five things about a company's business that really matter. We're constantly getting anecdotes or press releases from companies and upgrades and downgrades from analysts. We try to drink from the fire hose as much as we can, but we pursue or dismiss information relative to the key drivers to the company's business."

Maybe your investment philosophy is grounded in fundamentals but you can't resist soaring market momentum. Momentum investing is based almost purely on sentiment; so-called momentum stocks soared based mainly on their popularity. Despite its repeated quarterly losses, Amazon.com, a quintessential momentum stock, rose more than 6,000 percent from the day it started trading, in 1997, through mid-December 1999. (After the stock market decline of 2000, investors reverted to fundamental analysis and began looking again at P/E ratios; as a result, Amazon came crashing down.)

Momentum investing is all about market timing, about catching the wave as other investors begin to pile in and getting out before the wave crashes. It can happen to any type of stock, from industry stalwarts to Internet start-ups.

In 2000, we saw the momentum shift from e-commerce to energy. For years, utilities were a dependable but ho-hum group of value stocks whose main attraction came from their regular dividends, themselves a kind of thank-you for paying your monthly bills. Then came the boom in the Internet and telecommunications services, which created a huge demand for electricity. The market sentiment shifted; investors' interest began to home in on stocks like Calpine, Duke Energy, and Enron; money began to pour into the sector consistently and considerably; and the wave began to build. The utility index in 2000 looked like the Internet index of a year ago and vice versa: while the Nasdaq was down 40 percent, the utility index was up 39 percent.

Is there a lesson here? Sure. You can't just come up with an investment philosophy and then stick your head under a rock. You have to follow the news so that regardless of whether you are a "value" or "growth" investor, you'll be able to take advantage of waves of market momentum that might have an impact on your investments.

There's another lesson that's equally important. I believe you need to look at the fundamentals of a company, regardless of what kind of investor you are. Ignore the fundamentals at your own risk. But when I talk about fundamentals, I don't mean focusing only on the P/E ratio. Although it's a crucial data point, it's just one data point. You need to look at many data points to get a sense of the entire investment picture.

You need a checklist of company fundamentals. Your personal style of investing dictates what you're interested in, such as underpriced value stocks versus potentially expensive high-flying growth stocks. Whether it's a growth or a value story, the fundamentals don't change. There are no excuses; you cannot invest in a company without doing the fundamental analysis on it. You must find out how the company makes its money; how its most important area of business is doing; what the predictions are for revenue and earnings growth, debt, and other expenses; how experienced the management team is; and what its potential is for future success.

You should look at the chart of the company you're interested in, as well as its main competitors, to see where the highs and lows are and gauge the momentum within the sector. You'll want to confirm your findings against the hard facts of money flows.

You need a checklist of industry sector fundamentals outlining what the market forces are affecting this sector, who the top players are, what their strengths and weaknesses are, what kind of growth the sector is experiencing, and what could happen to derail it or push it higher.

This analysis brings up a few questions, which you need to consider: Is this stock priced for perfection? Does it have wiggle room to live through slower growth, weather a weakening economy, and compensate for a slowdown in orders from customers or a buildup in inventory? How many customers does the company have, and does it rely too much on one or two companies to bring in orders? All these issues point to unforeseen events that could jeopardize that argument that this company is going to continue growing at such a level to support such its valuation.

"You can do comparison shopping for equities, just as you do comparison shopping for consumer products," says Jonathan Cohen, managing director at Wit Soundview Capital. "If one company trades at ten times next year's earnings and the other at twenty, but the 10X company has a stronger growth rate, better margins, a better balance sheet, a better management team, and a more compelling business model, then all things being equal, investors should buy the 10X multiple company, because it's a higher-quality product and it's half the price.

"That's a dramatic oversimplification," he concedes. "Things are rarely clear-cut. Equities are not commodities and you can't compare them the way you compare bananas or airline seats. Every company is the product of individual human endeavor. But financial results are statistical representations and they can be compared very directly. And the parameters for analysis are not sophisticated—they're profitability, revenues, growth rates, and the quality of the balance sheet, all of which reflects the quality of management."

Putting the News in Perspective

Wouldn't it be nice if investing decisions really were this unemotional? The fact is, Wall Street may be an efficient pricing mechanism in the long term, but in the short term, it's very inefficient. People oversell and overbuy, and it takes a long time to find the medium. The reason for this behavior is an emotional overreaction to market news. The market gets to an overpriced scenario and then bad news hits and the market is down 400 points by 11:00 a.m. It works its way out in the long term, but if you tuned in at any one point during that period, you would think the sky was falling.

That's why you need to put the news in perspective. "When the sky really *is* falling, it won't be a single event," says Arthur R. Hogan III, chief market analyst for Jefferies & Company. "Nobody is going to flip the apocalypse switch and say, 'Okay, it's over.' When the sky is really falling, it will be a chain of events—companies going out of business, companies filing for Chapter 11, companies not making payment on their debt in sectors of the economy that should be doing well."

Most companies never have a one-quarter problem. Typically, whatever problem they're experiencing—a slowdown in orders, inventory buildup, glitches in the product cycle, out-of-control accounts receivable—has been building up over a couple of quarters. Lehman Brothers's semiconductor analyst Dan Niles calls it "the cockroach theory." Anyone who has ever lived in New York City knows that there's no such thing as one cockroach; you may see only one at first, but there are always many more.

Even without the threat of the sky falling or cockroaches crawling out of the woodwork, it makes sense to evaluate stocks and sectors within the larger context of broader economic trends. That means keeping an eye on news that comes from the U.S. government, especially inflation rates and indications of consumer sentiment, because if people are feeling optimistic about the economy, they will buy more goods.

"I tell people to take the PIL: profits, inflation and liquidity," says Tom Galvin, Credit Suisse First Boston chief strategist. "On a company-by-company basis, profits have to do with fundamentals—market share, good management, keeping costs in check, expanding profit margins. In terms of inflation, you want to identify the structural forces in the economy, which promote low inflation, which is positive for return on equity capital. Lastly, you want to have a handle on the monetary supply, so you can see when the supply-demand conditions are affected by inflows into mutual funds or outflows to fund IPOs. If you're able to identify positive momentum in profits, if you can recognize the structural forces that keep inflation low, and you can watch the liquidity both for individual sectors and stocks as well as for the market in general, you'll upgrade the quality of noise and will feel much better about your investments."

If you think of the context within which you evaluate your investment portfolio as a series of concentric rings, then the outermost ring is being aware of what's happening in the world markets. Globalization means that the world markets are increasingly linked in ever more intricate ways. "A rule of thumb is that what happens to foreign economies could have some near-term significance to the U.S. stock market," says Lawrence Kudlow, chief economist for ING Barings. However, he points out, the U.S. economy has been such a powerful juggernaut that it tends to just plow through whatever waves foreign crises send our way. "Nine-and-a-half times out of ten, the U.S. stock market is governed by U.S. developments." The U.S. economy is valued at $10.3 trillion, versus $32 trillion for the global economy.

"During the 1997 Asian crisis, everyone panicked and the U.S. market fell sharply," Kudlow continues. "But it didn't cause a recession here. The U.S. economy was still growing at 4 percent. It was bad for Asia but it didn't hurt us. It was the same with Russia and the same with Mexico and Latin America. Some sectors of the American economy can be affected, but the entire American economy today is so large and so diverse that death blows cannot be inflicted on us by foreigners. ""

CSFB's Galvin agrees. ""It seems that about every nine or twelve months, we get a scare, like the Asian flu or local wars in Indonesia or something disquieting out of Europe. It's the U.S. economy, stupid, so to speak. You have to realize that the U.S. is a net-importing, not a net-exporting country. So when Asia is having problems, we can usually benefit because we import cheaper goods from those countries and the U.S. is the biggest buyer out there. It's not true for every company, and you have to be aware of those companies and sectors that are overexposed, but you can't get overwhelmed by it. ""

On the other hand, it doesn't mean you can ignore world events. What you need to do is put them in context. ""Is this a three-day event or a three-year event?"" Kudlow always asks. ""If it's a three-year event, then it's worth looking at. If it's a three-day event, then forget about it. ""

Loest goes a step further: ""If Russia devalues the ruble, how will that affect the ability of U.S. companies to drive down the cost of bandwidth? How will the presidential election affect the value of my investments? It may have some nebulous overall effect, but it's not something you can quantify in terms of investing intelligently. Focus your attention and ignore the other stuff. ""

Monitor Your Stock Regularly

Once you own a stock, the bare minimum means monitoring it: monitoring everything that led you to buy it. You constantly have to ask yourself, Has the story changed? Has revenue growth slowed down or earnings growth slumped? Has the management team changed? You need to highlight the red flags that could endanger your portfolio.

""The game can change on any given day,"" says PIMCO's McKechnie. ""New anecdotes can uncover a new business driver. We've owned Cisco for a long time. At one point, the accounting was an important driver; at another, acquisitions were important. One of the most important changes in business drivers was when Cisco started penetrating telecom service companies. For a long time, it made most of its money from Fortune 500 companies. Now, it does at least 35 percent of its business in the telecom market. That definitely changed our view. ""

In 2000, the game changed again as telecom spending all but dried up. One wonders whether McKechnie's view changed in time.

Monitoring the stock means doing a delicate dance between the macro economic and industrial picture and the micro company-specific picture. You can't shortchange either. Companies can hit all their milestones and develop their technology on time, only to see the world pass them by. Satellite phone companies, for example, have been trying to prove their technology for ten years. But now that they've proved that their technology works, cell phones are cheap and are ubiquitous. So focusing with precision on technology alone would be missing the point.

Similarly, when wireless data companies set out to deliver high-speed data, the pricing umbrella was about $1,000 a month. They proved that their technology works, but meanwhile cable modems and DSL have become ubiquitous and the price is about $100 a month. So even though the stocks of wireless data companies like Teligent and Winstar moved every time they won a contract with content providers, the overall growth picture for their sector has diminished dramatically.

The buy and hold theory does not mean "buy and hold and forget about it." Nor does it mean "buy and hold and just blindly trust your broker." Let's not forget that the majority of fund managers and brokers were down in 2000 and have been underperforming the S&P 500 for some time. Furthermore, many are employed by investment firms doing business with the companies they want you to invest in.

Back in Chapter 1, I used the analogy that when you buy a car, you check the tires. Well, just because you've bought that car doesn't mean you shouldn't periodically continue to check the tires.

At a minimum, you should check all your signs every quarter. You can't do much better with earnings and revenues, because they're reported on a quarterly basis. I remember Roger Ackerman, the CEO of Corning, telling me that Corning used to report orders on a monthly basis until the analysts complained that they were being deluged with information and they didn't need to get such frequent reports. If you're like me, you'd be tempted to monitor the business on a monthly basis. But it's up to you.

Your Ultimate Investing Tool

How will you know when you've got enough information? Every person has his or her own criteria but it comes down to this: You've got to feel that you've exhausted every aspect of your research. You have to feel that you know this story intimately so that you can explain it clearly and concisely.

When I'm on the air talking about stocks, I try to speak not only to the savvy investor but also to my mother. She's not a savvy stock picker. If I'm not explaining it well enough that my mom can understand it, then you can't understand it. And if you can't understand the company, why should you assume other people will do the research and buy after you at a higher price? That's the way you have to know your investments. Use your common sense; remember, it's not brain surgery.

I often interview analysts who are very much in their own world and talk in technical jargon. I'll say, "Stop, you lost me. Tell me this story as if I know nothing and explain why it's such a great investment idea. Talk to me as if I'm your grandmother."

Okay, maybe your grandmother is a wizard with investments. If so, then here's another approach: explain in three sentences what this company does and why it's worth your money. That's what TV journalists often do, and if you can't figure out their story in the first three sentences, then they didn't write the story well.

To be a responsible investor, you must be a reporter. No matter whether you are a "value," "growth," or "momentum" investor, or any combination of the three, there's one common trait you all should share: you're looking for any important news that changes the story, any red flags that signal a shift in fundamentals. Only rarely will these signals come to you loud and clear; most of the time what will come through is a combination of news and noise. The trick is to be selective and, like any reporter, extract the right information that will help your investment story.

And remember: it's all too easy to fall in love with a stock—and get blindsided. Be suspicious; always ask yourself what could go wrong.

The information explosion has made some individual investors feel that they are being used by the news. They feel overwhelmed by waves upon waves of data, factoids, analyst reports, and headlines. They feel as if they're drowning in noise.

Noise is a good thing as long as you know how to process it. But you can't interpret and respond to every bit of information that is dumped on you daily. You have to screen out the unimportant details. News is the result of information that goes through the screening process.

By the time that information has gone through your screening process, you'll understand the accuracy and limitations of the data. If it's part of a series of numbers that comes out regularly, you'll know its limits and what it can and cannot accurately forecast. You'll hone your focus to see the details beneath the surface numbers, whether those numbers are presented in an earnings report from a company or statistics from the government. As you amass those details, you will build a picture of the condition of the business.

But there's still one more step before the picture is fully finished. Turn off the news, turn off the noise, turn off everything, except maybe the overhead light. Tune out the shock waves of the information explosion, the hype that makes you want to reach for the red "buy" or "sell" button and make a rash decision that you'll later regret.

Step back and think.

I'm a firm believer that common sense goes a long way on Wall Street. You know my story. I do not have an advanced degree in economics, but I "get" it. Over the years I've increased my knowledge of the markets, and I continue to learn something useful not just every year but every month and every day.

I make judgment calls all the time. I and many of my colleagues have to decide which stocks to talk about, which CEOs to interview, which sectors to explore.

How do I judge that what I learn is useful? I screen it through my accumulated knowledge; I bounce it off my common sense.

In this book I've tried to help you build your own screen by giving you what I've learned over the years. But your ultimate investing tool is your own good judgment.

That is how you separate news from noise. And now that you know how to do it, you'll be able to use the news, avoid the noise, and invest with confidence.

Appendix: Maria's Recommended Websites

I'm frequently on the Internet, digging up information about companies and checking the activity of particular stocks and industry sectors. When I first started in this business, I had to get the information I needed by telephoning traders and analysts. Today it's just a couple of mouse clicks away—and most of it doesn't cost a cent.

All of the websites that I've listed here are free. In some cases you may have to register but you won't have to pay a penny—a true example of how the information explosion has leveled the playing field for individual investors.

That said, I want to mention one of my favorite sites that is, as yet, not free. Bridge Information Systems (www.bridge.com) gives me access to real-time exchange data, including equities and commodities; fundamental stock data, including tabular information and earnings estimates; technical charting for all stocks; and an incredible amount of news, ranging from daily market reviews for G7 countries to press releases for individual companies. You can, however, replicate many of their services for nothing at a combination of the sites below.

General Market News and Information Sites

ADR.com, Bankofny.com/adr If you own Nokia, Vodafone, Taiwan Semiconductor, the high-flying Irish pharmaceutical stock Elan Corporation, or any one of more than fifteen hundred foreign stocks from fifty different countries, you hold not the actual share but an American Depositary

Receipt, or ADR. These sites enable you to keep a pulse on your international portfolio with global headline news and world market commentary as well as tools that let you track foreign stocks by geographical region and industry sector. On the ADR.com site, which is sponsored by J.P. Morgan Chase, there's also a comprehensive calendar of U.S. government economic data releases for the previous week, with helpful explanations of their significance to investors.

Bloomberg.com   Bloomberg is a good all-around market news site. Because I'm in the news business, I don't need to get my news from Bloomberg, so I use the site to get the most actively traded issues (information you can get almost anywhere, by the way). If a new stock shows up among the usual suspects—Cisco, Intel, Microsoft—then seeing it among the volume leaders tells me something is going on. I can also check the percentage gainers and losers, although this may not be that important. Altrex Inc. may be up 354 percent, but its price is $2.50 and the volume is thirty-one hundred; I'm not interested in something that's not liquid enough.

I check on the world indexes as well. I can see what the main indexes did in Europe and Asia overnight, and what's going on in Latin America. Since Wall Street sometimes takes its cue from the international markets, the world indexes might give you a hint of what could happen in the U.S. market that day.

CBSMarketwatch.com   This site has market information that's similar to what's on Bloomberg. What I particularly like is that this site gives information about upcoming stock splits. The calendar of splits goes out four months in advance, so you can see what's happening a couple of months ahead. It lists foreign splits also. If you don't want to check in all the time, you can sign up for its stock split alert, a free service that tells you when particular companies have announced stock splits.

CBSMarketwatch has good IPO information. It lists the IPOs scheduled for the week, as well as the results after the stock goes public.

The site also notes stock buybacks. This is useful information because when a company starts buying back its stock, it's signaling that it feels its stock is undervalued. It also means that the company has extra cash on its balance sheet and is looking for ways to enhance shareholder value. The one drawback of this site's buyback coverage is that, unlike with splits, it only covers buybacks on a week-by-week basis.

CNBC.com   Okay, I'm biased. In my opinion, this is the best website for market analysis. I don't think anyone else has the access to CEOs, market strategists, and analysts that CNBC has. And if you miss the live interview on air, you can pick it up later on the web.

Another plus: CNBC.com's real-time ticker runs up-to-the-minute stock quotes, instead of the delayed ones you get on most financial websites. The "portfolio tracker" function allows you to personalize the ticker, so you can see every little glimmer of movement in your stocks.

IndividualInvestor.com   Another bias—my husband is the CEO, and I write a monthly column for the magazine. Still, one of the greatest values of II, I think, is its "screens." The site screens out various stocks based on a particular earnings growth, insider buying, low valuations, and similar guidelines. It is nice to have one complete list of the stocks that grow 100 percent over the year-ago quarter as a starting-off point.

Reuters.com   Reuters is another good source for international news and the world markets.

Yahoo.com   Yahoo's Finance site does almost everything except give me real-time quotes. Its two biggest strengths are the headlines about the stock and the company profiles. What I like about the profiles is that they not only tell you who the management team comprises, but they also mention how much stock they own, what their pay is, and how many stock options they've exercised. You get a good sense of the vested interest the executives have in the company.

On the financial side the profiles give a daily range of the stock price, the overall market capitalization of the company, and the history of when the stock split. That's particularly useful because if there's a trend that the stock splits whenever it reaches $100, then investors can plan accordingly.

You can also get a sense of the short interest (i.e., the number of shares being shorted and how that compares to the number of outstanding shares). Short interest is significant because it's an indication of Street sentiment about the stock.

It's good to find out how Wall Street views the company and the site also gives a broad picture of the analyst community's sentiment about the stock. The research summary may say that four analysts have a strong buy recommendation, seven have a moderate and seven have a hold.

Finally, what I especially like about this site is that you can see how the company ranks within the context of its sector and the stock performs compared to its competitors.

Many financial magazines have informative websites. Some of the best are *Smart Money* (www.smartmoney.com), which is very good for news commentary, and TheStreet.com (www.thestreet.com), which offers a comprehensive listing of the latest stories from the wire services. I also like the website for my husband's magazine, *Individual Investor* (www.individualinvestor.com), especially the "Saturday Group" feature focusing in-depth on a specific stock each week. I also write for the magazine and can often do more in-depth articles than is possible in the CNBC format.

Here are some other websites with good coverage of the global markets, as well as regular interviews with CEOs and analysts: Quote.com (www.quote.com), StreetSide Investor (www.streetsideinvestor.com), and 123Jump.com (www.123jump.com), which specializes in the tech, biotech, and Internet sectors. Thomson Financial, the giant provider of global market news and analysis, sponsors two general-interest websites for individual investors: Market Eye (www.marketeye.com) and Thomson Financial Network (www.thomsonfn.com), whose I-Watch feature offers individual investors a nifty glimpse into the world of institutional trading by posting institutional trades that diverge from their thirty-day average.

Sites for Specific Market Activities

AMGdata.com, TrimTabs.com   These websites offer weekly, monthly, quarterly, and annual money flow data on mutual funds, including flow data on specific sectors. Investment Company Institute (www.ici.org) lists monthly mutual fund assets, money flows, sales, and analyses, also for free.

BestCalls.com   This site lists the times and websites for companies broadcasting their quarterly conference calls on the web. Especially useful: Many conference calls are archived on this site, so you can check in at a time that's most convenient for you. How do you know when analyst meetings and industry conferences are going to occur? Check out www.streetevents.com, www.bestcalls.com, and www.smartmoney.com, which also does its own look-ahead. CNBC.com also posts a list of upcoming conference calls.

Earningswire.com   This website provides one-stop shopping for earnings announcements and preannouncements, with useful commentary from the staff of First Call.

Federal Filings Online (www.fedfil.com)   This site notes when insiders file to buy or sell company stock, as well as providing analysis about insider activity.

Insiderscores.com, insidertrader.com   This site provides the skinny on insider buying and selling and includes such trivia as companies with the largest-ever insider buys and sales. It's also a good site for information about IPO lock-up expiration dates.

IPOFinancial.com, ipopros.com   Everything you want to know about IPOs can be found on these websites.

IPOlockup.com, unlockdates.com   These websites contain a month-by-month calendar of lock-up expiration dates. You can click on a specific ticker symbol for details that include a company's profile, shareholders, and underwriters. At unlockdates.com, you can register for free e-mail alerts on up to ten stocks.

Quote.com   What differentiates this good all-around market information site from others of its kind is the amount of information it has on IPOs: indexes, latest filings with the SEC, underwriters, number of shares in the IPO, headlines, analysis, quiet-period expirations and lock-up expirations.

This site also offers a robust charting package that enables investors who are interested in technical analysis to explore a stock's relative strength and its money flows.

Splittrader.com   At this site you'll find everything you ever wanted to know about stock splits, including predictions of the stocks mostly likely to split before the split is announced.

Whispernumber.com, earningswhispers.com, streetIQ.com   Look here to find whisper numbers for individual stocks, IPOs, and government reports. While whisper numbers by their very nature aren't official (the official consensus numbers are published at FirstCall.com and ibes.com), these sites are where you can see a calendar of upcoming IPOs and get a sense of how they'll break out of the gate.

Sites for Market Analysis

Many Wall Street firms guard their research like the crown jewels. For years, the only way to get access to it was to either pay a hefty fee or invest your money with them. Now individual investors can get inside research and analyst reports from certain firms for free on the web. Check out gotoanalysts.com for US Bancorp Piper Jaffray, epoch.com for Epoch Partners, sanfordbernstein.com for Sanford Bernstein, witsoundview.com for Wit Soundview Capital, rsco.com for Robertson Stephens, and standardandpoors.com for Standard & Poors.

Bulldogresearch.com, validea.com   These two sites analyze the analysts, with records of their upgrades and downgrades as measured against the actual performance of the stock. Both sites also reveal the latest stock suggestions from the most successful analysts, so investors can get the skinny without bothering to catch them live on television.

FirstCall.com   Individual investors who don't ante up the hefty fees can't access First Call's research, but market commentary by research director Chuck Hill and insider sales expert Bob Gabele is available for free.

Forrester.com   This is one of the top market research firms analyzing sectors from automotive to travel, but with a particular emphasis on technology, telecommunications, and financial services sectors.

MediaMetrix.com   Your source for measuring Internet and digital media trends is found here. Whether you want to know how successful the holiday season was for e-tailers or how women use the web, this is the place to visit.

Sites for Economic and Federal Government Information

Searchgov.com   This site provides one-stop shopping for finding which government agency handles which data.

Fedstats.gov   Can't remember which agency publishes which information? This site organizes official statistics collected and published by more than seventy Federal agencies in easy-to-find alphabetical order. One caveat: While you'll find such obvious statistics as the CPI and PPI on this site, you still have to go to the Bureau of Economic Analysis's site to find the latest reports on personal consumption expenditures (PCE).

Bureau of Economic Analysis (www.bea.doc.gov)   The Bureau of Economic Analysis publishes the PCE deflator, which has grown in importance ever since Fed chairman Alan Greenspan said he preferred this inflation tracker over the CPI. It's also where to find the latest information about the gross domestic product and personal income and outlays.

Bureau of Labor Statistics (www.bls.gov)   The consumer price index, the producer price index, the employment cost index, as well as reports on consumer spending, average hourly earnings, unemployment rates and productivity rates—they're all available at this site.

Census Bureau (www.census.gov)   What is the underlying growth rate of the economy? That's essentially retail sales, personal income, factory orders and unemployment statistics. This information, as well as data on monthly housing starts, U.S. international trade, advanced retail sales, and manufacturers' shipments and inventory, is available from the Census Bureau.

Conference Board (www.conference-board.org)   The Conference Board publishes the Consumer Confidence Index every month as well as the Index of Leading Economic Indicators.

Commodity Research Bureau (www.crbindex.com)   The Commodity Research Bureau publishes the commodity futures index, which measures futures on bulk goods such as grains, metals, and foods. It's a good inflation indicator.

Federal Communications Commission (www.fcc.gov)   This site provides headline news from the FCC, as well as reports on the latest telecommunication technologies.

Federal Reserve (www.federalreserve.gov)   At the Federal Reserve's website, you can read the Beige Book (the nickname for the quarterly *Summary of Commentary on Current Economic Conditions*), an evaluation of the economic conditions in twelve regions around the country by Fed staffers (available at Federalreserve.gov/FOMC/beigebook/2001/default. htm). The Beige Book is pretty dense reading, but there are summaries and highlights at sites such as Yardeni.com.

Federal Trade Commission (www.ftc.gov)   One of the most useful aspects of this site is the economic reports it publishes on a variety of industries, ranging from e-commerce to the financial impact of the proposed tobacco industry settlement to antitrust issues in the pharmaceutical industry.

Food and Drug Administration (www.fda.gov)   Here's where to find progress reports of the FDA trials for prospective pharmaceutical products.

Internal Revenue Service (www.irs.gov)   A wealth of statistics about how Americans pay their taxes is available a this site.

International Trade Administration (ITA.doc.gov)   Get the latest information about tariffs here.

Securities and Exchange Commission (www.sec.gov)   You can check a company's 10-Qs and 10-Ks at the EDGAR section of the SEC's website (www.sec.gov) or at Freedgar.com (www.freedgar.com).

Analysts' Favorite Industry-Specific Sites

American Petroleum Institute (www.api.org)   Lots of information about the oil and natural gas industry, although it tends to be told from a decidedly biased point of view (e.g., one article is titled "Quality of life. Brought to you by tankers").

Bankstocks.com Analyst Tom Brown's irreverent take on banking companies.

Information Resources, Inc. (www.infores.com) Where to find the latest trend information in the consumer packaged goods industry.

Minerals Management Service (www.mms.gov) More information about oil and natural gas exploration and drilling, with special emphasis on off-shore production, brought to you by the U.S. Department of the Interior.

Securities Industry Association (sia.com) A good overall source for issues affecting the securities industry.

CNET (cnet.com), Techweb (techweb.com), and ZDNet (zdnet.com) Technology information sites with the news and reviews of hands-on technology and the companies that manufacture it.

Index

About the Author

The first journalist to report live from the floor of the New York Stock Exchange, **Maria Bartiromo** is anchor of CNBC's fastest growing show *Market Week with Maria Bartiromo*, and anchor for the first hour of CNBC's *Street Signs* and second hour of *Market Wrap*.

In addition, Bartiromo covers breaking news from CNBC's New York Stock Exchange bureau during *Squawk Box*, and regularly provides business news reports to NBC affiliates nationwide as well as MSNBC and the *Today* show.

Bartiromo joined CNBC in 1993 after five years as a producer and assignment editor with CNN Business News. Additionally, she writes a monthly column for *Individual Investor Magazine*. She was chosen for the 2000 Upside Elite 100, *Upside Magazine*'s list of high-tech's most influential "high rollers of 2000." In 1996, Bartiromo was nominated for a CableACE Award for her three-part series on the Internet and its implications for investors. In 1997, she received the Coalition of Italo-American Association's Excellence in Broadcast Journalism Award.

Baritromo grew up in Brooklyn and graduated from New York University, where she majored in journalism and minored in economics. She lives in New York City with her husband of two years, Jonathan Steinberg, founder and chief executive officer of Individual Investor Group.